To Sarah Joseph
for whom 'liberation through work' was
closer to the spirit of Karma Yoga
than more recent panaceas.

Contents

Preface

This study originated from my interest in the interplay between sex and race at the work place in this country and in the wider, international implications of the allocation (or usurpation) of economic, cultural and intellectual roles between the rich and poor worlds. An examination of sex differences in the nature and status of work in this country provides a useful starting point. And this book is the result.

Fairly early in my research, a decision was made to concentrate on some of the issues raised by the dramatic post-war increase in the number of women going out to work. This soon meant a crossing of interdisciplinary barriers, bringing with it the attendant risk of incurring the displeasure of those who (rightly) feel that a book of the size contemplated would barely be sufficient to cover even a few of the specific areas examined here. There is also undoubtedly a measure of arbitrariness present in the emphasis and selection of topics contained here.

In extenuation, I can only plead that my main objective in writing this book is to present a composite, overall picture of some of the salient issues relating to women's work to a broad readership — not only to students of a number of disciplines, but also to a wider public who may find the task of searching for and assimilating literature contributed by demographers, economists, social historians, sociologists and political scientists in their various (and largely separate) pursuits fairly formidable.

This book also presents *facts* relating to trends in female participation in paid employment during this century, the nature of their attachment to the labour market and their occupational distribution and earnings relative to male workers. Their demographic profiles are mainly drawn from Population Census data going back to the turn of the century; the present unavailability of suitable data from the 1981 Population Census has left no other alternative but the use of administrative and survey data in studying the patterns of changes during the seventies. The sex/race nexus, which was the original source of interest, has been relegated to a few end-of-chapter notes scattered through this book, and awaits future treatment.

I should like to thank Louise Joseph and Barbara MacLennan for their constructive comments on parts of the manuscript in draft and for pointing out some of the verbal infelicities and obscurities. Ann Hirst provided valuable editorial assistance in eliminating bibliographical omissions and inconsistencies and in improving presentation generally. I am also indebted to Margaret Irvine for computer programming assistance and to Jean Ashton, Janice Hammond, Hilary Thornber and Marie Waite for typing parts of the manuscript.

Acknowledgments are due to Macmillan, London and Basingstoke, for permission to incorporate Tables 1.1 and 2.28 from *Occupation and Pay in Great Britain* by Guy Routh; to the Controller of Her Majesty's Stationery Office for data from the *Department of Employment Gazette*, November 1978, Table 6 (p. 1267), the *Employment Gazette*, April 1981, Table 4 (p. 171) and the *Statistics of Education*, 1971 and 1978; and to the Royal Statistical Society for information from the *Journal of the Royal Statistical Society*, Series A, 137(1), 1974, Table 3 (p. 64).

Manchester   George Joseph
January 1983

1

Introduction: A General Review of Issues and Evidence

During the last three or four decades, a revolution has occurred! But, in spite of the considerable public attention given to the feminist movement, this revolution — the entry into the work force of millions of women — has been largely ignored until recently.

In 1951, women constituted 31% of the working population of the UK, and by 1971 they accounted for 37% (an increase of 2.2 million women). According to a Department of Employment forecast made in 1974, this increase will continue, and by 1991 women will constitute 39% of the labour force. However, most past predictions of female labour force participation have proved to be underestimates. (In fact, according to the 1979 Labour Force Survey, the female share of the labour force had already reached 39.4%.) In any case, a striking feature of this trend towards greater participation in the work force is the rapid growth of *married* women; they increased their share of the female labour force from 38% in 1951 to 63% in 1971. It is expected that this figure will exceed 75% by 1991.

The reasons for this rapid growth in the number of working

1

women, especially working married women, are difficult to identify precisely. Economists have argued that paid work has become increasingly attractive as real wages have risen and suitable job opportunities have expanded. Sociologists have pointed to changes in sex role attitudes, rising divorce rates, smaller families, availability of domestic labour-saving gadgets, rising levels of education and the career aspirations of contemporary women as factors favouring the greater participation of women in the labour force, without paying undue attention to the difficult problem of disentangling the causes and effects of these factors.

A particular problem in examining the labour force participation behaviour of married women is the range of disciplines that converge on the subject. To an economist, the primary focus of interest is the fact that the growth in numbers of married women workers has represented the major dynamic element in the growth of labour supply since the end of the Second World War. While the numbers employed from the indigenous male population aged 16 to 64 years fell by about a million between the 1961 and 1971 Population Censuses, this deficit was more than made up for by an increase of 860,000 indigenous female workers and 610,000 total immigrant workers. And, except in the unlikely event of a lowering of the minimum school leaving age or an increase in the age of retirement, the traditional main source of labour supply — male workers — will not significantly augment the total labour force in the foreseeable future.

For a sociologist, the primary interest lies in an examination of the changing social conditions that have permitted the widespread employment of married women. One of these, a result of industrialisation and urbanisation, concerns the changing role of the family and the consequent change in the social role of women. The sociologist may be joined here by the psychologist in examining the motives underlying the growing desire among married women to take up paid employment, the impact of such employment on marital relationships and on the psychological and social development of children.

A demographer's interest is two-fold. First, there is need to examine the impact of various demographic factors such as fertility, nuptiality, mortality and migration on changes in the size and composition of the total labour force. Second, an attempt must be made to disentangle the web of complex inter-relationships that exist between fertility and the labour force participation of married women.

There is an 'ideological' dimension to the growing participation of married women in the labour force which is not often recognised. The role of women as merely 'marginal' or 'secondary' workers is given currency by a number of academics and politicians even today, when they constitute about one-third of the labour force. When labour is short, women are 'encouraged' to enter the labour force and the value of their contribution is emphasised. When jobs are in short supply, they are 'persuaded' not to enter the labour force and compete with the male breadwinners. The 'cult of the mother', the system of taxes and allowances, the eligibility for Social Security Benefits, the household division of labour and discrimination in the labour market all contribute to the relegation of many women to the position of an unskilled manpower reserve — an 'underclass' paid less than their male counterparts and often on less favourable terms of employment. Their situation is not dissimilar to that of immigrant workers in this country or the 'guest workers' on the Continent. The parallels between these groups and the ideological nature of the 'marginal' role of female workers will only be touched on in this study.

In this chapter, an attempt is made to evaluate in general terms the non-economic factors affecting labour force participation of married women with the economic dimensions being discussed in the next chapter. However, it would be useful to provide a historical perspective for the impact of the changing role of the family on the decision by women to take up paid employment outside their households.

The Family and Participation Decisions of Women: A Historical Note[1]

The coming of the Industrial Revolution affected a woman's role in her family in three major ways. First, in a pre-industrial family, a woman's role — in addition to the bearing and rearing of children — included the performance of numerous productive and managerial functions entailed in the location of the work place in the home. The movement of production from the household to the factory and a change in emphasis from employment of individuals rather than families had the twin effects of diminishing the community of interests between family members and polarising the domestic and employment roles of the 'gainfully' occupied members of the family. As a result, an 'inactive' woman lost the degree of self-esteem and worth which had existed before the Industrial Revolution from her active participation in wealth creation and income generation within the household. It may be argued that underlying the motives leading to an ever-increasing number of women seeking employment outside their homes is the desire to recapture their lost sense of usefulness and self-esteem.

A second direct result of industrialisation has been the growth of institutions to provide goods and services formerly produced within the household. Shorn of a substantial part of its traditional economic and educational functions and reduced in size by the absence of grandparents, maiden aunts and the presence of fewer children, the modern family's functions are sufficiently slim-line to permit increasing labour force participation of all its adult members.

A third factor in assessing the impact of changing family functions on labour force participation decisions of married women is the effect of the family structure on the social role of its women. The contemporary family is still an economic unit insofar as it is engaged in the production of meals, processing and completing production of semi-finished goods (e.g. dress-making or beer-brewing) and the repair or maintenance of houses and domestic equipment which has become increasingly a family activity because of the growing shortage of labour and rising costs of such services when supplied by outside agencies. Home 'production' has certain characteristics which distinguish it from similar activities in factories. First, home production is almost invariably undertaken for consumption within the household. Second, the value of these activities is often seen in terms of money saved rather than money made. Third, these activities are often impervious to market forces in the sense that the relationships defined as 'economic' between cost and output, wage and effort, and productivity and value have little relevance to home production activities. However, the basic functions of the contemporary family remain the rearing of children and acting as the primary social unit.

It is in this context of a family denuded of certain crucial functions that its effects on the perceptions and actuality of women's social role must be sought. The role that a woman *habitually* plays reflects not only on other roles she may be called upon to play elsewhere, but affects her status, attitudes and general outlook. Industrialisation created two classes of women with fundamental differences in their life styles, sets of values and codes of conduct.

A woman from the growing, though numerically small, middle class, whose prosperity was derived from the enormous expansion of industry and trade resulting from industrialisation and colonial exploitation, was expected to cultivate (within the spacious confines of her home) leisure as a mark of affluence, and idleness as a status symbol. Cosseted by an army of domestic servants, protected from the rigours of life and cultivating frailty as the hallmark of her sex, she was prepared for the ultimate status of a married woman when an eligible male could be persuaded to bestow it upon her. The marriage hardly changed her life style, except that she would then be engaged over the childbearing decades in giving frequent and regular birth to numerous offspring. Encapsulated within the confines of her family and her class, work outside the home was rarely contemplated. There already existed, however, certain forces which would gradually bring about fundamental changes in the position of women in this social class. There was a growing surplus of educated women who, due either to the emigration of eligible males to the colonies or to a tendency to marry later in life, had to earn their living. Expanding opportunities for employment as clerks, office workers, teachers and nurses, helped to absorb this surplus until the beginning of the Second World War.[2] The other class of women originated from the rural areas, leaving their cottage workshops and the land on which their families had worked in the past to join the ever-increasing army of those prepared to sell their labour for wages and live in a state of chronic destitution in the crowded tenements of the inner city areas.[3] From the early period of industrialisation, working-class women had found employment in relatively large numbers in cotton mills, potteries or at home on piece rates for garment manufacturers and the like. Domestic service absorbed about 35% of the total women in employment in 1911. The need to pass legislation in the middle of the nineteenth century to protect these women workers and their children was symptomatic of the existence of a problem of considerable magnitude. In general, the attitude of the 'informed' public to these working women was unfavourable. The high mortality among children and old people in urban areas was frequently attributed to the absence from their homes of working mothers. Factors such as poverty, malnutrition, overcrowding, lack of hygiene and sanitation and their contribution to mortality were not much emphasised.

Increased prosperity and greater concern for public welfare brought attendant improvements during the closing decades of the nineteenth century and the early decades of the twentieth. This was reflected in better working conditions, improvement in housing and health, better sanitation, smaller families and higher incomes among the working class. There was a fall in the relative number of women going out to work, possibly indicating that improving living standards among the working class led to the absorption of middle class aspirations and norms of behaviour, including the social stigma associated with working married women. Only after the outbreak of the Second World War has there been a reversal of this trend; and it has resulted in the labour force participation rate of married women (i.e. the proportion of married women in the labour force) in Britain rising from 22% in 1951 to 43% in 1971.[4]

Finally, in the last three or four decades, the gradual replacement of the traditional patriarchal family by a new, more democratic institution has, to some extent, undermined the Victorian stereotype of the family and reduced the gap in class attitudes to women going out to work. Yet many women face dilemmas — such as conflicts between the demands made by their jobs and their homes — which are often resolved in favour of the latter, thus making working women less reliable long-term employees than men who usually resolve such conflicts in the reverse direction. Another problem relates to the extent of the sharing role of the husband in assisting with domestic work which shows significant class and international differences.

Determinants of Labour Force Participation of Married Women: Classification Schemes

Most attempts at classifying the determinants of labour force participation of married women have made the basic distinction between motivation on one side and facilitating conditions on the other. The motives for taking up paid employment could include financial gain and psychological satisfaction to be derived from work outside the household, while the 'facilitating' or 'enabling' conditions include size and age-composition of the family, education and work experience of the married woman, and availability of suitable work in or near the area of residence. Sobol (1963) uses a more detailed scheme where he distinguishes between *enabling, facilitating* and *precipitating* conditions. A modified Sobol scheme would include the following headings:

1. *Enabling Conditions*
    (a) Ages and number of children
    (b) Future family-building plans
    (c) Number and age of other adults in the household (if any) and their attitudes to working wives
2. *Facilitating Conditions*
    (a) Type and level of educational attainment
    (b) Previous work experience
    (c) Availability of suitable work (e.g. part-time work near home)
3. *Precipitating Conditions*
    (i) *Structural aspects*
    (a) Husband's labour force status (i.e. employed, unemployed, not in the labour force) and income
    (b) Family's 'other' income: i.e. earnings of other members of the family excluding husband and wife, 'unearned' income, gifts and welfare payments
    (c) Wage rates of female workers
    (d) Planned purchase of consumer durables (e.g. cars or freezers) or special services (e.g. private schooling for children or expensive holidays)
    (ii) *Attitudinal aspects*
    (a) Desire for achievement and self-fulfilment as an individual outside the family
    (b) Desire to allocate time more productively

A basic flaw in this classification scheme is its tendency to mix different *levels* of analysis. Both financial factors which are of structural origin and 'aspirations' which have an attitudinal basis are classified as being at a similar level of analysis. This could be quite misleading. For example, an income of £12,000 per annum may be more than satisfactory for some couples, while others with higher economic aspirations may view the same income as merely adequate. The problem is how to discriminate between the labour force participation decisions of these two groups. Gordon and Kammeyer (1980) have proposed a typology which distinguishes clearly between (i) economic need (e.g. level of husband's income) (ii) obstacles and facilitators (e.g., wife's employment history before marriage, educational level of wife, age and number of children) and (iii) social psychological orientations and attitudes (e.g., beliefs about 'mothering' on part of both husband and wife, sex-role orientation of husband and wife).

The Sobol classificatory scheme does, however, serve two main purposes. First, it provides in general terms a list of factors that have some influence on whether a married woman goes out to work. Second, it provides an initial framework for ordering a number of disparate variables into categories (which are by no means mutually exclusive or of equal importance). An economist might emphasise the importance of financial factors, while work by social psychologists such as Hoffman (1963) and Morgan et al. (1966) has been focused on attitudinal and personality factors. Yet again, Sweet (1973) in his study of labour force activity of American wives placed considerable emphasis on the presence in the household of children and family history (i.e. age at marriage, marital stability, length of first and subsequent birth intervals).

The problem remains: is it possible to analyse household decisions with respect to labour force participation, amount of time and goods to be expended on housework, family size and spacing, allocation of time for leisure and other household activities within a single framework? A 'household choice' theory originating from work by Becker (1960, 1965) distinguishes between paid (market) work, unpaid (household) work and leisure, within a framework in which a family acts together as a single entity maximising its welfare under certain constraints.[5] In this theory, households exercise freedom of choice and behave rationally to maximise their welfare (or utility). The two major economic constraints on the maximisation of utility are income and prices. Since it is believed that the essence of rational behaviour is independent of time, class, race and culture, this 'neoclassical' view of human behaviour sees a limited number of economic variables determining the decisions made with respect to optimal allocation of a household's scarce resources (mainly time). Also, since for a neoclassicist a problem is economic if scarcity is involved and scarcity requires choice, then marriage, motherhood, household production and even a family visit to the zoo can be given an economic interpretation. The details of this theory and its implications for the labour force participation of married women will be presented in a later chapter. It would, however, be useful to begin with a discussion of the changing role of a married woman as a housewife and mother in an archetypal British household during this century and how this change has affected her ability and desire to take up paid work outside her home.

Married Women and their Domestic Role: Impact on Labour Force Participation

A number of factors have affected the nature and importance of the role of a housewife and mother in a contemporary household. Three characteristics of the present phase of Western capitalist development have had some impact on a married woman's domestic role. First, the mass production of cheap ready-to-wear clothes and convenience food has taken over an ever-widening range of functions from the housewife. Second, the development of labour-saving domestic appliances and convenience goods (e.g., non-iron clothes, detergents, extensive use of plastics) may have reduced the amount of time that needs to be spent on housework, so that a growing number of housewives, unless they have young children, feel underemployed. Third, the creation of a number of new jobs connected with the production, distribution and advertising of an increasing variety of goods and services, which is the hallmark of a consumer society, has served both to stimulate the desire to acquire an ever-increasing flow of goods and the means to satisfy such a desire, at least during much of the post-war period (a period characterised by a contracting male labour force and demand for labour outstripping supply) when the employment of older married women rose at a rapid rate.

A further factor in reducing the importance of the domestic role in the eyes of a number of married women is the low esteem in which domestic work is now held. In this regard, an important contribution of the feminist movement has been a critical examination of the ideological implications of the work done by housewives. The cult of home-maker and mother is often a disguise for both the inferior social standing of the housewife (whose status is often derived from that of her husband) and the unpaid drudgery that housework often entails. Socially isolated as a consequence of the pervasive urban ethos of privacy and the restricted communal activities found within the confines of a modern nuclear family, a housewife is often thrown upon her husband as the only source of mental and emotional sustenance. This sometimes builds up marital strain because of the incompatibility between the growing demands made upon marriage for sociability and leisure on the one hand and the great divide between home activities and work activities generated in contemporary society on the other.

There is a demographic dimension to the changing domestic role of married women. During the last hundred years female life expectancy has nearly doubled in this country, mainly due to an enormous decrease in infant mortality and, to a lesser extent, in maternal mortality arising from improved medical care and hygiene and a reduction in the incidence of childbearing. A clear indication of this advance is seen in the fact that while in 1850 about half of the female population of Britain died before reaching the age of 45, about 90% survive to that age today, with 70% reaching the age of 65. In other words, a woman who marries now can, on the average, expect to survive half a century or more.

Accompanying this increase in life expectancy has been a reduction in the relative length of the period of childrearing. This may be defined as the time between the birth of the first child and the departure of the last from home. Research in the United States (Glick, 1977) shows that the average length of the childrearing period has fallen by about 3 years since the turn of the century. At that time too, an average woman spent 15 years of her considerably shorter life on actual childbearing and nursing; the corresponding figure today is about 4 years. The 'family' function of women has diminished rapidly.

There is another aspect of the family life cycle which has some bearing on the domestic role of women. As a consequence of a relative increase in the number of women surviving their husbands (because of higher male mortality over the whole age-range), and the increasing rate of divorce, separation or desertion, there might be a growing tendency for women to attach less importance to their domestic role *vis-à-vis* their role as workers outside their families.

The importance of the domestic role to married women is to a considerable extent indicated by the number of hours that they spend on housework.[6] Studies by Nickols (1976), Vanek (1974) and Walker (1973) of American households showed that the average number of hours devoted per week by full-time housewives to housework ranged from 35 to 60 hours. Walker found that the proportional time allocation for four major housework activities were:

(a) *Meal preparation*:   30%
(b) *Cleaning*:   30%
(c) *Care of children and other family members:*   15–25% (depending on age and number of children)
(d) *Care of clothing and general housecare*:   15–25%

The amount of time a housewife spent on housework is, as expected, related to the time she spent on outside work, her level of education, the age and number of children and extent of help from other family members. Walker also found that on average a 'working' wife spent 19 fewer hours (i.e. 35% of her total 'working' time) on housework than a full-time housewife. However, when the number and ages of children were allowed for, the actual decline in the time spent on housework by a working wife was less than the average indicated.

To sum up, the amount of time allocated to housework is in the long run a function of availability of substitutes for home goods and services, society's valuation of the status and usefulness of housewives and uncertainties with respect to the permanence and length of marriage ties. In the short run, the influential factors are the employment status of the housewife, the ages and number of children and the efficiency of home production which is partially dependent on education and partially on the opportunity cost of not taking up paid employment.[7] There are certain changes which could make it easier for married women to combine their dual roles as housewives and working women. These include flexible shopping and working hours, changes in government attitudes to women working (which is directly reflected in exhortations to withdraw when labour supply is plentiful and enter when labour shortage is inhibiting production, as well as implicit indicators such as tax policies, child allowances, policies on school meals and day nurseries), and a more equitable division of labour at home.

Married Women and Children: Impact on Labour Force Participation

A useful starting point in an area filled with hidden minefields is the existence of a negative association between the number of children and the likelihood of being engaged in paid work outside the family. For example, while fertility (i.e. the actual number of children born alive) varies with age, socio-economic status, education, religion and ethnic background, there is considerable evidence that working wives have lower fertility than full-time housewives in almost all developed countries[8] (Andorka, 1978, p. 292). Four principal explanations have been proposed for this negative association between paid work and fertility:

(1) The presence of children makes women less willing or able to take up employment outside the home.

(2) This reverses the causal chain indicated in (1) and suggests that desires and plans concerning children, or attitudes concerning birth control, are influenced by attitudes towards labour force participation.

(3) Factors such as education and family background are emphasised here, as it is felt that they could be the determining factors in a woman's decision to have children and/or enter the work force.

(4) A final explanation suggests that decisions about employment and childbearing are made simultaneously and are to be regarded as causally interdependent.

The acceptance of the first explanation which has involved the inclusion of family size and birth interval measures in models explaining the employment of married women (Bowen and Finnegan, 1969; Oppenheimer, 1970; Sweet, 1973) is based on the following rationale:

Time is a scarce resource with competing uses. Care of children makes demands on the mother's time. Allocation of more time to child care leaves less time for other activities, including paid work. Thus, at any given moment in time, women who have more children or younger children are less likely to work than those who have fewer or older children.

The second explanation favoured by some demographers (Dixon, 1975; Hawthorn, 1970; Ryder and Westoff, 1971) considers married female employment as a determinant of family size and interprets the direction of causation from the perspective of role incompatibility. Some females will specialise in childbearing while others, particularly those in attractive jobs, will concentrate in the main on their jobs and consider childbearing a secondary activity. If this line of argument is valid, it would be shown in the nature of the association between *actual* and *desired* completed family size (i.e. total number of observed or desired live births per woman of a cohort by the end of their reproductive lives) and labour force participation of married women. A study by Ridley (1959), based on data from the 1955 Growth of American Families Study, used a sample of fecund women (i.e. women with unimpaired physiological ability to bear children) at the end of their childbearing period, to investigate the relationship between actual or desired completed family size and labour force participation of these sample women. The main relevant conclusions of her study may be summarised as follows: the duration of work after marriage has a positive association with completely planned families and infecundity; working women have and expect smaller completed families than non-working women, regardless of socio-economic status; present labour force status is a better predictor of whether there will be any future births than the *number* of future births desired; plans to work in the future are associated with current family size and desired completed family size; and the length of past work experience is directly associated with the past and expected use of contraceptives.

It is clear from these conclusions that the basic methodological dilemma is unresolved for, as Ridley (1959, p. 281) points out, it is difficult to decide whether families are smaller because wives wish to work, or whether they work because their families are smaller. There is some evidence, however, of a greater prevalence of and efficiency in using contraceptives among working women than non-working women. Does this imply that women limit their family size because they want to work for direct satisfaction obtained from such work, or that small families and higher living standards (which require women to take paid employment) are means to achieving an end which is upward social mobility? If the latter is the case, then this is consistent with the third explanation that the association between fertility and work is through a third factor which, in this case, would be the desire for upward social mobility.

There is, however, an economic rationale underlying the third explanation. The opportunity cost of children is the income foregone by having to stop or reduce the amount worked. Where a family is faced with unexpected economic pressures, a wife may decide to take up work if the marginal utility of earnings from work is greater than the marginal disutility of not having a child.[9]

Economic pressure works as the extraneous factor negatively affecting fertility and positively affecting the desire to work. It could also be interpreted in terms of the new microeconomic synthesis of labour force decisions and fertility decisions being made simultaneously as the fourth explanation would indicate. The framework of the microeconomic theory of fertility will be elaborated in the next chapter.

Despite the difficulties in explaining the nature of the negative association between married women's work and fertility, there are certain practical implications which need to be spelt out. From the association, it can be inferred that increased employment of married women could have an impact on the size and age-distribution of the British population. Again, if the association is through their link with a third variable, would, say an improvement in child-care facilities or a diminution of the social disapproval of working mothers, result in an increase in labour force participation without an accompanying fall in fertility? Finally, could future technological innovations on the domestic front, increasing acceptance of convenience food, greater involvement by fathers in housework and childrearing, greater flexibility in work schedules (including availability of part-time employment) and better provision of maternity leave reduce the negative association that exists between married women's employment and fertility?

In the discussion so far, birth spacing and its association with work has not been examined. In a recent study of family formation in Britain, Dunell (1979) found large differences existed in the length of the first birth interval (i.e. the duration between marriage and the birth of the first child) between women of different occupations. One quarter of the women in professional and managerial groups had their first child within the first two years of marriage compared to about half of the rest of working women and nearly three-quarters of those who were not working. In the case of later birth intervals, about a quarter of women, irrespective of occupation, worked during the second and third intervals, possibly indicating that the age of the youngest child is a more crucial factor than the number of children. Finally, for women with completed families, labour force activity rates were similar for women with one to three children, with the size of family becoming an important factor only for women with four or more children.

Namboodri (1964) investigated the relationship between length of time worked after marriage and length of birth intervals using the data on the Growth of American Families. His conclusions were not surprising. There existed a positive association between length of work experience and length of birth intervals irrespective of marriage duration and a negative association between probability of pre-marital pregnancy and work duration after marriage. Certain implications of the positive association between length of first birth interval and work duration for family income and wealth have been drawn by Freedman and Coombs (1966a and b). The shorter the first birth interval and subsequent birth spacing, the shorter the work duration after marriage and the lower the level of current income and asset accumulation. Also, the effect of this lack of work experience early in marriage affects the wife's ability to add to family income and wealth later through paid work when children are no longer a constraint on her labour force participation.

The analysis so far has sought association between fertility or family spacing and labour force participation of married women. The question remains: what is the *reduction* in the average number of years a married woman can be expected to work with one child, two children, three children, and so on? Garfinkle (1967) used a Multiple Decrement Table[10] to investigate the numbers of years lost to employment because of mortality and childbirth among American married women. His conclusion was that the birth of the first child reduced the average working life expectancy by ten years and by two or three years for each successive child. A similar exercise repeated by the author for Britain using data from the 1971 Population Census gave a reduction of 8 years in the case of the first child, 3 years for the next child and a reduction of 2 years for each subsequent child.

To sum up, the fundamental difficulty that arises in almost all studies relating to the fertility and labour force participation of married women is that of establishing a causal chain between them. Suggested causal links without any definitive empirical support are:
  (a) The desire to work leads to restricted fertility through use of contraceptives and/or lengthening of birth intervals.
  (b) Restricted fertility makes it possible to work through a reduction in the time spent on childbearing and rearing.
  (c) Work and fertility decisions are made simultaneously, probably influenced by extraneous factors such as desire for financial and social advancement.

It is sometimes argued that availability of longitudinal or retrospective data which follows age cohorts of women through their experience of work, marriage and childbearing could help to resolve the problem of the causal links. Yet this data would provide little indication of the influence of desired completed family size on participation behaviour *or* the importance of chance, choice or fecundity impairment in determining the length of birth intervals *or* how to allow for changes in socioeconomic status over time which have an important bearing on fertility and work decisions. An implication of this argument is that sufficiently detailed and appropriate data would resolve theoretical puzzles, i.e. a theoretical framework will somehow spring out of data. The only attempt to integrate the theory of fertility into an economic theory of household production and consumption following the line of Becker (1960) will be developed later. But despite the criticism that this approach is devoid of normative content and the immense problems of operationalising the variables of such a theory for purposes of empirical tests, the chief merit remains that it is a theoretical model with well-defined causal chains which could be adapted in empirical work.

Women and Marriage: Impact on Labour Force Participation

To a large majority of women, until recently marriage was the ultimate career. The combined influences of the patriarchal legacy (according to which women were considered incapable of managing their own affairs) and the effect of the breakdown of the extended agrarian family unit (which resulted in the wife being left in sole charge of the household and children) had the result of reducing any incentive to rationalise household work or re-introduce a more collective and widely-distributed responsibility similar to that which was prevalent in the multi-generation agrarian household.

The impact of marriage on the labour force participation of a woman is partly a function of her socio-economic status and partly dependent on the type of work she is engaged in. Economic necessity and a sense of independence often resulted in continuing paid employment for married working class women. Amongst the middle and upper classes, the social mores demanded that the woman be 'supported' by her husband. Indeed, the abililty to 'support' was in many cases a prerequisite for consent to the marriage in the first place. It is in this context that one should place the growing campaign for female emancipation found among women of this class. For the worker's wife who had to enter employment at least periodically to support the family or become self-supporting, *or* a farmer's wife who performed a 'productive' function in the household, the 'liberation through work' did not have the same compelling force.

At the level of an individual household, the decision to work or refrain from work cannot be taken in isolation from the views and needs of the family. The needs of children were highlighted and have already been discussed. From the vantage point of the married woman herself, there are two sets of relevant factors concerning her perception of family ideals and role norms. On the one hand there are questions as to what she feels is appropriate to her role of housewife and how she perceives the ideals and interests of persons in close proximity to her. On the other hand, the opportunities and attractions of alternative roles and role environments that she perceives, as well as the obstacles created by other persons in the family in taking up the alternative role, would influence her decision on taking up work outside the home.

It would appear that the attitude of the husband is often of decisive importance in the wife's decision as to whether to take up paid employment or not. In an American study (Weil, 1961) it was found that the husband's attitude was the factor that had the most important influence on the labour force participation decision of the wife. A British study (Klein, 1965) reported that 58% of a sample who wanted to work gave 'unconditional' disapproval of husbands as the reason for their not working. Both studies found significant class differences in attitudes of husbands to working wives — the higher the social class, the greater the percentage of married men approving of wives seeking paid employment. The negative attitude of husbands can be attributed in part to their ideological concepts of 'the family', the importance they attach to social prestige and partly to a fear that household production of goods and services will be diminished. Underlying a favourable attitude to working wives is the possibility of higher living standards and greater contentment from work outside on the part of the wives.

A very contemporary issue which may arise is whether work and marriage are considered as alternatives by a growing number of women.[11] There is some evidence to indicate that working women are more likely to postpone marriage, but little to show that they tend not to marry at all. Employment has several competing types of effects on marriage. On the one hand, women who are working may not marry because they are financially independent and socially fulfilled. On the other hand, women who are working are more likely to marry early either because they have more opportunities to meet 'eligible' men, or because their earning ability makes them more attractive, or because they can afford to marry earlier and set up homes. Empirical results have not helped to resolve the net effect of work on marriage. Preston and Richards (1975) found that among women aged 22–24 years there was a relatively larger proportion of women who were unmarried among those who worked compared to those who were not working. They interpreted their findings as supporting 'employment as an alternative to marriage' thesis, though it could just as well be interpreted as employment leading to the postponement of marriage. Sawhill *et al.* (1975) found an 'independence' effect reflected in an inverse association between marriage and income or possession of assets, though this effect wore off in two years among those receiving social welfare payments. There is, therefore, some support for the thesis that employment leads to a postponement but not necessarily a rejection of marriage. Marriage rates over the last two decades indicate that the proportion of 'never-married' women is rising among those under thirty and falling among those over thirty. It may be conjectured that increasing employment of women has been responsible for pushing the average age at marriage upward. Employment does not, however, seem to lead women to develop tastes or life styles that preclude eventual marriage. Only a slight increase is expected in the proportion of women who never marry among those who turn 20 during the 1980's. Rather than indicating a rejection of marriage, this increase will probably reflect either an increase in the number of those who postpone marriage to find suitable partners when they are ready for marriage, *or* an increase in the number of couples living together rather than getting married.

Changes in the expected duration of marriage have some effect on the labour force participation of married women. It was seen previously that one effect of increasing life expectancy is that a woman can expect to survive her husband for a longer time. In addition, an increasing number of marriages break up by divorce, separation, or desertion. The uncertainties engendered by both these tendencies could lead to a greater number of women wishing to have a measure of financial independence by working. Cain (1966) found a positive association between labour force participation and marital instability (measured by whether or not a woman was married more than once). Work as an insurance against the possibility of another breakdown of marriage is suggested as the explanation for this association.

If one now examines the impact on marital stability of a woman working, the effects can be either positive or negative. On the one hand, a woman with a job has an alternative means of support if her marriage is unsatisfactory. On the other hand, a wife who works can raise the family's living standard and perhaps improve their quality of life, thereby increasing the benefits of remaining married. Here again, there is inconclusive empirical evidence of the strength of the competing effects. Sawhill *et al.* (1975) found that wives with relatively high earnings in 1968 were more likely to separate or divorce by 1972 than wives with lower earnings. On the other hand, Hannan and Tuma (1977) and Hoffman and Holmes (1976) reported that under certain conditions receipt of welfare or supplementary income payments had a depressing effect on marital stability.

The size and stability of total family income may affect labour force participation through its effect on marital stability. Becker *et al.*(1976) found that divorce was generally less likely as the husband's income increased to a certain level, but above that level the likelihood of divorce rose. The relative earnings of the spouse have also been found to have a significant effect on marital stability. Cherlin (1977) and Moore *et al.* (1978) found a greater probability of divorce or separation among households where the wives earned a higher fraction of the household income than the husbands. Finally, stability of family income (Mott and Moore, 1977) and unemployment (Sawhill *et al.*, 1977) have been found to have a significant negative and positive association with the probability of divorce respectively.

To sum up, the impact of marriage on labour force participation of women is dependent on class, labour force status at marriage, family income and wealth. Marital disruption in the form of divorce, separation or desertion will have a positive effect generally, though the economic position of the 'divorced' woman will have an important bearing. If the direction of causation is reversed, the principal known effect on the formation and dissolution of marriage is to delay formation and encourage dissolution, though the empirical evidence on the latter is mixed. The size, composition and stability of family income have an effect on marital stability, though empirical evidence on the nature of the effect is inconclusive.

Women and Education: Impact on Labour Force Participation

The 1971 population census of Great Britain shows that 63.5% of all 'qualified' women and 57% of qualified married women were economically active, compared to 43% of total women and 42% of total married women.[12] There are two main explanations for the positive effect of education on labour force participation of married women. First, the effect is a reflection of the positive association that exists between educational attainment and earning potential or employability. Second, education often predisposes women to work with a career structure. In other words, the two factors underlying the positive association between education and labour force participation are the need or desire to find work and the ability to do so.

The need to find work has both an economic and social dimension. A negative relationship exists between family economic need and the educational attainment of the wife, arising from a tendency for educated women to choose educated mates with relatively higher current incomes or earning potential. Indeed, the higher average family income of educated women and its associated lower labour force participation often tends to mask the higher participation rates of these women.

There is, however, a countervailing social dimension. There is empirical evidence to indicate that highly educated working wives are significantly more satisfied with their marriages than comparably educated full-time housewives (Burke and Weir, 1976). An earlier study (Nye, 1963) found no significant difference in marital satisfaction between highly educated working wives and full-time housewives, though less educated full-time housewives were found to be more satisfied than the less educated working wives. There may be other critical factors at work reflecting on the relationship between work and marital satisfaction of married women. These include criteria such as whether there is an economic need to work, whether the jobs are interesting, whether husbands approve and help with housework and whether part-time work is available and easily accessible.

Insofar as the contribution of education to the ability to work is concerned, there are three factors of some importance. First, there is evidence (Yohalem, 1968) to show that the reduction in the working life of an average highly educated woman is more than compensated for by the shorter period that this woman spends at home on childbearing and childrearing. Second, education raises the productivity of market work *vis-à-vis* housework and thereby raises the opportunity cost of staying at home.[13] Third, education in general raises the employment potential and therefore makes it easier to find suitable job openings. Yet in the ultimate analysis it is the *type* of education received which determines the facility to obtain paid employment. In a later chapter we shall consider the role of education and training in determining the occupations that are popular with women.

Notes

1. This section is based on the lucid examination of the impact of early industrialisation on the status of women in Britain contained in Klein (1965, pp. 1–20).
2. It is interesting in this context that while the percentage of women in 'middle class' (white collar) occupations — teachers, nurses, shop assistants, civil servants — increased in England from 13% in 1881 to 24% in 1911, the percentage of women in 'working class' occupations — domestic service, garment makers, textile workers — fell from 87% to 76% over the same period.
3. Pinchbeck (1969) has painted a vivid picture of the appalling conditions of the working people between 1840–1880. Children from 5 years upwards worked for 14 hours a day. Working class families were on the average badly fed, ill clothed and lived in unsanitary dwellings ridden with disease.
4. The Second World War represented a watershed in female participation in the labour force in more than one way. Removal of restrictions on employment of married women in certain occupations, provision of child-care facilities and location of factories in areas with untapped resources from mothers with children were aimed at mobilising labour for a war-time economy.
5. It is interesting that this framework for household choice was formulated with married women in mind. The paid work–leisure dichotomy which forms the basis of the traditional labour supply theory is more apposite for a situation where male labour supply is the prime consideration.

6. In examining the relative amount of time spent on housework compared to work outside the home, Tarras Saellfone, a Swedish management consultant, made the calculation that 2,340 million working hours were spent annually in Sweden on shopping, cooking and washing up, while, by comparison, Swedish industry used only 1,290 million hours on production (quoted in Myrdal and Klein, 1968, p. 34).

7. Since the concept of *opportunity cost* is important in the economic theories of labour force participation behaviour discussed in the next chapter, a definition of the term would be useful. The opportunity cost of not taking up paid employment is the income and satisfaction from outside work *foregone* by remaining at home.

8. By the same token it is found that a larger proportion of women who are childless are found in the 'working category'.

9. This simply implies that a family, faced by unexpected calls on its resources, may feel that a working wife's contribution to family income is so important as to postpone (or even curtail) its family building plans. The use of economic jargon here is deliberate. It is a foretaste of the terminology that is prevalent in the neoclassical version of microeconomics.

10. A Multiple Decrement table is a statistical device which traces a hypothetical population born at the same time which through the passage of time is diminished by two or more causes of decrement. In this case a hypothetical cohort of working married women is subject to two causes of decrement — mortality and withdrawal from the labour force as a result of childbirth.

11. Effectively, the demands made on top civil servants, doctors, lawyers, etc. preclude marriage in many cases. But marriage, as an institution, has been changing partly in response to the growing need to reduce conflicts generated by career aspirations and domestic role for an increasing number of women.

12. 'Qualified' women are those possessing qualifications above GCE A-level or equivalent.

13. There is little empirical evidence on the impact of education on the productivity of housework. It may be argued that educated women are likely to afford and experiment with new technology at home, thereby raising the productivity of housework. At the same time they may avoid convenience food (or junk food) and devote more time to the physical and mental stimulation of their children. Further, husbands of educated women tend to participate more in housework than those of less educated women (Liebowitz, 1974).

2

Labour Supply and Married Women: The Economic Dimension

Introduction

When economists talk about labour supply, they may use the term in two distinct senses. In a precise sense, it indicates the quantity of labour supplied (often measured in hours) at a specified wage rate at a particular moment in time. In a looser sense, the term may be used to describe the numbers who are economically active or participate in a labour force. In our discussion so far, the latter usage has prevailed, so that the labour force participation rate (often referred to as the economic activity rate) measures the proportion of those in paid employment or actively seeking work (i.e. the unemployed) among the population who are capable of work. The numerator of this measure consists of the economically active population or the labour force, and the denominator consists of the working-age population less those who (due to disabilities or incarceration in penal institutions) cannot join the labour force.

Neither the numbers involved in the labour force, nor the hours spent on market work alone, give a complete picture of labour supply. The former ignore an essential quantitative element, the number of hours worked, especially in the case of labour supplied by part-time married women workers, by concentrating only on whether an individual is a labour force participant or not. The latter include only those who are in paid employment. Often data problems and difficulties of devising measures for theoretical concepts which have no empirical equivalents result in unsatisfactory measures of labour supply being used in empirical studies. As we shall see later, evidence from American studies indicates that different measures can alter drastically the nature of the conclusions that can be drawn with respect to the sensitivity of labour supply to changes in the economy and the determinants of labour force participation of various groups.

Labour Supply and Household Choice Theory: An Attempted Synthesis

The most widely known of the recent approaches to the study of labour force participation decisions is deeply embedded in the neoclassical theory of household choice and resource allocation.[1] The following assumptions are central to the development of the theory:

(1) The Maximising Utility Assumption: this depends on the existence of a decision unit — an individual, family or household — which is primarily interested in maximising the welfare (or utility) it derives from the range of activities it undertakes.[2] A married woman, in all probability, is a member of a decision unit consisting of a household or family. As a unit, its principal activities may be categorised as:
   (a) undertaking the production and consumption of household goods (including children or, more precisely, child services);
   (b) production and consumption of market goods, which require that the household be linked to an external labour market environment that provides the means of transforming household resources into market goods; and
   (c) the production and consumption of leisure.

The question arises: how does a household determine what and how much to produce and consume? The answers are found in the next two assumptions.

(2) The assumption that each decision unit has a given and stable set of preferences which do not vary significantly from those of other decision units faced with similar resource constraints, wherever and whenever such decision units may be identified. This set of preferences is not to be interpreted as a set of preferences for specific goods and services or actual physical objects, but as characteristics of those goods and services which provide utility to the household (satisfying certain fundamental aspects of life, such as food, shelter, health, desire for children, prestige, etc.). The importance of this type of specification of household preferences lies in its easy incorporation into a household utility function. By considering the attributes or characteristics of different types of market goods and services and physical commodities, the relationship between these goods and the needs that they satisfy are better established than if the utility function consisted of different and non-aggregatable categories of goods and services.

The basic resource constraints for a household consisting of a married couple and children are:

(a) the stock of material wealth obtained through public and private transfers such as inheritances, gifts and public welfare benefits: and

(b) the time available to the husband and wife for household production, market production and leisure.

Since, for most households, wealth gained through transfers is of minor importance, the basic household resource is time.

(3) The assumption that there is, within each decision unit, a single rational decision maker who achieves an optimal allocation of the unit's resources through the Price System.[3] Prices, whether they are 'money' prices of market goods or services *or* imputed 'shadow' prices of non-market activities, both measure the opportunity cost of using some scarce resource(s). For example, the opportunity cost of a married woman not working is the income lost by her as a result of her absence from the labour force. This would also be the shadow price of her disengagement from paid employment.[4]

It will have been noted that the process of *how* preferences and tastes are formed has not been mentioned; they are simply taken as 'given'. It has always been contended by positivists of the neoclassical school that an understanding of how preferences and tastes are developed is not vital to subsequent analysis.[5] The neoclassicist's implicit view of the household is of one permeated by care and love with no conflicts, so that everyone's preferences are 'swept' into one household utility function. Divorces, battered children and wives and violent family disagreements are but 'distortions' which do not affect the normal tendency for different household members to weigh each other's preferences in arriving at household decisions. There is clearly a certain lack of dynamism in this approach, or, as Boulding (1970, p. 118) put it, the economist's indifference curves (representing an individual's preferences) must have been 'immaculately conceived'. There are certain complex technical problems in formulating dynamic utility functions which are well discussed by Morishima (1970).

On a more general level, let us apply the household choice theory to family formation and observe the questions it leaves unanswered. Neoclassically speaking, the first step in household formation is an act of marriage. The newly formed household is faced with the question of the number and spacing of children. The children, once born, become co-determiners of the utility function, whereas previously they were mere arguments. Given this fairly general situation,

1) can sequential sets of decisions be condensed into a single, static, timeless utility function?
2) at what stage does the utility function of the household as a unit become operative?
3) can the entire process of household formation be separated into two (or more) independent parts (e.g. (a) from the act of marriage to the birth of children, and (b) the subsequent period)?

Allocation of Time: The Basic Resource

Leaving aside these unanswerable questions (within the context of this theory), it remains to show how a household, with a given set of preferences, which wishes to maximise its total utility, can bring about an optimal allocation of total time, which is initially assumed to be its only input or scarce resource.[6]

(a) Time: Market versus Household Work

A basic decision here is the extent to which household members should offer to participate in *market* work. There are three dimensions to the supply of household labour for market work. The two quantitative dimensions consist of the number of members who supply labour and the number of hours they supply. The qualitative dimension indicates the intensity of work offered during these hours. The multi-dimensionality of labour supply decisions is given a sharper focus if they are analysed within the framework of the socio-demographic environment within which the household operates.

Each woman in a household has a range of attributes which influences her labour force status, the number of hours worked inside and outside the household and the degree of intensity with which she works. The attributes include *personal characteristics* such as age, marital status, education, and family responsibilities; *economic characteristics* such as the minimum wage rate she needs to be offered to induce her to take up paid work *or* increase the hours spent in paid employment; and a number of unquantifiable factors, which are nevertheless important, such as customary attitudes to work and leisure, bringing up children and caring for old people. A combination of these factors influences labour supply decisions on the part of a household.

The traditional economic approach to labour supply has been by way of an individual choice to allocate a fixed time (usually the number of hours in a day) between work and leisure in a manner that maximises the individual's utility function, assuming a positive price for time (i.e. marginal utility of time is positive). More recent work by Mincer (1962) and Becker (1965) has emphasised the need to examine labour supply decisions of married women, to analyse (paid) market work, (unpaid) household work and leisure within the framework of a family (or household) operating as a utility maximising entity under certain resource constraints. These constraints consist of a *budget constraint* which states the obvious fact that household expenditure cannot in the long term exceed household income and a *time constraint* which implies equally obviously that the time allocated to various household activities cannot exceed the total time available for the household to expend. The maximisation of household utility now recognises not only allocation of time between different competing uses, but also between different activities of the household (including paid work outside the household, unpaid work within the household and

leisure). The mathematical development of this argument is
contained in the Appendix at the end of this chapter.

(b) Time: Allocation Between Husband and Wife

For an optimal allocation of time between husband and wife with
respect to market work, household work and leisure, it is necessary
to specify measures of the relative efficiency of these household
members in performing these activities. The efficiency of different
members of the household in market production and household
production (including rearing and educating children) may vary
significantly enough for greater gains in utility to result from
household division of labour. For example, conventional wisdom
would have us believe that a wife is more efficient in household
production and in rearing children, while the husband is more
efficient in market production or earning a relatively higher
monetary income. Evidence for this is deduced from the higher
market wage rate per hour of the husband and higher household
output per hour of the wife's time.[7] If one discounts the problems of
measuring household output, the existence of wage discrimination
between the sexes and the importance of sex role stereotyping in
most societies, the logical conclusion is that, for a household to
maximise its utility, it allocates the available time of its members
according to certain given efficiency indices.

There is an interesting implication for labour supply that arises
from the household choice model outlined above. Since any activity
which utilises market goods and services or time involves the
allocation of scarce resources among competing alternatives, it
follows that a wide range of activities from household formation
through marriage and family building, church attendance, crime
and even suicide can be given an economic interpretation within the
framework of the above model. Of the activities listed, fertility
behaviour has an important bearing on the labour supply decisions
of married women. The incorporation of fertility into the household
choice model will now be discussed briefly.

(c) Incorporation of Fertility and Other Considerations

A household has available a time budget which it allocates not only
to produce market and household goods, but also to produce 'child

services', devoting whatever time is left to leisure. There are two elements in the production of child services. The first element involves the *number* of children produced, whose inputs consist of the household time expended on the *physical* aspects of childbearing and childrearing on the one hand and the market inputs (such as prams and baby food) on the other. The other element which involves improving the *quality* of children also requires time inputs (e.g. teaching a child to read) and market inputs (e.g. purchase of children's books). The household is both a producing unit of child services and a consumer of child services from which it derives utility or satisfaction.[8]

To sum up, there are four elements in the household choice theory of optimal allocation of household resources among competing uses:[9]

1. A utility function (with a single decision maker for the household) whose arguments are not physical goods and services but bundles of attributes.
2. A technology of household production incorporated in production functions whose inputs are time and market commodities.
3. An external labour market environment which provides the means by which part of the household resources (mainly time) are transformed into market commodities.
4. A set of household resource constraints.

The theory provides a framework for these elements to be combined to provide an optimal allocation scheme for limited household resources to be distributed among a number of competing ends. More particularly, it provides a theory of optimal allocation of time between market work and other activities for all adult household members including the wife or mother. Mathematical extensions of the theory to take account of different household compositions and activities are easily achieved.

Implications of Household Choice Theory for Female Labour Supply

Before the theoretical framework outlined above can be used to consider the labour force participation behaviour of married women, the following further assumptions need to be made:[10]

1. Child-care activity is relatively highly time-intensive for the mother and this intensity falls with a child's age.
2. The male partner is more efficient (i.e. has a comparative advantage) in obtaining market commodities through market work than the female. Therefore the male tends to be almost completely specialised in market work.
3. Market wage rates are reasonable indicators of the opportunity value of market work or the opportunity cost of not working.

If the above assumptions hold, the following implications of the household choice theory for female labour supply can be drawn:

1. A rise in female wage rates will raise the opportunity cost of the time allocated by the wife to home production and consequently lead to a movement away from time-intensive basic commodities, such as children and home-baked bread, to those requiring more market inputs.
2. Family composition, through its effect on the value of the mother's time at home, is strongly associated with her labour force behaviour.
3. The value placed by the household on the wife's time is to an important extent determined by her labour force status. Gronau (1973) has shown that the value of time of housewives exceeds the average working wage of working women in the USA by less than 20%, while in the case of women who opt for market work, the value of their time falls short of the average wage rate by about 20–30%. He found that the practice of equating the value of the time of housewives with that of working women yielded an error of the magnitude of about 20% in the case of white housewives and an even larger margin in the case of blacks. This margin varied with the housewife's characteristics such as her age, education, income, number and age-composition of her children.
4. While child care tends to be more time-intensive than any other home production activity, withdrawal of mothers from the labour force is strongly associated with their level of educational attainment. A study by Ben Porath (1973) of Israeli women with young children found that initially labour force participation fell as the level of educational attainment rose, but above a certain level of education of the mother

participation rates started to rise.[11] Educational levels were having different effects on the relative efficiency of home and market production, particularly with respect to the interactions between education and quality of children.

5. A promising area of empirical research has been opened up on the determinants of fertility behaviour. Previous work has concentrated on the impact of such correlates as religion, social class, race, income, education and place of residence (e.g. rural or urban) in 'explaining' variations in completed family size. Apart from the *ad hoc* nature of such work, recent data, particularly in the USA, have shown that the explanatory power of these variables has decreased considerably (Andorka, 1978). A useful contribution of the household choice theory is that it has shifted the emphasis from such social correlates and focuses on fertility behaviour as the outcome of one among a number of household resource allocation decisions. In the process, a new list of variables has become relevant. It includes:

(a) the relative demand for child services *vis-à-vis* other 'commodities';

(b) the desired allocation of time among various activities (including market work) by both husband and wife;

(c) the perceived opportunity cost of children which could be defined *either* in narrow economic terms as the income lost through the job interruption effect, *or* broadly in 'psychological' terms as all satisfactions foregone;

(d) the perceived costs and benefits of contraception and abortion.

There are major problems in empiricising the economic model of fertility. They include unavailability of suitable data, difficulties in obtaining empirical equivalents of the variables listed above and problems in specifying the dynamic nature of the reproductive process.[12]

Limitations of Household Choice Theory

There are certain limitations inherent in the theory itself which restrict its validity both for describing labour force participation decisions of married women and for the projections of the female labour supply in the future. They are:

1. The specified utility function ignores the presence of at least two decision-makers in a standard household whose 'interactions' (or disagreements!) have important implications for the formation of household preferences and the desired allocation of resources between activities. For example, the interactions of husband and wife and possibly older children in a household will often affect subsequent fertility, irrespective of the effect of other factors. A static and timeless utility function incorporating the preferences of a single decision-maker is hardly an accurate representation of the sequential and dynamic nature of household functions. Even if the utility function is assumed to be a reasonably accurate reflection of reality, the fundamental question remains: If household formation is dependent on resource allocation decisions, who makes these decisions and at what point does the utility function come in?

2. An important implicit assumption in the household choice theory is that each 'commodity' entering the utility function is assumed to be produced independently of each other commodity. For example, in the incorporation of fertility as an additional argument, its components — number of children and quality of children — are assumed to enter separately in the household utility function, produced by independent production processes. (This formulation not only ignores the obvious negative correlation between number of children and quality of children — however measured — but by neglecting the sequential and dynamic aspect of household investment in child quality, it cannot explain a tendency in most poor societies to invest heavily in the education of the eldest male child compared to younger children.)

An important consequence of assuming that production activities (and the utilities resulting from them) are separable and independent is that certain complementarities between the activities are neglected. A number of dimensions of child quality — health, physical development and intellectual growth — which are inextricably interrelated, considered in the dynamic setting of a growing child, cannot be validly represented.

3. It is in the representation of the assumptions underlying the transformation of household resources into market commodities to be used in household production that the static nature of the model has serious repercussions for fertility and labour force participation of married women. A whole range of factors such as timing and spacing of births, opportunities for part-time work, accumulation of

paid employment experience and even the extent of investment in education for future employment are determined by the changing terms (influenced in the short run by the state of the economy and in the long term by the acceptability of women in a wide range of jobs) under which women can participate in the labour market.[13] The static nature of the model precludes the incorporation of the cyclical and secular changes in labour force participation of married women. These changes will be discussed in some detail later in this study.[14]

4. The relationship between household production and the inputs entering into the production process is not as simple as envisaged in the model described above. Certain products — such as sleep and food — are themselves inputs into the production of household resources and are passed on from generation to generation. In a study by Liebowitz (1972) using the data of Terman's 1921 sample of Californian school children, it was found that the amount of time invested by a mother on her child and the quality of the investment (as measured by the mother's education) had a significant effect on her child's (or children's) learning potential.

The whole problem of inter-generational links cannot be handled within the static framework of the model. Not only is the question of the effects of one generation's inputs on the output of the next generation at issue, but the whole problem of inter-generational change in household preferences brought about by new technology and changing attitudes of people to their environment (e.g. growing concern with pollution and health) cannot be captured by the model.

5. There remains the criticism made specifically about the economics of fertility which could also be applied more generally to the household choice theory. Household decisions are assumed to be made *in vacuo*, independently of outside influences and events. It is its neutrality from the political and sociological considerations and its neglect of the 'normative' side of individual behaviour that has led some social scientists to dismiss it as naive (Blake, 1968; Ryder, 1973). For example, labour force participation decisions of married women are to a considerable extent determined by their position in society, which in turn depends at least partly on the organisation of production (including who owns the means of production) and the class divisions that exist. To the extent that married women workers are still considered by many as a 'marginal class', and are concentrated in a limited range of jobs and suffer

from both job and wage discrimination, decisions on their participation even at the household level cannot be free of these considerations.

Economic Factors in Participation Decisions of Women: Modelling for Empirical Implementation

The household choice theory has helped to identify a number of factors which influence the labour force participation behaviour of married women. Some of these factors, as we have seen, pose serious difficulties in any empirical work, either because of the unavailability of suitable data or because of the problems of translating certain theoretical concepts into empirical measures.[15] Often when the original variable is difficult to measure, a proxy variable which is expected to correspond closely theoretically or statistically to the original variable is used. For example, De Tray (1973) used expected school investment per child as a proxy measure of the quality of children variable and difference in the years of schooling as a proxy measure of the relative efficiency of husband's and wife's work in household production.

Primary Factor: Income

Among the measurable variables which affect the labour force participation behaviour of married women are:

1. *Household income*: This consists of the sum of all real earnings (net of tax) plus any 'unearned' real income (net of tax but including welfare benefits) of a household. There has been some argument on whether it is the level of current family income or the 'permanent' family income which is the more appropriate measure of income.

   An increase in the family's other sources of income (excluding wife's earnings) would increase the demand for wife's leisure and home goods, so that eventually the wife could drop out of the labour force altogether and devote her time exclusively between home production and leisure. This effect of income on labour supply is often called the 'income effect'.

2. *Wife's earnings*: If a wife's potential earnings from supplying one unit of market work are measured by the overall female wage rate, a rise in this wage rate could be an important

stimulus to participation in the labour force by raising the relative price of the time spent on her leisure and home production *vis-à-vis* market work. The effect of the wage rate on labour supply is often referred to as the 'substitution' effect. What is being substituted here is market work for non-market activities or *vice versa*, depending on whether the wage rate rises or falls.

There is no analytical means of ascertaining the relative strengths of the income and substitution effects. An important area of empirical research, particularly in the US, has been the impact of the two effects resulting from cyclical fluctuations in the economy on the labour force participation rate of different demographic groups. A discussion of some of these studies, particularly pertaining to the British economy, will be found in the next section. Derived from these two effects are two competing hypotheses capable of empirical verification.

The first hypothesis states that as the level of economic activity declines (i.e. the economy is in its downswing phase), some members of the household may lose their jobs and leave the labour force. It is implicit in this argument that the 'discouraged workers' could consist of both 'primary' workers (i.e. males in the working age-span) and 'secondary' workers (i.e. the rest, including married women).[16] This is the *'discouraged worker' hypothesis.*

The second hypothesis states that as the economy declines, a sufficient number of 'secondary' workers (the major component being married women) will enter to offset reduced household income as a result of a fall in earnings (e.g. no overtime work) or loss of job by the husband. This is called the *'additional worker' hypothesis.*

An immediate problem that arises in empirical work is to devise measures to capture the impact of the economy on household income or wife's earnings. An obvious income measure would be the difference between current (or actual) household income and the 'permanent' household income. A shortfall in the 'permanent' household income, measured by this difference, will have an 'additional worker' effect through the operation of the income effect. Similarly, an earnings measure is the deviation of female earnings from some previously defined *norm.* An increase in this deviation, through the 'substitution' effect, will have a 'discouraged worker' effect.

In any empirical work, direct measures of these two indices are well-nigh impossible. So often the unemployment rate, which is a widespread proxy measure of the level of economic activity, is used instead on the assumption that it is *positively* related to both the income and earnings measures defined in the previous paragraph. An increase in the unemployment rate could, through the substitution effect, discourage participation in the labour force; and at the same time it could increase participation by the need to maintain or augment household income. Depending on whether a significant positive or negative association exists between the labour force participation rates of married women and the overall employment effect, it can be inferred whether the 'net' role effect supports the 'additional' or 'discouraged' worker effect.[17] As will be shown later, studies both in the USA and the UK suggest that the 'discouraged worker' effect has predominated for much of the post-war period, probably implying that the female workers have borne the brunt of the recessions in terms of employment opportunities.

Secondary Factor: Number and Location of Flexi-Time Jobs

Most empirical work in this area has involved models in which the two main 'explanatory' variables (i.e. variables 'explaining' variations in the labour force participation rates) were 'income' and the unemployment rate (a proxy for the level of economic activity).[18] For married females, an important additional variable is the availability of accessible jobs with flexible hours. There have been a number of attempts to construct measures of this influence on labour force participation. Barth (1968) and Cain (1966) used proportions employed in the trade and service sectors in their examination of geographical variations in the labour force participation rates of secondary worker groups (including married women) in the USA on the basis that these workers would be concentrated in these sectors.

A better measure used first by Bowen and Finegan (1969) is an *Industry-Occupation Mix Index*. It measures the percentage of jobs in each area which can be *expected* to be held by a specific group (e.g. married women) on the basis of the industry-occupation mix of that area. For example if one wanted to construct the Index for married women for all 68 sub-regions of Great Britain using information contained in the 1971 Population Census, one would begin by computing the employment rates of married women for *each* occupation-industry sub-category nationally. The product of these rates and the corresponding numbers in total employment for each sub-region would give the *expected* number of married women employed in each sub-region. The ratio of the expected numbers in employment to actual numbers in employment in each sub-region would provide a measure of the 'attractiveness' of that sub-region as a source of suitable jobs for married women.[19] This measure could be extended to reflect additional attributes, such as part-time job availability and proximity of jobs to places of residence.[20]

Specification of a Labour Force Participation Function for Married Women: The Initial Stages

Apart from the primary economic variables of income, wage rate, unemployment and to a smaller extent some measure of employment opportunities, there has been a tendency in a number of empirical studies to introduce a series of 'control' or 'non-economic' intruder variables more or less on an *ad hoc* basis. As an illustration, take a model specified by Bowen and Finegan (1969) to examine the determinants of the labour force participation of married women in the US. Writing it in the form of an equation where the left-hand side contains the *dependent* variable — labour force participation rate — and the right-hand side contains the *determining* or explanatory variables, the relationship is expressed as:

$$m = b_1 + b_2 A + b_3 C + b_4 S + b_5 H + b_6 OFM + b_7 LH + b_8 WF + b_9 U + b_{10} DF + b_{11} SF$$

where m (labour force participation rate) is expressed as a linear function of *personal characteristics* such as Age (A), colour (C), number of years of schooling (S); of *household characteristics* such as home commitments (H), number of children (CH), other family members (OFM), labour force status of husband (LH); and of *labour market characteristics* such as female wage rate (WF), overall unemployment rate (U), industry-occupation mix (DF) and female-male mix (SF).

Apart from WF, U and possibly DF and SF, all other variables are considered as 'control' or 'intruder variables. Their inclusion often serves one primary purpose which is to remove any variations in the

participation rates, that could be statistically attributed to them —
i.e. to 'clean' away the influences of these variables on labour force
participation. The focus of interest is mainly on the magnitude and
sign of the coefficients of WF, U and possibly DF and SF.

If one ignores the problems of meaningfully measuring the
variables specified above and the difficulties of providing valid
statistical interpretations for the estimated regression line of the
equation,[21] the estimated values of the co-efficients ($b_1, b_2, \ldots b_{11}$)
have precise economic meanings. The value of each coefficient is an
indication of the 'net' or 'partial' effect of its variable on m. For
example, b_8 measures the net effect of a 1% change in the average
female wage rate (WF) on the average labour force participation
rate (m). We would expect the coefficient WF to be positive.

It is clear that we have moved some distance from the well-
integrated household choice theory approach to participation
decisions where only traces of the microeconomic theoretical
underpinnings remain. The *ad hoc* nature of the empirical model
can be partly attributed to serious data problems and partly to the
difficulties of devising empirical measures for theoretical concepts
which have no direct empirical equivalents. This does not mean that
the empirical possibilities have been explored to any great extent.
For example, an important influence on the labour force
participation of married women is the presence of children in the
household. The empirical model of Bowen and Finegan (1969)
outlined above has one variable to take account of this influence,
i.e. number of children (CH). The specification implies that CH
affects m *independently* of home commitments (H), labour force
status of husband (LH), other family members (OFM), number of
years of schooling (S), etc. The household choice theory emphasises
the inter-relationships between these variables and shows them as
part of household allocation decisions.

A specification of the relationship between presence of children
and labour force participation decisions closer to the spirit of the
household choice theoretic approach would consider prices of
different kinds of 'commodities' (P_N, P_G, P_X, P_{G_M}), the male and
female wage rates (W_M, W_W), efficiency indices of males and
females in various household activities and the ease with which
members of the household can substitute between production of
monetary income, household commodities and child services as
being important determinants of the number and quality of children

and ultimately of the labour force participation behaviour of married women. (The symbols refer to the mathematical development of the household choice theory contained in the Appendix at the end of this chapter.) The mis-specification errors arising from the Bowen and Finegan formulation are considered to be mainly a consequence of its *ad hoc* nature which in turn is a result of the general neglect of the microeconomic decision framework.

Labour Force Participation and Married Women: A Review of Empirical Work

During the last four or five decades, economists in the USA and Britain have concentrated much of their attention on finding empirical answers to the following questions:
1. If the working population of a country is divided into distinctive demographic groups by age, sex and marital status, are there any significant variations in their labour force participation behaviour in response to changes in the economy (or to what are often referred to as *cyclical* changes)?
2. For any given group at a particular point in time, what and how important are various factors in 'explaining' differences in the participation behaviour of its members?

Answers to these questions are sought for a number of reasons. If the group in question consists of married women, the answers may be useful in illuminating past trends in the labour force participation of this group and in assessing its future patterns of labour activity. Second, and this reason applies particularly to married women and other 'secondary' workers, the true numbers of the unemployed should consist of the sum of recorded (or registered) unemployed and the unregistered (or hidden) unemployed. Estimates of the potential labour force, an important part of the exercise of stock-taking of the available human resources in a country, would require account to be taken of both these components. Third, estimates of certain labour supply parameters (such as income and wage elasticities) are useful to a government in predicting the effects on labour supply of changes in taxes and social security benefits (assessed on earned and unearned incomes of different household members).[22] An examination of the efficiency of a country's tax structure presupposes the knowledge of such elasticity estimates.

The Two Approaches

In examining either cyclical responses or the determinants of labour force participation of a particular group, two main approaches have been used in empirical work[23] In seeking to answer the first question, a *time-series* approach is generally used; this concentrates on an examination of how labour force attachments change over a trade cycle. Do a larger number of women join or leave the labour force when an economy is on the downturn compared to the numbers on the upswing? This approach makes fewer demands on statistical data, using mainly two labour market indicators — numbers employed and numbers unemployed — which are made to act as proxies for a host of cyclical factors that affect short-run labour force participation.

In seeking to answer the second question a *cross-sectional* approach is usual; the objective of this type of analysis is to examine the determinants of the labour force participation behaviour of various groups at particular moments in time. It often uses data on a large number of explanatory variables derived mainly from Population Censuses or labour force surveys. The large number of variables is needed to provide a reasonable 'explanation' of household or geographical differences in labour force participation. A statistical consequence of the resulting large regression models is to diminish the reliability of the estimates.[24] A further difficulty with this approach is that all variables are measured at a particular point in time (i.e. the date of the census or survey) and therefore important questions concerning the impact of timing and duration of unemployment as well as its seasonal variation will not ordinarily enter into the analysis of labour force behaviour.

There are also certain thorny questions of comparability between estimates obtained from the two approaches such as:

(a) do estimates from time-series studies measure the same responses as those from comparable cross-sectional studies, particularly with respect to unemployment?

(b) do differences in the nature of the relationship between husbands' earnings and wives' labour force participation indicated by time-series and cross-sectional studies show, as Mincer (1962) argued, that the impact of household income and prices on labour force participation of wives is qualitatively different from that on husbands?

These and other questions, discussed in great detail in Mincer (1966) which incidentally provides one of the best surveys of earlier empirical studies in this area, will not be gone into in the present study.

The Time-Series Approach

A: Early American Studies

In 1940 Woytinsky sought to measure the number of 'additional' workers pressurised into entering the labour force as a result of wide-spread unemployment among primary workers (i.e. male workers within the working age-span) during the Great Depression in the 1930s. His conclusion that the secondary workers (predominant among whom were married women) would exaggerate the numbers unemployed during periods of high unemployment was soon challenged by Humphrey (1940) who argued that the 'discouraged' workers leaving the labour force during those periods would more than offset the additional workers entering the labour force to supplement household income. While the reverberations of this controversy still echo in recent studies, the general conclusion to emerge from American studies is that the net discouraged worker effect is dominant for all secondary workers, especially married women. What this implies is that labour force participation of secondary workers is pro-cyclical in the sense that the lower the unemployment rate, the higher the labour force participation and *vice versa*.[25] A number of attempts have been made to use estimates of cyclical fluctuations in the labour force to derive the numerical magnitudes of labour 'reserves' of hidden unemployment. Joseph (1978) estimated hidden unemployment among married women in Britain, taking the 'natural' rate of unemployment of 5.1%, amounted to about 200,000 in 1971. The following reservations should be made about estimating labour reserves from 'unemployment' models of labour force participation.

(1) Most studies use the unemployment rate as a measure of demand and, therefore, of the state of the economy. Strictly speaking, the unemployment rate measures excess labour supply as a ratio of the labour force. It can only be used as a proxy for demand on the assumption that a stable negative relationship holds between excess labour supply and level of demand.

(2) Mincer (1966) has pointed out that in the absence of some

alteration in the 'allocative efficiency of the market', it is not
valid to treat a figure derived from an estimation based on a
fixed, arbitrary level of unemployment (which reflects the full
employment level) as an accurate figure for the labour reserve.
(3) There is an implicit assumption that the relative (market)
productivities of the hidden unemployed and the recorded
unemployed are the same. Since the hidden unemployed are
found mainly among secondary workers, who tend to be
concentrated in part-time work in low productivity occupations,
the assumption is not valid.

In general, estimates of labour reserves tend to be overestimates.

B: British Studies

Hunter (1963):   All the work mentioned so far has dealt with the
American experience. An early study by Hunter tested the relative
strength of the additional and discouraged worker hypothesis
during the recessions and upswings in the British economy for the
period 1951–60. The analysis was carried out in terms of comparing
the movement and timing of unemployment rates with the total
labour force participation rates between cyclical peaks and troughs
for four periods during 1951–60. It was found that the labour force
in Britain had reacted to changing market conditions in such a way
as to dampen fluctuations in the demand for labour. In
expansionary periods there had been relative increases in
participation, whereas in recessions there had been contraction.
The fact that the study did not distinguish between responses by sex
and marital status, as well as the comparative mildness and brevity
of recessions during the short sample period under study, should not
detract from the value of this early attempt to test the cyclical
sensitivity of labour supply in Britain. The discovery that, despite
institutional differences, labour supply reacted in the same way as in
the USA, provided some impetus to further empirical work in this
area.
Other British Studies: A number of studies in this country have
focused on the nature and stability of the relationship between
employment and registered unemployment as a means of assessing
the relative strength of the additional and discouraged worker
effects. Godley and Shepherd (1964) found, from the incorporation
of the unemployment rate and a trend factor (to pick up long-term

changes in participation rates) as explanatory variables, and total civilian employment as the dependent variable, within the framework of a linear regression model a highly significant negative unemployment coefficient. They concluded that this implied a net discouraged worker effect for the period 1951–1961, though the highly aggregative nature of the data used would tend to subsume any differences in the responses of various demographic groups.

In a later study, Shepherd (1968) concluded that a non-linear relationship existed between unemployment and employment, and deduced that a rising level of unemployment was associated with the falling importance of the net discouraged effect as measured by the unemployment coefficient. Similar conclusions were reached by Anyanwa (1969) using 'pooled' time series and regional data. Using similar data, Webb (1970) found that from the end of 1966 or beginning of 1967 a change had occurred in the relationship between employment and recorded unemployment, though whether such a change was due to a fundamental shift in the decision to register as unemployed, or whether it was a manifestation of the non-linear nature of the relationship between the two variables as new levels of unemployment were reached, remained a matter of conjecture. Bosanquet and Standing (1972) and Taylor (1972) produced evidence to suggest that a structural shift in unemployment had taken place while Bowers et al. (1972), using labour turnover statistics for manufacturing industries as a measure of employment changes, found from an examination of the intercept terms and the slope coefficients of different regression equations (estimated for different sample periods chosen from quarterly data for 1952–1972) no evidence of any fundamental shifts.

Some Limitations of the Time-Series Approach

1. None of these studies allows for any differential effects between various age/sex/marital status groups. This is partly due to difficulties of obtaining disaggregated short-run data series on labour force and population. But more importantly, there exist considerable (though largely unmeasured) differences in the extent to which different groups register as unemployed. For example, among married women, since there is no financial incentive for most to register when they are not entitled to unemployment benefits, there can exist considerable discrepancy between those actually

seeking work and those who register as unemployed.[26] Recent studies by Joshi (1978, 1981) have investigated the relationship between registered and unregistered unemployment among secondary workers (and particularly pensioners and women) over different phases of the employment cycle for the period 1961–1974. Godley and Shepherd (1964) and Tarling (1976) have indicated that on the aggregate, for every worker who moved between employment and registered unemployment, or *vice versa*, there was another 'hidden' or missing worker who moved between registered unemployment and unregistered unemployment or out of the labour force. Joshi examined the magnitude of the 'missing worker' effect for four groups who had different attachments to the National Unemployment Insurance Scheme: uninsured married women, uninsured older workers, insured older workers and the rest of the work force. Some of her main conclusions were:

(a) The 'missing worker' effect was relatively more pronounced among uninsured work categories, indicating that they belonged to the margin of the *true* labour force (i.e. including unregistered unemployed) rather than to the registered labour force.

(b) The groups among the uninsured workers who showed greater sensitivity to cyclical movement in employment (as measured by the relative volatility of the numbers of missing workers) were all pensioner groups and women under 35 (a predominant number of whom consisted of married women re-entering the labour force between the ages of 25 to 35). The experience of women aged 45–59 with respect to cyclical changes in employment was not significantly different from that of men, in that both groups exhibited considerable cyclical stability.

(c) Of those groups exhibiting the greatest volatility, their role as 'auxiliary labour supply to the economy' operated through a dynamic process of 'acceleration and postponement of entries and exits (from the labour force) rather than drawing on a reserve pool of individuals who are prepared to work sporadically' (Joshi, 1981, p. 40).

(d) There is little support for the thesis that there would be a significant difference in cyclical variation between the numbers claiming unemployment benefit among married women and the rest of the labour force if unemployment benefits were made available to all married women. This follows from the result that the majority of married women workers (i.e. as a percentage of the total married female labour force) were aged 35 or over and fell into the less volatile group. A slack labour market will not, therefore, bring about a proportionately greater claim on unemployment on the part of married women compared to the rest of the labour force.

2. There is no attempt to examine the effect of variations in unemployment duration on the labour force participation behaviour of different groups for different phases of the cycle. The last decade has seen many studies of the *determinants* of unemployment duration in this country. They have concentrated either on experiences of cohorts of redundant workers (Mackay and Reid, 1972), *or* on a cross-section of unemployed workers (Daniel, 1974), *or* on the negative relationship between unemployment duration and probability of re-employment (McGregor, 1978). There has been little empirical work on the effect of unemployment duration on decisions to stay in or withdraw from the labour force. A study by Joseph (1982) using a Markov chain model found that, for the period 1950–1965, the discouragement effect of long-term unemployment on females was slightly greater in the upswing of the cycle than in the downswing, indicating the greater importance of the income or additional worker effect when the level of economic activity is declining. For males, the evidence of a discouragement effect is mixed. For the period until the late fifties, the effect was negative insofar as there was greater discouragement to participation arising from short-term unemployment compared to long-term unemployment. A positive discouragement effect operated for subsequent periods. There is also evidence that responses to cyclical changes have become more muted for both sexes in the seventies.

3. In the studies discussed before, no attempt was made to differentiate between the considerable variation among different groups as to their proneness to unemployment. Nickell (1980), in an examination of male unemployment in Britain based on data from the 1972 General Household Survey, found that certain groups were over-represented among the unemployed due either to the excessive duration of their spells of unemployment, or to their above-average chances of becoming unemployed. The groups identified consisted of the 'young', the 'old', the 'unskilled', those with large families, and people living in council houses in the

northern half of Britain. His main policy conclusion, particularly
relating to the older unemployed, is that employers should be
provided with special subsidies for taking the long-term
unemployed into their work force. A similar examination of female
unemployment using household survey data would be useful.[27]

4. An important relationship which is of topical concern is that
between duration of unemployment and level of unemployment
benefits. The ratio of unemployment and related benefits to after-
tax earnings (often referred to as the *replacement ratio*) in Britain
increased from about 22% in 1956 to about 39% in 1967 and has
remained stable ever since. As a consequence of this increase and
the absolute rise in the number of claimants (predominantly male),
these benefits have become an increasing item of government
expenditure. This has prompted the question: do increased benefits
encourage unemployment through individuals opting either for
voluntary unemployment or for increasing the length of spells of
unemployment by becoming more choosy about the new jobs that
they will accept? There is little evidence that the former channel is
of any major importance. The rate of the monthly flow into
unemployment since 1967 bears little relation to the level of
unemployment and has remained stable in spite of the substantial
increase in the numbers unemployed. On the other hand, estimates
by Lancaster (1979) and Nickell (1979a) indicate that a 1% increase
in some measure of the replacement ratio is associated with a 0.6%
increase in male unemployment duration. In other words, a relative
increase in unemployment benefits could lead to the unemployed
'searching' for a longer period before accepting a new job.
However, Nickell (1979b) has found that the impact of the
replacement ratio declined as the unemployment duration
increased, so that there would be 'negligible efficiency losses' from
increasing the benefits of the long-term unemployed (i.e. 26 weeks
or more).

The impact of the duration and timing of unemployment on the
labour force participation of different groups is an area in which
considerable work remains to be done. While the recent increase in
the proportion of women who register as unemployed is likely to
make the participation behaviour more sensitive to unemployment
duration and less sensitive over the cycle, the movement of females
between registered unemployment, unregistered unemployment

and out of the labour force in response to cyclical factors is very difficult to quantify. Further, the discrepancy between the true labour force (*including* unregistered unemployed) and the recorded labour force (*excluding* unregistered unemployed) should make one cautious of the validity of conclusions drawn in empirical work using administrative statistics (i.e. statistics collected at Employment Exchanges).

Approaches Incorporating Cross-Sectional Data

The main focus of the discussion so far has been on empirical work relating to labour force participation decisions in response to cyclical fluctuations. We now examine empirical work done in this country in response to the second question stated at the beginning of this section: what are the *determinants* of labour force participation behaviour of specified groups, particularly married women?

Corry and Roberts (1970) and (1974)

A study of the determinants of short-run fluctuations in the labour force which is close to the spirit of a number of cross-sectional American studies[28] is that of Corry and Roberts. The authors used regional annual data for the UK for the period 1951–1966 to test:

(a) whether a significant inverse relationship existed between regional unemployment levels and labour force participation rates;
(b) whether differential responses to unemployment operated between different age and marital status groups;
(c) the nature of the timing of labour force participation rates to changes in unemployment rates.

They found little evidence for (a), and for (b) they found that a 1% rise in registered unemployment was associated with a fall of $\frac{1}{3}$ % and 1% of the labour force participation rates of males and females respectively. Finally, in response to (c), they found that the introduction of an unemployment variable lagged one year improved the significance of the unemployment coefficient, possibly indicating a delay in the timing of labour force responses to changes in the demand for labour (as measured by unemployment). The main limitations of this study are: (i) the use of small samples,

(ii) poor statistical fits of the estimated regression equations (as measured by the low values of the statistic R^2), and (iii) certain specification problems arising from difficulties in distinguishing between *true* and *measured* variations in labour participation rates. There were also doubts about the appropriateness of using single equation models where identification problems and simultaneous bias were present.

Reservations about the reliability of results from work by Corry and Roberts are further highlighted if they are compared with those obtained in an earlier work by Galambos (1967). Galambos used the Analysis of Variance approach to examine data on labour force participation rates by age and sex for Great Britain for the period 1951–1964. His main conclusions were:

(a) the presence of significant differences in participation rates between regions;

(b) the existence of a significant (rank) correlation between regional labour force trends and both regional unemployment levels and net migration levels (or net migration rates), possibly indicating a movement of sections of the labour force away from high unemployment regions; and

(c) significant rising trends in the female labour force for all regions.

Wabe (1969)

An early cross-sectional study of male and female participation rates by Wabe used 1951 and 1961 population census data on 122 suburban London boroughs. Individuals in any one of these boroughs have the following choices open to them with respect to labour market activity. They can either find employment within the borough in which they reside, *or* travel to central London for employment, *or* travel to another suburban borough in search of a job, *or* remain economically inactive. Each option has costs and benefits associated with it. For example, if they opt for the first alternative — i.e. find employment within their home borough — they are likely to receive a wage rate lower than in the centre, though this has to be balanced against the savings in costs in terms of time and money as a result of avoiding travelling to the centre, as well as the lower rents to be paid for accommodation the further they are away from the centre.[29] Wabe suggests that a negative association exists between labour force participation rates and journey times for the following reasons:

(a) Only those households where travel to work outweighs the higher property prices to be paid to live near the centre will choose to live close to the centre. These households will exclude old age pensioners and households where wives are likely to be economically inactive because of family responsibilities.

(b) The opportunity cost of economic inactivity rises as the costs of travel fall and the wage differentials between the centre and outer boroughs increase. This would affect both the choice of married women between market work and housework and the decision of older workers to retire or not.

Wabe distinguishes between two sets of variables affecting labour force participation of male and female populations of the boroughs studied. First, there are the 'economic variables' consisting of wage differentials, journey time to work, cost of travel to work and availability of jobs measured by the ratio of population working in the borough to the resident population. Second, the 'structural variables' consist of the age and social class composition of the population, the proportion of young children in the borough population and the proportion of institutional inmates in the borough.

Empirical results for females showed that over 80% of the variation in labour force participation rates for 1951 and 1961 were 'explained' by these economic and structural variables. The coefficients of journey time and price of travel were significant and negative; the single most important variable, the borough's job opportunities index, was positive and highly significant; and the structural variables which were significant had the 'right' signs. The results regarding social class were interesting. While the explanatory power of the social class variable fell over the two years, it was still significant and positive, indicating the existence of greater economic activity among women in the upper social classes. It is a moot point whether the differences in educational attainment and occupational structure *or* inherent class differences are more reflected in preference for market work between classes. The study also showed that women are much more influenced by the amount of time taken in travelling to work than the price of travel, given the constraints imposed by their other household commitments.

Greenhalgh (1977) and McNabb (1977)

Two more recent examples of census-based cross-sectional studies of determinants of labour force participation of married women in this country are those of Greenhalgh and McNabb. Both use 1971 census data with Greenhalgh's sample consisting of 106 towns and McNabb's of 63 subregions in Britain. In McNabb's model, variations in labour force participation rates are attributed to average hourly earnings of male manual workers, male and female unemployment rates, a measure of 'industry mix' to reflect female labour-intensive industries, a measure of educational attainment, a measure of the number of 'New Commonwealth' immigrants,[30] and finally the relative number of households with family responsibilities. The above list of explanatory variables can be readily translated into the list of variables incorporated in the generalised empirical model given in the last section. The average hourly earnings of female workers is a proxy for a wife's wage rate. A rise in wage rates could be an important stimulus to participation by raising the relative price of the time spent on leisure and home production *vis-à-vis* market work. The effect of the wage rate on labour supply is positive through the operation of the substitution effect.

As a measure of the 'other' household income, the average hourly earnings of male workers is taken as a proxy. This is unsatisfactory, since no recognition is given to the importance of 'unearned' income, nor are male hourly earnings a suitable measure of 'other' earned income of a household. Unemployment rates are incorporated as proxies for demand for labour, and would as a consequence measure the net impact of added worker and discouraged worker effects.

Estimates of 'own' income elasticity of 1.25, an insignificant 'other' income elasticity and a net discouraged effect indicated by the difference between an elasticity with respect to female unemployment of −2.5 (interpreted as showing discouraged worker effect) and a male unemployment elasticity of 1 (interpreted as showing added worker effect) are the main conclusions of McNabb's study.

The major innovation of Greenhalgh's study is the introduction of two proxies for 'unearned' income. The first, the median income of taxable units in each of her sample towns, turned out to be statistically insignificant. However the other, consisting of the proportion of houses with basic amenities (which has little more than a tenuous association with unearned income or wealth), was found to be significantly negative. Unlike McNabb, Greenhalgh only incorporated a male unemployment variable whose significant negative coefficient was interpreted as reflecting a discouraged worker effect. A new variable measuring 'deficient demand' unemployment is incorporated to capture the added worker effect.[31] Its significant positive coefficient exceeded the negative coefficient reflecting the discouraged worker effect and the conclusion was reached that, unlike McNabb, the added effect predominated. Greenhalgh also found that the presence of 'New Commonwealth' immigrants had a significant positive effect on the labour force participation rates of married women.

A comparison of these two studies with a similar data base highlights some of the difficulties inherent in empirical work of this nature. Diametrically opposite conclusions were reached on the effect of demand (as measured by unemployment) on the labour force participation behaviour of married females. Measurement of certain variables (e.g. unearned income) pose serious problems and the use of proxies leaves some doubts as to their efficacy. Conflicting results on the statistical significance of certain variables (e.g. the presence of 'New Commonwealth' immigrants) cast further doubts on the credibility of the results. Finally, assumptions regarding mutual statistical independence of the explanatory variables and the form of the relationship specified in the estimating equations are difficult to justify.

Limitations Common to Both Approaches: Available Options

Given these difficulties and the inconclusive or conflicting results obtained from these studies, there are three courses of action open to an empirical researcher. First, he can discontinue empirical work of this nature, conceding that it is not practicable to make a statistical translation from fuzzy theoretical concepts to empirically derived measures or proxies for these concepts. Second, the *ad hoc* nature of much of the empirical modelling which constitutes the substance of such studies needs to be eliminated by developing a well-integrated microeconomic model of labour supply, such as the household choice model discussed in the previous section. On the other hand it may be equally well argued that, if serious data problems and difficulties of devising empirical measures for theoretical concepts which have no direct empirical equivalents can be resolved, the *ad hoc* nature of much of the empirical work in this area would be diminished. Third, it is argued, an important reason for the unsatisfactory nature of most of the results arises from the highly aggregated nature of the data used in the studies discussed so far. Disaggregated studies using an individual household as the unit of observation offer certain real advantages. The main one is that since labour supply decisions are made at the household level, a household data base offers estimates of empirical measures (such as elasticities) which have a direct interpretation in relation to the theoretical model and at the same time avoids vexing aggregation problems in the estimation procedures. Other advantages of using disaggregated data are greater statistical precision in estimates arising from the availability of larger samples and much greater variation in observations, particularly with respect to more elaborate hypotheses.

Recent British Studies Using Individual Household Data

Two recent studies of married female labour supply by Greenhalgh (1980a) and Layard *et al.* (1980) use individual household data from the General Household Surveys of 1971 and 1974 respectively.[32] In these studies two measures of labour supply are used, labour force participation rates and number of hours worked. The use of household data with respect to number of hours worked raises two fundamental problems which need to be sorted out before estimation is possible. First, the treatment of after-tax earnings as exogenous to the model ignores the dependence of the number of hours worked on the tax rates at the margins of the earnings limit.[33] The biases arising from ignoring simultaneous determination of taxes paid with hours of work and earnings may be sufficient to reverse the direction of effect of such variables as wage rates and incomes on the labour supply of married women. Second, the existence of various tax rates for different income bands introduces non-linearities into the budget constraint equation usually specified in linear form as in Equation (3) in the Appendix to this chapter. Solutions involve either estimating parameters of the resulting non-linear model by maximum likelihood techniques which can be a computationally   burdensome   procedure,   or   using   linear approximations to non-linear functions. The former approach has been used by Ashworth and Ulph (1977) and Wales and Woodland (1979) and the latter procedure by Greenhalgh (1980a) and Layard *et al.* (1980)

Greenhalgh found a positive 'own' elasticity with respect to labour force participation of 0.36 and an 'other' income elasticity of -0.35. These results are similar to those obtained by Layard *et al.* (1980), using different estimation procedures for data from the year 1974. A variable introduced by Layard *et al.* as a measure of the relative strength of added worker and discouraged worker effects found that wives with unemployed husbands were 30% less likely to work, indicating a strong discouraged worker effect. They attributed this result to the way that the supplementary benefits system is operated in Britain, where the benefits are reduced by the same amount as the additional earnings of the wife beyond a given earnings threshold.

It is with respect to the presence of children and the inhibiting influence on labour force participation that some of the more impressive results are obtained from using individual household data. There is agreement between the studies on the inhibiting effect of young children on the labour supply of wives, with the effect falling in magnitude as the age of the youngest child in the family rises, so that in those households with the youngest child over ten, the association between age and labour supply becomes non-significant or even slightly positive. As for family size, Greenhalgh estimated that the reduction of average family size by one child would have the total 'life-time' effect of raising labour force particpation rates by 4% and the number of hours of work supplied by 12.5%. The fact remains: the specification of the 'fertility' influences on participation is fairly simplistic from a demographic angle. Studies by Sweet (1973) and Dickinson (1976) indicate that the participation behaviour of mothers significantly affected birth order, spacing and timing of births, and the pattern of family formation in the past.

An important factor identified by both Greenhalgh and Layard *et al.* as having a depressing effect on labour force participation for all ages is poor health. In the case of wives, it is not only their ill-health that is relevant but also the additional home responsibility borne as a result of the ill-health of the other family members, especially children. Greenhalgh found that ill-health of wives reduced individual participation by 15% and poor health of dependents reduced the average number of hours worked by 11%.

In a previous section, a factor identified as pertinent to labour force participation decisions of married women was the availability of accessible jobs with flexible hours. A recent study by King (1978) tested the effects of greater flexibility in the hours of work on female labour force participation against an industry mix variable relating to type of jobs available. It was found that the variability of hours appeared more important for mothers with pre-school children, while the type of work available was more significant for women without children or with children of school age.

Empirical Studies and their Limitations: A Summing Up

To sum up, empirical work on female labour supply, whether seen in terms of participation or numbers of hours worked, has suffered from certain serious drawbacks.[34] Work on labour force participation has been bedevilled by the difficulty of obtaining time-series data on the numbers unemployed (including unregistered unemployed). There is some evidence that the proportion of women seeking work who register has risen noticeably over the last ten years. There is further evidence that the relative numbers who register are sensitive to cyclical changes. It is therefore clear that 'unemployment' models of labour force participation that ignore the unregistered unemployed would introduce a bias in the estimates whose nature, size and direction are difficult to assess.

On cyclical responses of the married female labour force there is fairly substantive evidence that the discouraged worker effect is dominant. A simple implication of this result is that there is a growing army of 'hidden' unemployed among secondary workers whose inclusion would make the present unemployment situation even more gloomy. But a note of caution needs to be sounded even here. Evidence from American studies shows that the cyclical sensitivity decreases as more comprehensive measures of labour supply are used. Even cross-sectional studies which overwhelmingly indicate a negative relationship between labour supply and unemployment have been questioned by Fleisher and Rhodes (1976). They argue, at least over space, both labour supply and unemployment are correlates of differences in the characteristics and work environment between different areas, and that as long as these differences persist, the positive effect on unemployment and negative effect on labour force participation will hold, irrespective of the cyclical phase of the economy.

An important objective of the cross-sectional studies in general has been to estimate labour supply elasticities with respect to wage rates and household income. If one examines the estimates made by different studies, one is struck by the marked variation that exists in these estimates. Greenhalgh's (1977) estimates based on town data from the 1971 Population Census gave a high wage elasticity of 1.35; while a later study by the same author (1980a) using household survey data for 1971 gave an estimate of 0.36. Again, using number of hours worked as a measure of labour supply, estimates of wage elasticity varied from 0.08 in the study by Layard *et al.* (1980) to 0.68 in the study by Greenhalgh (1980a), with the former using household data for 1974 and the latter for 1971. Further, the typical result in many of the studies using household data provides an explanation for only a small part of the variation in labour supply. Whilst differences in the results may be a reflection of differences in model specification, estimation procedures and data base, there is little unanimity as to what are acceptable results to use for policy prescriptions and labour supply predictions. There is some unease as to whether certain mis-specification errors have arisen as a result of not sufficiently emphasising the relationship that exists between decisions with respect to market work, housework and leisure in the case of married women, as well as the tendency to treat family structure as exogenous and determining labour supply when, as we saw in the last section, decisions relating to family creation and labour supply are simultaneous to some degree. No empirical study in this country has to date attempted to take account of these complications.

Other Approaches to Women and Work: Some Concluding Remarks

In this chapter, which attempted to provide an economic perspective to changes in the labour force participation behaviour, particularly of married women, the neoclassical paradigm has held sway.[35] In this approach, increased labour force participation of married women since the Second World War is explicable mainly in terms of two primary economic variables — price of labour and income of household — which in turn subsume a whole host of factors, including changes in 'tastes'. This reductionism (to a mere two variables) is seen by some as providing the key for statistical testing of various hypotheses regarding labour force participation decisions. The approach prides itself on the fact that it allows comparisons over space, time and social strata, since its subject of study is an individual who makes decisions without temporal, spatial or class constraints. It is this ahistorical characteristic and its neglect of the nature and relevance of power in moulding institutional and individual behaviour that makes the neoclassical paradigm an unsuitable vehicle for analysing long-term changes in the labour force participation behaviour of different groups.

There are two other paradigms which have relevance to a long-term analysis of women and work. The first views the increases in women's participation as a consequence of certain institutional changes. Two such changes are often identified. We have noted that the family as an institution has changed, particularly with respect to its decision processes and certain structural features, which in turn influence whether its members can take part in labour market activity or not. Again, as Oppenheimer (1970) shows, increased entry of women into the labour force has been facilitated by the greater availability of 'women's' work, both in terms of the growth of segmented labour markets and more flexible-hour jobs. The institutional paradigm provides an important basis for our discussion in a later chapter of occupational concentration by sex and the relatively low female earnings.

The second paradigm, the Marxist paradigm, offers a total contrast from the neoclassical view. In place of the operation of the market, the Marxist substitutes organisation of production. The primary variables, prices and incomes, of the Neoclassicist are, to the Marxists, merely ephemeral quantities underlying fundamental decisions about capital accumulation. What the Neoclassicist sees as household decisions on production and consumption taken on the basis of free choice, the Marxist views in terms of class conflict. Class relations depend on the mode of production; individual behaviour depends on class membership. Consequently, change to the Neoclassicist has a primarily quantitative dimension; to the Marxist, quantitative changes are necessarily followed by qualitative 'leaps'. Finally, while 'tastes' remain 'immaculately conceived' in the neoclassicist approach, the Marxist sees them neither as exogenous nor stable but a function of the organisation of production and the disposal of surplus value.

Gender was not a category that Marx considered in his theory of capital. But it is possible to infer from the works of Engels (1884) and Bebel (1883) a Marxian view of the family which has a direct bearing on female labour force participation behaviour.[36] In Marxian literature the inferior position of women in the market economy is interpreted as a result of sex inequality within the family. With industrialisation and an increasing number of women going out to work, the equality between the sexes will be gradually established as the earnings potential of women is first recognised and then realised. But the existence and even aggravation of sexually differentiated employment patterns, which we shall establish in a later chapter, throws doubt on this position. Humphries (1977) argues that existing sex-based relations of domination and subordination can be understood only in terms of successful attempts by the working class family to achieve a family wage (i.e. a wage sufficient to support a man, his economically inactive wife and children). The use of the family as a means of raising wages by the working class men would imply a discouraging attitude on the part of husbands towards their wives' entry into the labour force during the nineteenth century. Hence, the male workers' refusal to grant equal status to women is seen as arising from their perceptions of capitalists bent on appropriating greater surplus product by exploiting women workers.[37]

The substantial growth in the female labour force since the Second World War may be seen either as the lessening of the need to restrict the labour supply given the persistent labour shortages that characterised the 1950s and 1960s, *or* as a result of the growing feminist demand for the right to work. In either case occupational segmentation results. This effect of increasing participation of women in the labour force will be treated in a later chapter.

Notes

1. There are other approaches — the institutional or the Marxist — which start with different premises and have different methodologies. The neoclassical approach has certain undeniable attractions which can make it irresistible. It is challenging, rigorously deductive and empirically 'productive'. Its paradigm has a certain unifying power and its reductionism a universal appeal. Yet its ahistorical and asocial character, devoid of normative content, explains everything and nothing. These points will be spelt out later in this section.

2. A household need not be conscious of its efforts to maximise its utility, nor does it have to calculate systematically the utility derived from each activity. Given a set of preferences, the household will strive to satisfy these preferences, subject to the constraints of the resources available.

3. The economic concept of rationality is of utilitarian origin and therefore the decision-maker chooses that set of allocations which maximises the household utility.

4. The concept of opportunity cost should be broadened to include all foregone satisfactions, including intellectual and social satisfaction from work. For the sake of making it a less elusive and more measurable concept, the narrow economic definition is often used.

5. A Marxist approach, on the other hand, would not only disagree with the assumption of the immutability of preference over time and space, but would emphasise the importance of the organisation of production in preference formation.

6. Within a mathematical framework, it can be shown that the problem is one of maximising household utility subject to the constraint imposed by household resources which in this case is time. In this process of constrained maximisation of household utility, an optimal allocation of total time available among a number of competing uses takes place on the basis of evaluating the relative costs of and the relative satisfaction derived from these uses. The full mathematical development is contained in the Appendix to this chapter.

7. There is a theoretical circularity in this argument which should be noted. If the division of labour within the household is taken as given, wives will fail to acquire as much training and skills as their husbands and will therefore earn less than men in the labour market. However, if male-female differentials are taken as given, then the division of labour within the household appears logical. As Sawhill (1977, p. 121) asks: Have the economists "done anything more that describe the *status quo* in a society where sex roles are 'givens' – defined by culture, biology or other factors not specified in the economic models?"

8. The incorporation of fertility into the household choice model is achieved by including the quantity of child services as another element of household utility and incorporating the time expended on 'production' of child services as a further demand on household resources. The mathematical development is contained in the Appendix at the end of this chapter.

9. This listing is based on Nerlove (1974, p. S210)

10. A point worth reiterating is that it is the labour force participation of *married* women that is the object of explanation. Children, even when they exist, must remain for most part as arguments in the utility function. Considering married women as a separate category has 'ideological' implications which will be considered later in this book.

11. Ben Porath found that the relationship between education and labour force participation can be approximated by a U curve.

12. A couple's preference for children and other activities changes with

the varying perceptions of the opportunity cost of children. The data and the theoretical model should reflect this dynamic element. For a further discussion of these points and a summary of empirical work in this area, see Turchi (1975).

13. The life-cycle effects (i.e. effects over different stages of life) of labour force participation on the factors listed above could be more easily incorporated into the model following the approach adopted in human capital literature by Mincer (1963) and Ben Porath (1973). The household choice model, however, cannot 'explain' the lesser investment in education for girls or women.

14. A notable attempt to dynamise this model has been made by Ghez and Becker (1975) and Heckman (1974). Their versions are dynamic only in a restricted sense of utility maximisation over a number of time periods without introducing the uncertainty resulting from cyclical changes.

15. Gardiner's (1973, p. 103) comment that 'the theory on the economics of family size has outrun the data available to test it' is particularly apposite.

16. The ideological implications of this distinction between 'primary' and 'secondary' workers will be discussed in Chapter 5, p. 199–204.

17. There is some uncertainty as to when the 'additional worker' effect operates. Is it operative only when a husband is unemployed or would the entry of a wife in anticipation of probable unemployment of the husband count as the 'additional worker' effect?

18. The 'unemployment' variable is not only a proxy for the state of the economy, but may affect wage levels through the operation of market forces. A rising unemployment rate is symptomatic of a decline in the level of economic activity, with too many hopefuls chasing a decreasing number of jobs, and thereby exerting a downward pressure on prevailing wage rates. The consequent effect of a fall in wage levels may to some extent be counterbalanced by discouraged workers leaving the labour force.

19. This variable not only indicates the nature of the jobs available for married women but is often sensitive to changes in the level of economic activity, since it contains some persons employed in those occupation-industrial categories who are sensitive to such changes. It would follow, therefore, that while the unemployment variable reflects the level of demand for labour, the occupation-industry mix variable represents a measure of the differentiated demand for labour.

20. Bowen and Finegan (1969) have a separate Residence Index to measure the effect of job proximity to residence. The availability of part-time work could also be considered as a separate variable. Population Census data could be used to construct all these indices for the UK (see Joseph, 1978).

21. The problems of estimation and statistical interpretations constitute a vast subject and can be mentioned only briefly in a note. The problems arise mainly from the assumptions made to obtain a 'good' estimate of the regression equation. These assumptions include:

    (a) the variables on the right-hand side of the equation are independent (or uncorrelated) with one another;

    (b) labour force participation rates (i.e. the dependent variable) are determined by the 'explanatory' variables on the right-hand side and *not vice versa*;

    (c) all 'important' determinants of labour force participation have been included on the right-hand side of the equation;

    (d) the *form* of the relationship between the dependent variable and the explanatory variables has been correctly specified as a linear relationship. The violation of these assumptions would make the estimates unreliable. It is clear from the theoretical development of the previous pages that (a) and (b) are certainly violated.

22. The elasticity of labour supply with respect to wage rate is a measure of the percentage change in the quantity of labour supplied as a result of a 1% change in the wage rate, so that the higher the elasticity, the greater the response of supply to a unit change in the wage rate.

23. A combination of both approaches, as we shall see later, has been used in some empirical studies.

24. These are strictly econometric problems of *multicollinearity* and *errors in variables* whose presence diminishes the reliability of the statistical estimates. For a discussion of the nature and consequences of these problems, see Johnston (1972).

25. Recent American studies show much less cyclical sensitivity if a more comprehensive measure of labour supply is used, but the negative relationship between labour supply and unemployment persists in most cross-sectional studies.

26. The unemployment rate revealed by the 1966 sample census was about one and a half times as large as the registered unemployment rate.

27. While women in general suffer higher rates of unemployment than men at all times, the male-female differential tends to narrow during recessions. Explanations for this phenomenon have varied from the neoclassical argument that women's labour force participation is procyclical (Niemi, 1974), to the institutional view that recession hits hardest those jobs where women are under-represented (OECD, 1976).

28. For a useful summary of American work on the determinants of labour force participation behaviour, see Bowen and Finegan (1969).

29. This ignores the progressive deterioration in value and quality of inner city housing, which arguably was less marked during the years under study.

30. The rationale underlying the inclusion of this variable goes back to the studies for the USA by Cain (1966) and Bowen and Finegan (1969) who found significant differences between labour force participation rates of black and white women. The 'New Commonwealth' immigrant women are hardly a homogeneous group as far as their participation behaviour is concerned. In 1971, 74% of West Indians, 45% of non-Muslims and 17% of Muslim women were at work,

compared with 43% of women in the population in general.

31. A study by Metcalfe (1975) found that regional demand pressures (measured by taking the difference between the current regional unemployment rate and that which would occur at full employment) was an important determinant of local unemployment rate. This variable was used in this study to take account of the effects of involuntary male unemployment on female participation. Consequently, a significant positive coefficient could be interpreted as added worker effect.

32. A study of Elias (1980) examines labour force participation experiences of married women in the UK using Family Expenditure Survey data for the years 1968–75.

33. Leaving aside the estimation problems arising from the treatment of after-tax earnings as exogenous to the model, Greenhalgh (1981) has argued that the present fiscal structure operates against highly qualified women working, while at the same time increasing the supply of low paid and unskilled women workers. The impact of fiscal policies on the occupations and earnings of women needs further study.

34. Certain technical problems such as simultaneity bias, linearity assumptions with respect to dummy variable and statistical independence between explanatory variables, which are present in varying degrees in most empirical work in this area, will merely be noted in passing.

35. An important characteristic of any paradigm is that the paradigm is itself responsible for suggesting the problem and the questions that its adherents should investigate. A researcher working within the confines of the neoclassical paradigm will start from very different premises from a researcher working within, say, the Marxist paradigm. Each includes, for example, its own very different value judgments, and serves as the basis on which endogenous *versus* exogenous classifications are made and identifying restrictions imposed in the estimation procedures employed.

36. There still remain unresolved issues between the analysis of class exploitation and sex oppression. This point will be taken up in a later chapter.

37. Restrictive practices by trade unions aimed at excluding women from certain types of work were widespread until the Second World War. For a useful discussion of this point, see Lewenhak (1977).

Appendix

Given a set of preferences (represented by Z_1, Z_2, ..., Z_n basic commodities),[1] define the household utility function as:

$$U = U(Z_1, Z_2, ..., Z_n)$$

where Z_i is the ith basic commodity. The total amount of time (t) expended as inputs on the 'production'[2] of all n basic commodities is:

$$\sum_{i=1}^{n} t_i = t$$

We are assuming that the only input needed for producing Z_i is time, so that:

$$Z_i = Z_i(t_i) \qquad i = 1, 2, ..., n$$

where $Z_i(\cdot)$ defines the production function of Z_i.

Given the technology of household production described by production functions whose inputs consist only of time and a concave utility function, the problem of optimal allocation of scarce resources (time) among n activities may be described as:

Maximise: $\qquad\qquad U = U(Z_1, Z_2, ..., Z_n)$

Subject to: $\qquad\qquad Z_i = Z_i(t_i) \qquad i = 1, 2, ..., n$

and

$$\sum_{i=1}^{n} t_i = t$$

This is a constrained maximisation problem whose solution will give the first order equilibrium condition for optimal allocation of the scarce resource (time) among n competing uses as:

$$\frac{\partial U}{\partial Z_i} = \lambda \frac{\partial t_i}{\partial Z_i} = \frac{\lambda}{\partial Z_i/\partial t_i}$$

where $\lambda > 0$ is the marginal utility of time (i.e. utility obtained by expending one more unit of time).

$\partial Z_i/\partial t_i$ is the marginal 'shadow' price of basic commodity i (i.e. time required to produce a unit change in basic commodity i).

$\partial U/\partial Z_i$ is the marginal utility of basic commodity i.

Consequently, it follows that an optimal allocation of time between, say, Z_i and Z_j will result if the ratio of the price of these basic commodities equals the ratio of their marginal utilities, i.e.:

$$\frac{\partial U/\partial Z_i}{\partial U/\partial Z_j} = \frac{\partial Z_i/\partial t_i}{\partial Z_j/\partial t_j} \qquad \begin{matrix} i \neq j \\ i, j = 1, 2, ..., n \end{matrix}$$

Therefore, an increase in the price of commodity i relative to the price of commodity j will reduce the relative consumption of commodity i, since the marginal utility of commodity i will fall.

An economic approach to household choice theory would involve the combined assumptions of maximisation of utility and a stable set of preferences leading to market equilibrium which will ensure optimal allocation of scarce resources.

Let the household utility function to be maximised be written as:

$$U = U(G_{Mt}, G_H, L_M, L_W) \tag{A.1}$$

where U is a strictly concave utility function of a typical household consisting of a husband and wife who are potential suppliers of market work; G_{Mt}, G_H, L_M, L_W are the *arguments* of U representing market commodities, household commodities, time devoted to leisure by the husband and time devoted to leisure by the wife respectively.

Each member of this household is engaged in activities which result in the use of inputs of time and market commodities. These activities can vary from a highly time-intensive activity such as spending an afternoon in a public library, to a highly commodity-intensive activity such as eating out in an expensive restaurant. A household production function which relates the relative market and time inputs of the members of the household may be defined as:

$$G_H = G_H(X_H, T_H) \tag{A.2}$$

where X_H and T_H represent respectively market and time inputs into household production.

Now specify a *budget constraint equation* which states that the expenditure on market inputs (X_H) and final commodities (G_{Mt}) cannot exceed income earned from market work (i.e. the *product* of time spent on market work by members of the household (T_{Mt}) and the average wage rate of the members (w)) plus 'other' (i.e. unearned) income (Y):

$$P_X X_H + P_{G_{Mt}} G_{Mt} \leq wT_{Mt} + Y \tag{A.3}$$

where P_X and $P_{G_{MT}}$ are the prices of market inputs and final commodities respectively.

A *time constraint equation* which completes the resource constraints faced by the household may be specified as:

$$T_{Mt} + T_H + L = T_0 \tag{A.4}$$

where T_0 is the total time available and $L = L_M + L_W$.

The maximisation of the household utility function given in (A.1) subject to the conditions and constraints given in (A.2) to (A.4) will yield the optimal allocation of time between different *activities* of the household and the optimal allocation between market inputs and final market goods.[3]

The incorporation of fertility into the household choice model is achieved by including the quantity of child services (C) as an additional *argument* in the utility function given in (A.1). The two elements of C are incorporated through a child service function defined as:

$$C = C(N, Q) \tag{A.5}$$

where N is the number of children and Q is some measure of the quality of the children.[4]

If the household production of N and Q are specified by the following relations:

$$N = N(T_N, X_N; \alpha, \beta) \tag{A.6}$$

$$Q = Q(T_Q, X_Q; \alpha, \beta) \tag{A.7}$$

where T_N and T_Q are amounts of time expended on the 'production' of the number of children (N) and quality of children (Q) respectively. X_N and X_Q are market inputs in the production of N and Q; α and β are efficiency indices of the wife and husband relating to the production of N and Q respectively.

The *budget constraint equation* defined in (A.3) will now become:

$$P_X X_H + P_{G_{Mt}} G_{Mt} + P_N X_N + P_Q X_Q \leq W_M T_{Mt(M)} + W_W T_{Mt(W)} + Y \tag{A.8}$$

where P_N and P_Q are the prices of the market inputs for producing N and Q respectively. W_M and W_W are the market wage rates of male and female workers respectively. $T_{Mt(M)}$ and $T_{Mt(W)}$ are the time allocated for market work by husband and wife respectively, so that $T_{Mt(M)} + T_{Mt(W)} = T_{Mt}$.

The *time constraint equation* defined in (A.4) will now become:

$$T_0 = T_{Mt} + T_{H'} + L + T_N + T_Q \tag{A.9}$$

where the subscript H' represents time allocated to housework (excluding time used for the production of child services, C).

The maximisation of the household utility function (with an additional argument to incorporate child services) subject to the conditions and constraints given by (A.2) and (A.5) to (A.9) will yield the optimal allocation of time between husband and wife for different activities, including production of child services; and the optimal allocation of expenditure between market inputs into household production and production of child services and final market commodities.

The model presented above is fairly basic and should be seen only as an aid to the verbal exposition given in this chapter. It ignores a number of interesting theoretical and methodological innovations of recent years. Heckman and Macurdy (1980) have presented a dynamic model of female labour supply, extending the work by Ghez and Becker (1975) and Smith (1979), with a significant innovation in allowing for differences in the valuation of 'non-market' time (i.e., T_H and L) at different points in the life cycle of a typical woman. An extension of the original Becker model by Atkinson and Stern (1981) allows for the joint incorporation of labour supply and commodity demand decisions within a household production model. They do so by associating a given amount of leisure time with consumption of each commodity, so that it becomes possible to estimate a 'time-price' for each commodity. A recent extension of the incorporation of fertility into labour supply decisions by Nerlove and Razin (1981) has examined the effect of child-spacing (i.e. the average duration between sucessive births) on the mother's labour supply. By establishing a close direct relationship between child-spacing and child quality (Q), they have made it possible to examine the nature of the interaction between quantity (N) and quality (Q) of children, first discussed by Becker and Tomes (1976).

Notes on the Appendix

1. It should be emphasised that $Z_1, Z_2, \ldots, Z_n$ represent not goods *per se* but their characteristics or attributes which give rise to utility. Further they could include attributes such as child service (i.e. satisfactions derived from having children). Or again, a good can possess more than one attribute and goods in combination possess attributes which are different from those pertaining to the same goods consumed separately. A generic term, *basic commodities*, is used to describe the preferred attributes that give rise to utility.
2. Production is any activity undertaken to satisfy human wants for which payment either in money or time has to be made.
3. For a detailed discussion and mathematical derivations relating to this model, see Gronau (1973) and Gramm (1975).
4. A proxy that has been used in some American studies as a measure of the quality of the children is the expected school investment per child. For a discussion of various proxies, see De Tray (1973).

3

The British Labour Force During the Twentieth Century: A Demographic Analysis of the Growing Importance of Women Workers

Introduction

A number of descriptive studies examining long-term changes in the size and composition of the American labour force have been published over the last three or four decades.[1] Similar studies relating to British experience have been notably lacking. The American studies found that behind the apparent long-run stability of the overall labour force participation rate of the working-age population, there have operated conflicting and compensating changes in age/sex and geographical-composition of the American labour force. In this chapter, utilising mainly Population Census data, an attempt will be made to describe how labour force participation experiences of various groups, distinguished by age,

sex, marital status and family characteristics, have changed over the
period between the census years 1881 and 1971,[2] and how these
changes have affected the composition of the British labour force.
The later sections of this chapter will evaluate the relative
contributions of primary factors such as the size, age-composition
and marital status of the population as well as changing
opportunities for part-time employment, to the growth of various
groups in the British labour force. In all cases the extent of the detail
and the length of the period of study are dictated solely by the
exigencies of the data available for such an analysis.

The Demographic Dimensions of Labour Force Growth in Britain: 1881–1971

Over the 90 years between 1881 and 1971, the total labour force
increased from 13 million to 25 million, while total population rose
from about 30 million to 54 million.[3] Figure 3.1 represents the
growth in the two aggregates as well as their male and female
components. The growth has been continuous and not dissimilar in
character as far as the two aggregates are concerned. However, the
changing slope and undulating movement in the total labour force
curve shows an unevenness in the rate of growth with two trends
clearly discernible, a gradual decline in the growth rate before 1951
and a slight spurt subsequently, with a marked decline in the period
between 1966 and 1971. These trends are clearer if one examines
Figure 3.2 which represents percentage changes over successive
decennial intervals.

It is seen from the two diagrams that the post-war spurt in labour
force growth is primarily due to the accelerated growth in the female
component, and indeed an absolute fall in the numbers in the male
labour force between 1961 and 1971.[4] It is therefore evident that the
female component has become the *dynamic* element in labour force
growth in this country and will probably remain so in the
foreseeable future. It may be conjectured that it is unlikely that the
post-war labour supply in Great Britain would have been sufficient
to allow for expanding industrial production and services and the
extension of full-time higher education to a growing number of
young people if participation rates of women had remained at the
same level as prevailed during the first few decades of this century.[5]

During the past nine decades, the sex-composition of the labour

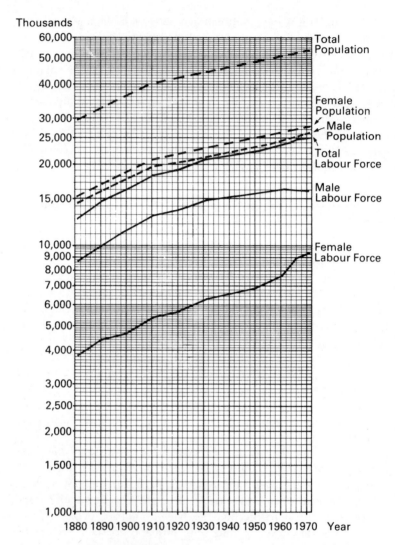

Fig. 3.1 *Growth in Labour Force and Total Population in Britain:*
1881–1971

Sources: Censuses of Population and British Labour Statistics: Historical
*   Abstracts 1886–1968,* Table 109.

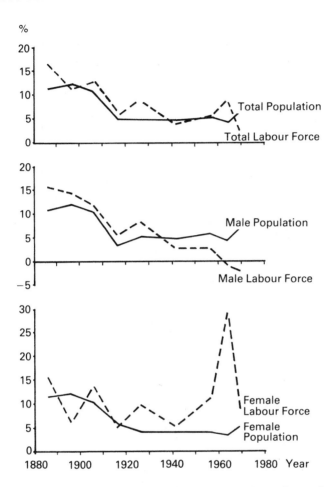

Fig. 3.2   *Percentage Change in Labour Force and Total Population in Britain over Successive Decennial Intervals: 1881–1971*

Sources: Censuses of Population and British Labour Statistics: Historical Abstracts 1886–1968, Table 109.

force has been changing in that the female share has increased from 27% in 1881 to 37% in 1971. Much of this increase is a post-war phenomenon; the female share fluctuated between the narrow bounds of 27% and 30% in the period before 1950, while a 7% increase was recorded between 1950 and 1971.[6] However, even during the period of relative stability, the composition of the female labour force changed significantly. Figure 3.3 shows the percentage of women in the labour force disaggregated by broad age-groups and marital status for four census years, 1911, 1931, 1951 and 1971.[7]

If one ignores the problems of data comparability of the first two years with subsequent years (arising from changes in minimum age of entry into the labour force), females under the age of 20 years, an overwhelming proportion of them single, constituted the largest share of the labour force, rising from 42% in 1911 to 47% in 1971. The share of the married females in this age-group rose from under 1% in 1911 to 3.5% in 1971. The proportion of married women aged 20–24 in the labour force of that age-group rose by about 6% over the same period. It is in the 46–64 age-group that the largest increase in the share of the female component, amounting to 16% is recorded. In this age-group, the share of married females rose from 6% to 26%, while the share of single, widowed and divorced females (SWDF) fell from 14% to 10%.

Figure 3.3 can be used to deduce sex-ratios of the labour force by various age-groups. It is seen that the share of males has been declining over the whole age-range, except in the case of the 'under 20s' and '20–24' age-groups for whom the decline has been halted since 1961. Earlier retirement trends among the '45–64' age-group may explain the dramatic fall from 80% to 60% between 1911 and 1971 in the share of males in that age-group.

So far, we have concentrated mainly on the changes in the sex composition of the labour force and our main conclusion is that the increasing participation of females, especially the married ones, has reduced the sex differential in labour force participation in recent years. It is likely that if the present trend of rising participation rates among females continues in the future, this differential will be diminished even further.

We now change our emphasis to the age-composition of the labour force. This involves, primarily, a discussion of the age-specific participation changes over the period, and then a consideration of the three main influences bringing about a shift in

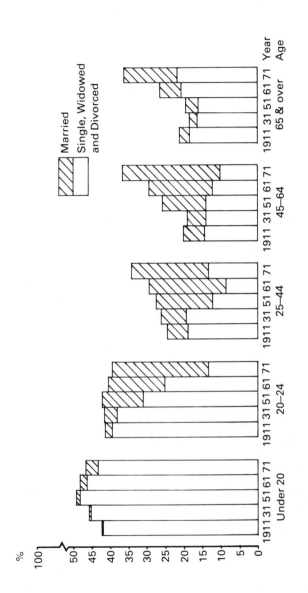

Fig. 3.3 *Percentage Share of Women in the Labour Force by Marital Status: 1911, 1931, 1951, 1971*

Source: See Table A in the Data Appendix.

the age-composition of the labour force over a specific period. The three influences were:

(a) an increase in the average age of the British population;
(b) an increase in the average age of first entry into the labour force, arising from the combination of successive raising of the school leaving age from 10 years in 1881, to 12 years by 1921, to 14 years by 1931, to 15 years by 1951 and longer periods of post-school education and full-time training to acquire skills needed in an increasingly sophisticated economy;[8] and
(c) a gradual fall in the average age of retirement.

Figures 3.4 (a)–(f) give the labour force status of the British population by sex, marital status of the female component and varying age-intervals for the six census years 1891, 1911, 1931, 1951, 1961 and 1971.

The minimal age of entry into the labour force is in doubt for the years 1891 and 1911, though it can be reasonably assumed that an overwhelming number of juveniles of both sexes who started or sought work were aged 10 years or over. For the male component, participation in the labour force is almost 100% for those aged 25 and 44. Therefore, the size of the labour force in these age-intervals for the two years is almost completely determined by the size of the male population in the same age-intervals. Where changes have occurred over the years is at the two ends of the age-spectrum. Statutory restrictions on the minimum age of entry and longer periods of full-time education and training have resulted in a gradual withdrawal over the years, though there is some evidence to suggest that in the post-war years better opportunities in a full-employment economy to earn good wages, coupled with earlier family building intentions, have partly restricted the operation of forces bringing about a later entry into the labour force.[9] At the other end of the age-spectrum, there is evidence to support the contention that, with the establishment of comprehensive state and private pension schemes, retirement is no longer a luxury enjoyed by only a few through fortune of birth or thrift, but a norm for a significantly large segment of the life cycle of most men.

The trend in age-specific participation of females is more difficult to discern from the diagrams. Unlike the male component, the female labour force age-pyramids do not fit neatly into the population pyramids. Hence, it is a reasonable deduction that

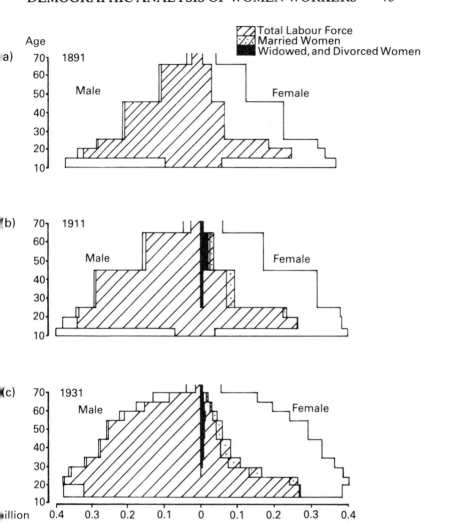

Fig. 3.4 *Labour Force Status of the British Population by Age, Sex and Marital Status (for females only): 1891, 1911, 1931, 1951, 1961 and 1971*

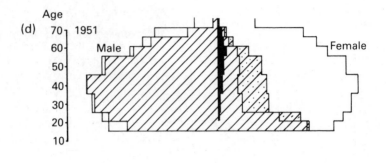

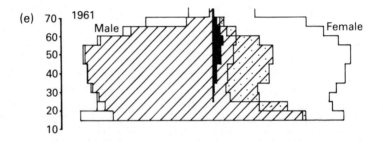

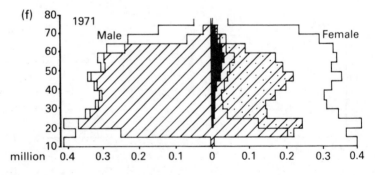

Fig. 3.4 *contd.*

population size in this instance acts more as a constraint than as an important determinant of the size of the female labour force. It is interesting to note that, if one excludes the married women component, the labour force age-pyramids of single women (and to a lesser extent those of the widowed and divorced women) increasingly, over the years, show a pattern similar to that of their respective population age-pyramids. This may partly be a reflection of the increased propensity of single women to follow life-time careers and the gradual disappearance of three generation households, which has meant that an adult single woman has a less satisfying role to play in the periphery of her own family. However, the growth of the married women component, the decline in the more predictable single women component and the increasing significance of the widowed and divorced women in the older age-intervals of the female labour force, makes any forecasting exercise a more difficult one, for such an exercise presupposes, among other things, that data are available for cross-classification of female labour force activity by marital status, family characteristics, education, etc.[10] The broad pattern that emerges, especially in the later years, is that the life cycle of female labour activity has two peaks, the first occurring between the time females leave school and the time they marry or, more probably, when they have their first child, when many withdraw from the labour force. They return between the ages of 35 and 45 when the last child is at school and this trend is accentuated by the increasing incidence of divorce. Finally, there is a period of decreasing participation as the cohort moves to old age.[11] This pattern of accession and withdrawal is becoming more and more typical and the level of participation of the cohort in its early years has some bearing on the life cycle participation pattern.

An extra dimension to female participation is provided by Table 3.1 which gives the distribution of women by marital status and family characteristics for the three census years 1961, 1966 and 1971. Unfortunately, such detailed information is unavailable for earlier years. The pattern that emerges for the three years is that there is a direct relationship between the number of children and female participation: that the older a child, the greater the tendency for its mother to participate in the labour force; and that marital status is a crucial factor determining labour force participation since the ratio relating to participation is uniformly higher for the

Table 3.1　Percentage Distribution of Ever-Married Female Population and Labour Force by Marital Status, Age and Number of Children in Britain: 1961, 1966 and 1971.

Marital Status, Number and Age of Children	1961			1966			1971		
	Labour Force	Population	Ratio	Labour Force	Population	Ratio	Labour Force	Population	Ratio
Total Ever-Married Women									
15 years and over	100	100		100	100		100	100	
Married	92.97	94.08	0.99	94.16	94.02	1.00	94.51	93.91	1.01
Widowed and Divorced	7.03	5.92	1.19	5.84	5.98	0.98	5.49	6.09	0.90
Nos. with 0 children	56.31	50.72	1.11	55.38	51.75	1.07	53.55	51.15	1.05
Nos. with 1–2 children	38.11	39.44	0.97	36.93	37.03	1.00	37.01	37.00	1.00
Nos. with 3 or more children	5.58	9.84	0.57	7.69	11.22	0.68	9.44	11.85	0.80
Nos. with youngest child aged less than 5	8.62	21.22	0.41	10.99	22.85	0.48	11.44	23.14	0.49
Nos. with youngest child aged 5–11 years	13.01	14.12	0.92	14.12	13.20	1.07	14.70	13.37	1.10
Nos. with youngest child aged less than 16 but more than 11	19.22	12.33	1.56	15.24	9.38	1.62	16.55	9.49	1.74
Nos. with youngest child aged 16 and over	2.84	1.62	1.76	4.28	2.81	1.52	4.65	2.85	1.63
Total Married Women Aged 15 & over (Husbands Present)	100	100		100	100		100	100	

Nos. with 0 children	56.51	1.14	55.41	50.51	1.10	54.43	50.83	1.07
Nos. with 1–2 children	37.73	0.94	36.70	37.82	0.97	35.98	37.06	0.97
Nos. with 3 or more children	5.76	0.56	7.89	11.67	0.67	9.59	12.11	0.79
Nos. with youngest child aged less than 5	8.85	0.40	11.28	23.92	0.47	11.53	23.76	0.49
Nos. with youngest child aged 5 to 11	13.34	0.91	14.29	13.07	1.09	14.60	12.98	1.12
Nos. with youngest child aged 11 to 16	18.77	1.53	15.00	9.62	1.56	15.33	9.56	1.60
Nos. with youngest child aged 16 and over	2.53	1.73	4.02	2.88	1.39	4.11	2.87	1.43
Total Widowed and Divorced	100		100	100		100	100	
Nos. with 0 children	53.66	0.75	54.95	71.36	0.77	50.71	67.38	0.75
Nos. with 1–2 children	43.17	1.69	40.69	27.57	1.66	42.94	26.51	1.62
Nos. with 3 or more children	3.17	1.03	4.36	4.07	1.07	6.35	6.11	1.04
Nos. with youngest child aged less than 5	4.95	1.13	6.29	6.05	1.04	6.89	6.90	1.00
Nos. with youngest child aged 5 to 11	10.61	1.58	11.48	7.42	1.55	12.56	8.45	1.49
Nos. with youngest child aged 11 to 16	23.73	1.76	19.06	12.75	1.77	20.85	12.24	1.70
Nos. with youngest child aged 16 and over	7.04	1.75	8.22	4.42	1.86	8.99	5.03	1.79

'widowed and divorced' compared to the 'married' group, with an exception in the case of women with no children. Any comparison over time is limited by the fact that only three sets of observations are available, though it is noticeable, with some important exceptions that there has been a slight increase in participation among all women, irrespective of their marital status and the ages of their children.[12]

Certain additional inferences could be drawn from an examination of the age patterns of participation of married women *with* and *without* dependent children for the census years 1961 and 1971, given in Table D of the Data Appendix at the end of this chapter. The group consisting of married women with no dependent children includes childless women, as well as women whose children have completed full-time education. A similarity between the age patterns of participation among women with no dependent children and those of single women (given in Table C of the Data Appendix) is clearly discernible, possibly indicating that the presence of dependent children rather than marital status is the important inhibitory factor on female labour force participaton. Also over the period 1961 to 1971, while increases in participation rates were recorded in all age-groups, for both married women with *and* without dependent children, the increases were more marked among mothers of dependent children. An obvious inference here is that the relative increase in married women in the labour force was to a significant extent a reflection of the increasing number of working mothers in the labour force.[13]

Table 3.1 provides further information on changing patterns of labour force participation among mothers with dependent children. A convergence in the ratios relating to married women with school-age children (i.e. those aged 5 to 16) and those relating to women with no children is apparent. The implication here is that, while an upward trend in labour force participation is evident among all groups considered in Table 3.1, a growing tendency is discernible for the labour force participation of mothers with older children to resemble those of women with no children. The wide differentials in participation between these two groups and mothers with pre-school children are clearly persistent.

A record of the changes in labour force participation rates of male and female components as well as those of married females during the period 1881–1971 is summarised in Figures 3.5 (a)–(e).[14] The

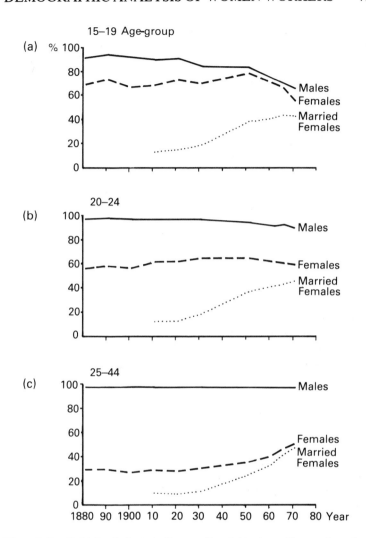

Fig. 3.5 *British Labour Force Participation Rates by Age and Sex: 1881–1971*

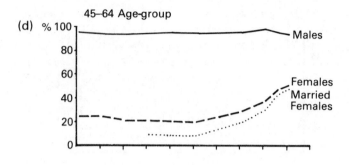

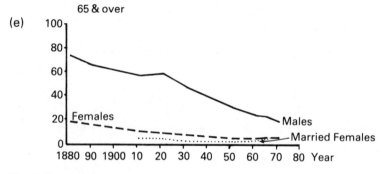

Fig. 3.5   *contd.*

Source: Table B in the Data Appendix.

choice of the age-groups is determined solely by the exigencies of
the data available in earlier years. For the male component, it is at
the extreme ages that the decline in participation rates is most
marked. This, together with the slight decline in the '20–24' and
'45–64' age-groups in more recent years, represents the lengthening
of the period of full-time education, on the one hand, and the long-
term trend towards earlier retirement in the case of the older
population. The same influences operate for the female
component, though the fall in participation rates of the 'over-65s' is
not as dramatic. It is, however, in the intermediate age-groups that
participation rates have shown the greatest increase in the last four
decades. This increase has occurred despite a fall of over 15% in the

participation rates of single, widowed and divorced females between 1931 and 1971. This fall was more than offset by a four-fold increase in the participation rates of married women from 9.6% in 1911 to 42.9% in 1971.

Table C in the Data Appendix gives the participation rates of various groups for the period 1931 to 1971 by five-year age-categories. The pattern that emerges for married females is an increase in participation rates over the whole age-range, with the largest increases being recorded for the age-groups 35–44 and 45–54, whose rates are over five times the level in 1931. It is these groups that have constituted the most dynamic elements in the total labour force growth, more than offsetting the reduced participation rates of the males. Further, an increasing trend towards a bimodal pattern in participation is discernible for married females which has, and will have, a significant effect on the age-composition of the female labour force. This tendency to raise the average age of the labour force is reinforced by the increase in the participation rates of the 'Widowed and Divorced' group who have a negatively skewed age-distribution and the fall in the relative numbers and participation rates of the 'single' females who have a positively skewed age-distribution.

An examination of the participation rates of various population groups given in Table B in the Data Appendix suggests that there are two distinct trends at work. These are those changes occurring during the period 1881 to 1951 and those occurring subsequently.

Figures 3.6 (a)–(c) represent the age-profiles of the average change in participation rates of males, females and married women in the labour force for the two periods. For the first period, the rate of change among males is near zero until the mid-fifties and falls below zero for subsequent age intervals. The female component shows a declining positive rate, reaching the zero level at about sixty years and a negative rate subsequently. The married females, during the first period (i.e. between 1911 and 1951), show a 6% growth rate in the youngest age-group, a decline thereafter in an uneven fashion, reaching the zero level after 65 years. For the second period (1951–1971) the male trend represents a negative rate of change for all age-groups, particularly marked in the extreme age-ranges. The female and married female trends are very similar except that a negative rate of change is discerned for the total female component, reaching the positive level only in the mid-fifties. For

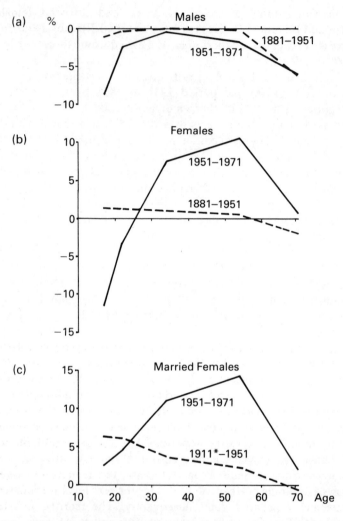

Fig. 3.6 *Age–Profile of Changes in Labour Force Participation Rates in Britain by Sex and Marital Status (for women only): Average of Decades 1881–1951 compared to that of Decades 1951–1971*

Source: Table B in the Data Appendix.

Note: * Reliable figures on the labour force by marital status are available only in censuses from 1911 onwards.

the married females, the changes in the rate are positive for all ages, reaching a peak around the mid-fifties and declining subsequently.

The following general features are suggested by Figures 3.6 (a)–(c):

(1) There is a tendency towards accelerated decline in participation rates for all groups at the upper end of the age-profile for both periods, showing a long-term trend to earlier retirement.

(2) For the second period, the lowest rate of change is recorded at the other end of the age-spectrum showing a tendency towards later entry into the labour force as a result of longer periods of full-time education and training.

(3) The main contribution to labour force growth in recent years has been made by older females, especially married women, which has more than offset the reduced male participation over the whole age-spectrum. This has marked a shift from younger single women who characterised part of the dynamics of labour force growth in the earlier period. As a result, it can be expected that the average age of the total labour force will continue to rise, but at a declining rate.

Four main factors have governed the ageing of the labour force. The trend towards earlier withdrawal has been more than offset by three main forces working in the other direction. First, as discussed above, the increasing participation of married women with their characteristic bimodal pattern of work cycle has contributed to a rise in the average age of the labour force. Second, the decline of the proportion of young people who enter the labour force before the age of 25 years has been another factor. Third, the average age of the population has been rising over the period, the indication being an increase in life expectancy at birth from 48 and 52 years to 69 and 75 at present for males and females respectively,[15] though the post-war fertility increase may, to some extent, work in the opposite direction. Table 3.2 gives the median ages of the working-age population and labour force by sex and marital condition (of females) for six census years. The pattern that emerges for all groups is a gradual rise in the median ages over time. A crude measure of the closeness of the relationship between the age-distribution of the population and the labour force is given in the last column of the table. The relationship is very close for males ($r =$

Table 3.2 Median Ages of Working-Age Population* and
Labour Force in Britain by Sex and Marital Condition
(of Females only)

Sex/Marital	Working-Age Population					
Status	1891	1911	1931	1951	1961	1971
Males	29.1	31.3	36.1	40.3	41.6	41.6
Females	30.2	31.2	37.4	42.4	44.3	45.0
Married Females	n.a.	39.0	41.3	41.8	42.7	43.1
Single Females	n.a.	19.1	22.1	26.5	24.7	22.3
Widowed & Divorced	n.a.	61.4	63.0	66.1	67.8	68.8

Sex/Marital	Labour Force						
Status	1891	1911	1931	1951	1961	1971	Correlation Coefficient (r)
Males	31.7	33.6	35.2	38.6	39.0	39.0	0.98
Females	23.0	24.3	25.1	32.4	36.5	39.1	0.94
Married Females	n.a.	39.0	35.2	37.9	40.2	41.6	0.44
Single Females	n.a.	21.2	22.3	23.0	22.2	22.0	0.93
Widowed & Divorced	n.a.	53.2	52.8	51.6	54.7	55.0	0.54

Source: Censuses of Population.

Note: * Working-Age Population: defined as 10 and over in 1891 and
1911; 14 and over in 1931 and 15 and over in subsequent years.

0.98) and single women ($r = 0.93$). However, the correlation
coefficient for married women is 0.43, and this is partly explained by
the fact that the proportionate increase in participation of married
women in age-group 35 to 54 years (see Figure 3.6(c)) was greater
than the proportionate increase in married women in the
population. This would also partly explain why the median age of
the female labour force rose faster than that of the male.

A further dimension to the ageing of the labour force is provided
by an examination of the proportion of the population (aged 15 and
over) and the labour force (aged 15 and over) in various age/sex/
marital status groups. For both males and females the most

significant discrepancy between labour force and population proportions arises at present for age-groups 25–44 and 45–64 where labour proportions are higher, and 'over-65s' where population proportions are higher. The decline in labour force proportions for those 'under 25' is quite marked, despite a slight rise recorded for the '20–24' age-group between 1961 and 1971. A similar decline is also seen in the case of population proportions. The stability in the labour force proportions of the 'over-65s' for all groups contrasts with the increases in the population proportions over the same period.

In summary, the general trend is towards an older labour force. This has a wide range of implications, among them being a reduced flexibility of labour force responses to changes in demand, a greater vulnerability to unemployment arising from greater geographical and occupational immobility and, in general, a perpetuation of regional imbalances.

Changes in Occupational Composition and Labour Force Growth

An examination of the changes in the occupational composition over the last six decades would help to explain the differences in the growth of the major demographic groups in the labour force.[16] Three relevant aspects are isolated and discussed briefly here. First, the phenomenal growth in labour force participation of women, especially in the post-war years, is reflected in shifts in the occupational structure favourable to an increase in the employment of women. Second, the same changes in the occupational composition have had an adverse effect on the employment of older workers. Third, changes in the skills required have postponed the entry of young workers, especially males, into the labour force.

Three forces relating to occupational trends have operated in reducing opportunitites for employment among older workers, especially those past their physical prime. First, the number of males employed in agriculture and allied industries fell by over a half from 1.5 million to 700,000 between 1881 and 1966. The corresponding figures for females were 116,000 in 1881 to 101,000 in 1966, though considerable doubts exist about the validity of comparing these figures because of the failure to describe much of female farm work as 'gainful' employment in earlier censuses. Since a large number of farm workers continue to work at relatively advanced ages, the occupational shift to non-agricultural pursuits may be an important explanation for the decline in labour force participation of men aged 55 and over during this period. Second, the growth of large industrial establishments at the expense of smaller businesses run by individuals, a significant number of them past their prime, may have been another factor in reducing employment opportunities for older workers. Third, changes in the skill requirements dictated by technological development over this period may also have worked against older men. The third point will be discussed later.

Table 3.3 gives the occupational distribution (in broad categories) of the labour force in Britain by sex for three years, 1911, 1951 and 1971. The figures for 1911, 1951 and 1971 are obtained from Table 1.1 of Routh's (1980, pp. 6–7) study of *Occupation and Pay in Great Britain 1906–1979*. The most noteworthy change in the occupational distribution of men between 1911 and 1971 has been the relative increase in the proportion of managers and professional men at the expense of both manual workers irrespective of their skills and, to a lesser extent, that of employers and proprietors. For females, the most drastic increase is shown among the clerical workers who constituted only 3% of the total 'occupied' population in 1911, but comprised over a quarter of the total female labour force in 1971. The largest number of females fell into the semi-skilled manual worker category, while in the case of males, the skilled manual worker category had the largest numbers during the post-war years. The pattern that emerges is that, over the period, there has been a phenomenal increase in the demand for female clerical workers, especially of the letter- and report-writing kind, and a slower growth in semi-skilled manual workers, which was initially met by a significant transfer of domestic service workers into manufacturing and distributive trades. Hence, the changes in the occupational distribution have favoured more female participation in the labour force. Among males, the occupational shift in favour of professional, managerial and supervisory skills at the expense of semi-skilled manual work, has meant longer periods of training and later entry into the labour force on the one hand and earlier withdrawal from the labour force on the other.

A crude measure of the extent to which temporal changes in numbers in each occupation group are due to changes in the occupational structure of the labour force, rather than a proportionate expansion of numbers in that group due to growth in the total labour force, can be obtained by standardising, say, the 1951 labour force on 1911 occupational distribution.[17] Columns 7 to 14 in Table 3.3 show the standardisation of the 1951 labour force with the 1911 occupational distribution and the 1971 labour force with the 1951 occupational distribution. Columns 8, 9, 12 and 13 allocate the increases in numbers in each occupational group for the periods 1911–1951 and 1951–1966 to either the 'labour force growth' component or the 'change in occupational distribution' component. Certain general conclusions about the impact of changes in occupational structure on labour force growth of both sexes for the periods 1911–1951 and 1951–1971 may be drawn.

(a) The increases in the number of males in professional, managerial and supervisory occupations over both periods were overwhelmingly due to the disproportionate expansion of these occupations. But in cases of males in the manual categories, the 'occupation' component had a negative impact on growth in numbers for both periods in 1971.

(b) The positive impact of the 'occupation' component is fairly dramatic for female clerical workers, whose numbers increased by almost seven times during the period 1911–1951. About 95% of this increase can be directly attributed to the 'occupation' component. There was a decline in the magnitude of this impact during the period 1951–1971. With the exception of three cases, the impact of the 'occupation' component was positive for all categories of female workers for both periods. The exceptions were skilled and semi-skilled manual workers, and employers and proprietors. The change in occupational distribution had a positive impact on labour force growth of unskilled manual workers in case of females for both periods, but a negative impact on males in the second period.

(c) It is interesting to note that the magnitude of the contribution of the 'occupation' component was smaller for females than males in the professional, managerial, administrative and supervisory occupations over the whole period. This is quite consistent with the findings that the female share of more senior and responsible jobs has not grown at the same rate as the male share. In a later chapter the whole question of inequality and female employment distribution will be explored in detail.

Table 3.3 Occupational Class and Sex of the Labour Force in Britain, 1911, 1951 and 1971; Numbers and Percentage (Nos. in 000's)

	(1)	(2)	(3)	(4)	(5)	(6)
	1911		*1951*		*1971*	
Occupational Class	Nos.	%	Nos.	%	Nos.	%
1A *Higher Profession*						
Male	173	1.34	399	2.56	774	4.87
Female	11	0.20	36	0.52	50	0.55
1B *Lower Profession*						
Male	208	1.61	492	3.16	946	5.95
Female	352	6.49	567	8.18	1000	10.96
2A *Employers and Proprietors*						
Male	1000	7.74	894	5.74	805	5.07
Female	232	4.28	223	3.22	251	2.75
2B *Managers and Administrators*						
Male	506	3.91	1056	6.78	1733	10.91
Female	125	2.30	189	2.73	321	3.51
3 *Clerical Workers*						
Male	708	5.48	990	6.35	1013	6.38
Female	179	3.30	1414	20.41	2466	27.00
4 *Foremen and Supervisors*						
Male	227	1.75	511	3.28	801	5.04
Female	10	0.18	79	1.14	168	1.84
5 *Skilled Manual Workers*						
Male	4264	32.99	4733	30.36	4619	29.08
Female	1344	24.78	884	12.75	775	8.48
6 *Semi-Skilled Manual Workers*						
Male	4346	33.63	4352	27.92	3307	20.82
Female	2898	53.42	2988	43.12	3005	32.90
7 *Unskilled Manual Workers*						
Male	1494	11.55	2158	13.84	1889	11.89
Female	274	5.05	550	7.94	1098	12.02
Total M	12925	100.00	15584	100.00	15884	100.00
F	5425	100.00	6930	100.00	9134	100.00

(7)	(8)	(9)	(10)	(11)	(12)	(13)	(14)
Expected Nos. in 1951 (given 1911 Occ. Dist.)	Expected Increase in Nos. Due to Growth of L.F. [(7)-(1)]	Increase Due to Change in Occupa-tional Distri-bution	Total Change 1911-1951	Expected Nos. in 1971 (given 1951 Occ. Dist.)	Expected Increase in Nos. Due to Growth of L.F. [(11)-(3)]	Increase Due to Change in Occupa-tional Distri-bution	Total Change 1951-1971
209	36	190	226	407	8	367	375
14	3	22	25	47	11	3	14
251	43	241	284	502	10	484	494
450	98	117	215	747	180	253	433
1206	206	-312	-106	912	18	-107	89
297	65	-74	-9	294	71	-43	28
609	103	447	550	1077	21	656	677
159	34	30	64	249	60	72	132
854	146	136	282	1009	19	4	23
229	50	1185	1235	1864	450	602	1052
273	46	238	284	521	10	280	290
12	52	67	69	104	25	23	89
5141	877	-408	469	4822	89	-203	-114
1717	373	-888	-460	1165	281	-390	-109
5241	895	-889	6	4435	83	-1128	-1045
3702	804	-714	90	3939	951	-934	17
1800	306	358	664	2199	41	-310	-269
350	76	200	276	725	175	373	548
15584			2659	15884			300
930			1505	9134			2204

Source: Guy Routh, *Occupation and Pay in Great Britain 1906–1979* (Macmillan, London, 1980), Table 1.1, pp. 6–7.

Changes in Part-Time Employment Opportunities and Growth of the Female Labour Force

Information on the number of women working part-time has become available only since the Second World War. There are three main sources of information. First, Population Censuses from 1961 onwards have contained information, but based on different definitions of part-time work.[18] The 1961 Population Census contained a question on whether the employed population was engaged in part-time or full-time work, 'part-time' being defined as work for 'less than the normal hours in employment'. An estimated 5% under-enumeration of married women in the labour force must have contained a large proportion of part-time workers who had declared that they were economically inactive because of the ambiguity in the definition of part-time work. The 1966 sample census had a similar question about the numbers of hours spent in part-time employment, but omitted the misleading definition of 'part-time'. The 1971 Census schedule simply asked: 'How many hours does a (person) usually work, excluding over-time and meal breaks?' This brought the 1971 Census more closely in line with the second main source of information on part-time work, the quarterly returns made by the manufacturing establishments to the department of Employment (and formerly the Ministry of Labour) called the 'L' returns. The dividing line between part-time and full-time work was drawn at 30 hours per week for the overwhelming number of workers, important exceptions being made for teachers and similar groups. The third important source, which encompasses all workers, and includes the seasonal workers omitted by Population Censuses, is the Family Expenditure Survey, which is based on a rotating sample design and therefore involves taking samples of households throughout the year. A slight definitional change of part-time work from 'over 10 hours and up to 30 hours' (a definition used for the period 1963–1967) to 'work of less than 30 hours' (a definition used in subsequent years), raises problems of time comparability, though, by assuming a temporal constancy in the ratio of part-time workers employed for less than 10 hours to those employed for 10 to 30 hours, a series has been generated for the years 1963–1972.

More recent sources of information on female part-time employment include the New Earnings Survey, first conducted in 1968, repeated in 1970 and subsequent years, and the annual Census of Employment taken every June since 1971. The New Earnings Survey, based on details supplied by employers and matched with National Insurance numbers, provides information on part-time workers among females of all ages and women (i.e., females aged 18 and over). Similar information is available for the Census of Employment which, however, excludes employees in private domestic service and counts the number of jobs rather than the number of persons doing these jobs. Finally, the General Household Survey, published annually, has information on the number of days and hours worked per week, disaggregated by age, sex, marital status and a number of other attributes.

Figure 3.7 represents the percentage changes in the number of females employed part-time for the period 1950–1975 calculated from these different data sources. The number of female part-time workers in manufacturing industries rose from about 10% in the early 1950s to about 25% in 1975, though the figures for 1974 and 1975 are not strictly comparable with those of earlier years, since they are derived from a new sample of manufacturing firms using different stratification factors. The next longest series comes from Family Expenditure Surveys which provide data on female part-time workers in all sectors. The trend in this case shows a rise from 37.5% in 1962 to 45.5% in 1971, with a fall subsequently to 41.4% in 1975. The short series from the Census of Employment data indicates a trend which is inconsistent with that of the Family Expenditure series. A possible explanation may be that while there was a decline in the proportion of female workers in all sectors during the period 1971–1974, there may also have been a relative increase in the number of part-time jobs available which, as mentioned before, is the basis of the count in the case of the Census of Employment data.

A more detailed examination of the trends in part-time employment would need some breakdown of this group by industry or occupation orders.[19] Since data is more available by industry orders for the earlier census years, Table 3.4 presents the breakdown of part-time employees by various industries as a percentage of all employees in these industries for different years from 1961 to 1975. An examination of the census-derived percentages for 1961, 1966 and 1971 shows an overall upward trend at all levels, though there is considerable variation in the proportions between industries. This is particularly noticeable in

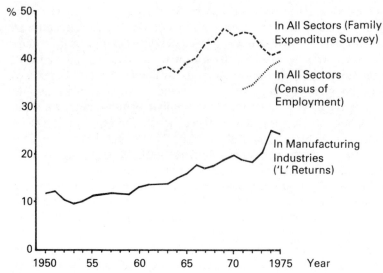

Fig. 3.7 *Percentage of Females Employed Part-Time in Britain: 1950–1975*

Sources: 1) *Historical Abstract of Labour Statistics*
2) *Annual Abstract of Labour Statistics 1970–*
3) *Family Expenditure Survey 1962–*

Notes: 1) Part-time employment is defined as ordinary employment involving *not* more than 30 hours a week.
2) In Manufacturing Industries ('L' Returns i.e. returns that employers have to provide each month to the Department of Employment) the 1974 & 1975 figures are derived from a new sample of manufacturing firms which took account of the rise in the size of manufacturing firms (as measured by the increase in the average work force). See note on page 736 of *Department of Employment Gazette*, August 1974.

the case of manufacturing industries (i.e., Industry Orders III–XVI), where the highest proportion of part-time employees, over one-third of the total female employees, was in 'Food, Drink and Tobacco' with all other industries, with the sole exception of 'Shipbuilding and Marine Engineering', recording one-fifth to one-third of their total female work force as part-time workers. It is also interesting to note that the two industries with a large female work force,[20] 'Textiles' and 'Clothing and Footwear', did not have more than the average proportion of part-time employees in their work

Table 3.4   Percentage of Female Part-Time Workers by Industry
Order: 1961–1975

	1961 Census	1966 Census	1971 Census	April 1972 New Earnings Survey	June 1975 Census of Employment
I Agriculture, Forestry, Fishing	25.6	36.5	43.4	40.2	42.9
II Mining and Quarrying	14.1	22.5	23.3	24.4	21.6
III Food, Drink and Tobacco	25.3	30.3	33.7	35.2	34.9
IV Chemicals and Allied Industries	15.0	21.4	22.0	19.4	22.1
V Metal Manufacture	17.2	21.4	22.1	17.4	20.7
VI Engineering and Electrical Goods	16.1	21.5	22.4	20.0	22.7
VII Shipbuilding and Marine Engineering	16.2	20.2	24.9	31.1	23.2
VIII Vehicles	11.6	15.6	15.7	12.8	13.3
IX Metal Goods n.e.s.	25.8	30.4	29.1	26.2	26.7
X Textiles	21.5	25.2	23.2	18.4	21.7
XI Leather, Leather Goods and Fur	29.0	33.0	31.9	19.9	27.9
XII Clothing and Footwear	23.4	25.0	23.2	17.6	19.5
XIII Bricks, Pottery, Glass, etc.	15.6	19.4	21.1	14.1	21.3
XIV Timber, Furniture, etc.	23.1	26.7	27.3	24.0	26.4
XV Paper, Printing and Publishing	16.9	21.4	23.4	20.4	23.7
XVI Other Manufacturing Industries	23.6	28.3	30.1	25.9	30.4
XVII Construction	24.4	31.3	37.0	30.9	34.4
XVIII Gas, Electricity, Water	15.0	18.9	19.8	19.2	21.9
XIX Transport and Communication	13.1	18.6	22.2	18.1	21.3
XX Distributive Trades	26.1	34.6	40.0	39.3	50.3
XXI Insurance, Banking, Finance	14.6	17.3	27.6	22.5	28.5

Table **3.4** *contd.*

		1961 Census	1966 Census	1971 Census	April 1972 New Earnings Survey	June 1975 Census of Employ- ment
XXII	Professional and Scientific	29.8	36.9	52.8	40.2	47.1
XXIII	Miscellaneous Services	35.0	45.4	51.3	47.9	55.5
XXIV	Public Administration and Defence	17.0	20.9	23.1	24.7	27.8

Sources: *1971 Population Census*: Great Britain Economic Activity Part IV, Table 26. *British Labour Statistics*: Historical Abstract, Table 143, p. 275. New Earnings Survey, 1972, *Department of Employment Gazette,* Vol. LXXXIV, No. 9, September, 1976, Table I, pp. 992–995.

force. However, it was in the 'Service' industries and 'Agriculture and related industries' that the highest proportions were recorded with more than half the female work force in 'Professional and Scientific services' of which about 50% were in the Educational services, and 'Miscellaneous services' of which about 40% were in catering trades and domestic services. No less than two-thirds of all female part-timers are to be found in three service industries, namely, Professional and Scientific Services, the Distributive Trades and Miscellaneous Services.

The most notable increase in the proportion of part-time female employees over time was in 'Insurance, Banking and Finance', which recorded an increase of about 90% in the decade between 1961 and 1971. Increases of 77% and 70% were recorded in 'Professional and Scientific Services' and 'Agriculture and related industries' over the same period, while a fall of about 1% was recorded for 'Clothing and Footwear'. While measures derived from the Census of Employment were not strictly comparable with those derived from Population Censuses, a fall in the proportion of part-time workers has been recorded in almost all industries in the last few years, providing support for the evidence in the Family Expenditure data. The 1972 New Earnings Survey tends to depress the proportions in all industries with the exception of 'Mining and

Quarrying' and 'Food, Drink and Tobacco'.

To sum up, the growth of part-time employment, particularly among married women, has been a major feature of female employment for the post-war period in this country. Part-time work has predominated in those sectors which lend themselves to such work, either because demand for labour is intermittent (e.g. catering, cleaning and entertainment), or in those sectors where full-time workers are in short supply. They are a clearly identifiable group who are often treated differently in terms of pay, fringe benefits, promotion and tenure. It will be seen in a later chapter that the disproportionate number of women represented among part-time workers has an important bearing on the 'inferior' status of women in employment.

Finally, to pinpoint the basic features of the changes in the British labour force during the last seven or eight decades described up till now, the following illustrations might be illuminating. At the beginning of this century, a typical British male worker was likely to be about 30 years old, live in a city, be an unskilled or semi-skilled worker who began work when he was about 12 years old. He could be expected to work for another twenty years. By the seventies, he had become a skilled worker, aged 40 years, working and living in an urban area, began working when he was fifteen and has a working life expectancy of another twenty years. The typical woman worker, at the turn of the century, was also a city dweller, a widow or spinster aged 25 years, employed as a domestic servant or in a textile factory. By the seventies, the typical female worker, aged 40 years, is married, has returned to work after some years of economic inactivity, and works part-time in a clerical job.[21]

Correlates of Long-Term Changes in the Size and Composition of the British Labour Force: A Demographic Analysis

In this section an attempt will be made to provide a quantitative assessment of the importance of age/sex compositional factors, as well as of changes in family responsibilities (shown by the age and number of dependent children) and the growth in part-time employment opportunities for women, in promoting or inhibiting long-term growth of the British labour force. The focus of interest here is on the long-term determinants of labour force growth and the method of analysis involves the use of a battery of standardisation techniques familiar in demographic analysis. However, before starting on such an analysis it would be useful to distinguish between the short-term and long-term determinants of labour force growth.

In the last chapter which reviewed empirical work on labour force participation, the main emphasis was on the short-term factors influencing labour supply. These included the usual wage and income variables as well as measures of the level and structure of labour demand. By incorporating these variables into the framework of the household choice, short-run labour force participation behaviour was examined and 'explained'. Certain demographic variables — notably, age, sex, marital status and family characteristics — were introduced as 'control' variables in a number of studies discussed in the last chapter. In the present section these demographic variables are considered as determinants of long-term labour force growth. The impact of immigration on labour force growth, despite its importance during the post-war period, will not be examined here, mainly because of the unavailability of suitable census data on the demographic characteristics of the immigrants.[22]

The size and composition of a country's labour force depends not only on the size of its population, but also on the composition of that population with respect to a number of characteristics which affect both the ability and desire to work of its adult inhabitants. These characteristics are primarily demographic ones, such as the age and sex composition of the population, as well as the marital condition and family responsibilities[23] of its female components. Changes in these characteristics have considerable implications for the long-term growth of the labour force.[24]

A primary factor determining the size of a labour force in any country is its total population. Not only does the population size impose a physical constraint on the growth of the labour force but also in any country experiencing rapid population change, the structure and size of its future labour force is continuously being modified by the dynamics of this change. Figures 3.8 and 3.9 indicate the strength of the relationship between population size and labour force numbers for a number of countries picked out at random from the UN Demographic Yearbook for 1974. It is seen that the relationship is very close and positive for males ($r = 0.98$). A correlation coefficient of 0.83 for females suggests a greater

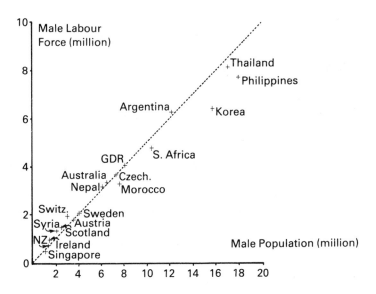

Fig. 3.8   *Total Population and Labour Force (Males)*

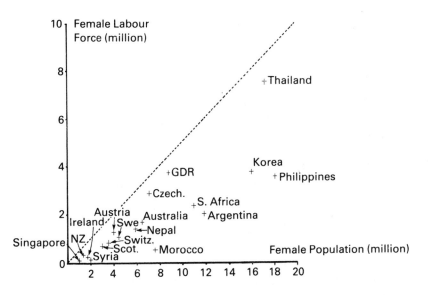

Fig. 3.9   *Total Population and Labour Force (Females)*

diversity in the social attitudes to working women, though the existence of marked differences in the reporting of women in paid employment between countries must also be taken into account.

While the most important effect of the total population is to shape the main contours of its working population, there are certain other variables which more specifically determine the size and composition of the labour force. These include the age and sex compositions of the population, its marital status, and family characteristics. It would be useful to examine briefly how some of these characteristics have changed in Britain over the last hundred years. Figures 3.10 (a)–(e) summarise the changes in age-composition between 1881–1971 for five demographic groups — total males, total females, single females, married females and widowed and divorced females. These diagrams are in the form of 100 percent surface charts, so that the changing width of the band for any age-group reflects the changing proportion of the population in that age-group. Principally, a decline in the percentage of the population under 15 years from 37.5% in 1881 to 25.2% in 1971 for total males, and from 35.5 to 22.6% in the case of females must have been a positive factor in labour force growth, though this trend was to some extent counterbalanced by the increase in the proportion of the population aged 65 years and over which grew from 4.3% to 10.4% for males and from 5% to 15.8% for females during the same period. To a smaller extent, changes in the numbers in the 20–24 and 60–64 age-groups for males may be pertinent insofar as they reflect in the first case later entry into the labour force as a result of longer periods of full-time education and training, and in the latter case a trend towards earlier retirement. If one examines the charts relating to the female population in different marital status groups, the following main features may be noted. In the case of single females, the proportion in the age-range 20 to 44 years, the ages of maximal labour force activity, has fallen and there has been a rise in the relative numbers aged 65 years and over. For both the widowed and divorced groups, and, to a smaller extent for married females, there has been an increase in the proportion among the older age-groups.

A useful way of assessing the importance of changes in age-composition on labour force activity of the principal demographic groups studied here, is to derive the labour force participation rates of these groups while holding constant the influence of age-

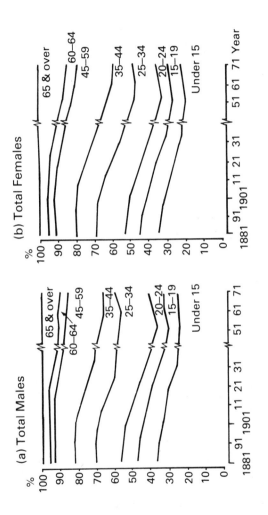

Fig. 3.10 *Percentage Changes in the Age-Structure of the British Population by Sex and (for females only) Marital Status: 1881–1971*

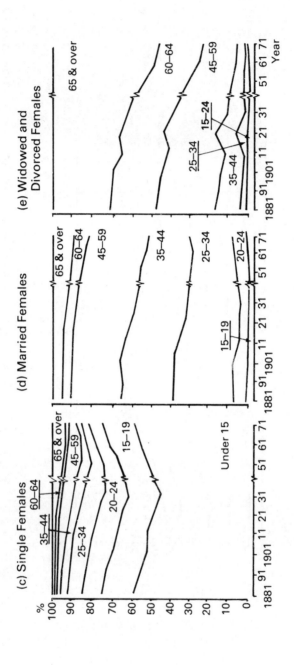

Fig. 3.10   *contd.*

Sources: Censuses of Population: England and Wales and Scotland 1881–1971

Note: Since no census was taken in 1941, no reliable data are available for that year.

compositional changes on the rates. By taking the age-distribution of the population in 1881 as standard,[25] the expected overall participation rates for various groups were derived and then compared with the actual rates. The magnitude and direction of these differences are shown in Table 3.5. For males, changes in age-composition had a progressively favourable effect on labour force participation until 1951, with the effect gradually becoming less important thereafter. In other words, the declining proportion of the population below working age (however defined) more than compensated for the increasing proportion of the elderly until 1951, so that this trend stimulated labour force growth; but after 1951, the disproportionate rise in the juvenile population led to a declining positive effect of age-compositional changes on labour force participation rates. For females as a whole, changes in age-composition have had a relatively smaller effect on labour force participation rates, though when disaggregated by marital status categories, age-compositional changes have had a gradually increasing negative effect on participation rates of married women, probably due to a falling average age at marriage and the earlier start to family building activity.[26] A rapid rise in the proportion of aged widows from 53% aged 60 and over in 1881 to 77% in the same age range in 1971, together with the rise in the average age of adult single females, has also depressed labour force activity in these groups.

The above analysis for various groups in the female population is not complete unless it allows for changes in the relative size of various marital status groups over the period. Following standardisation procedures similar to those used to control age-compositional changes, calculations were carried out, using the proportions in each marital status group in 1881 as the standard. The results are contained in Table 3.6. It is evident that from 1931 onwards the changes in marital-composition have inhibited labour force participation among the female population. The disproportionate growth in the number of married females, at the expense of single females, especially in the younger age-groups, has been the primary inhibitory factor. This tendency has, to a smaller extent, been counterbalanced by the relative increase of divorced females who have a higher participation rate than their married counterparts over the whole age-range, though here again the rise in life expectancy has raised the average age of widowhood, and

Table 3.5 Observed and Expected Labour Force Participation Rates for Various Demographic Groups in Great Britain: 1891–1971 (1881 age-composition taken as the Standard)

Demographic Group	Census Year							
	1891	1901	1911	1921	1931	1951	1961	1971
Total Males								
Expected Rates	62.5	61.8	61.2	61.3	64.9	56.4	55.8	53.5
Observed Rates	63.1	64.5	65.4	66.9	68.9	66.7	64.8	60.6
Difference	−0.6	−2.7	−4.2	−5.6	−4.0	−10.3	−9.0	−7.1
Total Females								
Expected Rates	26.7	24.5	25.4	25.5	29.0	27.8	29.5	32.5
Observed Rates	26.4	24.9	25.7	25.5	26.9	27.4	29.2	33.4
Difference	0.3	−0.4	−0.3	0.0	2.1	0.4	0.3	−0.9
Married Females								
Expected Rates	–	–	9.7	8.9	10.8	23.2	30.7	45.9
Observed Rates	–	–	9.6	8.7	10.0	21.5	29.9	42.9
Difference	–	–	0.1	0.2	0.8	1.7	0.8	3.0

Single Females

Expected Rates	—	—	—	38.3	33.4	32.9	23.9
Observed Rates	—	—	—	41.4	35.5	30.8	24.5
Difference	—	—	—	-3.1	-2.1	2.1	0.6

Widowed and Divorced Females

Expected Rates	—	—	—	—	30.1	36.0	39.6
Observed Rates	—	—	—	—	20.7	22.0	23.6
Difference	—	—	—	—	9.4	14.0	16.0

Notes: (a) Labour force participation rates are calculated with the denominator as total population rather than the more conventional denominator of working-age population, so as to make the data from different censuses comparable. This takes account of changes in the minimum age of entry, but does not allow for the great increase in the number of people leaving the labour force at ages 60 and 65 with the introduction of a comprehensive state pension scheme.

(b) Information on labour activity of females by marital status became available from 1901, though there is considerable doubt about the accuracy of those figures.

(c) Putting the 'widowed' and 'divorced' into one group is resorted to only becuse such a practice was prevalent in earlier censuses. However, from an analytical point of view, such a grouping subsumes certain basic differences between the two groups, namely, the significant differences in the age-composition of the two groups and the opposing trends over the period, with the widows becoming less important in the middle age-groups and a rise in the proportion of the 'divorced' over the age-range, but especially in the younger age-groups.

consequently reduced the labour force activity rate of widows.[27] To sum up, both changes in age-composition and marital-composition have inhibited labour force participation of the female population over the period under discussion.

The analysis so far has been conducted on the implicit assumption that changes in age-composition and marital-composition are independent of each other. However, there is a close dynamic relationship between these two variables. Any change in marital status, through its effect on fertility and to a lesser extent on mortality and migration, will be an important long-term determinant of the age-composition of a population. Similarly, changes in age-composition by their effects on the numbers exposed to risks of marriage, divorce and widowhood, would affect the distribution of a population into various marital status groups. The calculation of the numerical contribution of this 'interaction' effect is shown in Table 3.6. A large negative value for 1951 indicates that, despite changes in both compositional factors working independently of each other to inhibit labour force activity, the interaction of the two factors more than compensated for the downward trend.[28] However, a more likely explanation is that there has been a dramatic change in labour force activity of all groups since the War. One way of testing this hypothesis is to estimate the expected numbers in each age/sex/marital status group for the years 1951, 1961 and 1971 on two alternative assumptions:

   (a) age-specific participation rates for various groups remained at the 1931 levels, and
   (b) the age-specific rates for various groups remained at the 1951 levels for all subsequent census years.

The results of these simple standardisation exercises are summarised in Table 3.7. The method of calculating 'normalised' ratios is indicated at the foot of the table. The trends in the normalised ratios for different demographic groups (irrespective of whether the age-specific participation rates of 1931 or 1951 were used) show that changes in participation rates have tended to depress the growth of the male labour force and stimulate greatly the growth of the female labour force, especially its married component — a conclusion already discussed in some detail earlier in this chapter. It is, however, the 'differences' in the normalised ratios for each group contained in Table 3.7 that provide some indication of the transformation in labour force participation

Table 3.6   Observed and Expected Labour Force Participation Rates of the Female Population in Great Britain 1911–1971 (1881 age-composition and/or marital status-composition taken as the Standard)

	Census Year					
	1911	1921	1931	1951	1961	1971
Expected rates (controlling both age- and marital status-composition)	24.4	26.2	28.8	23.3	32.7	34.8
Observed rates	25.7	25.5	26.9	27.4	29.2	33.4
Difference [1]	-1.3	0.7	1.8	-4.1	3.5	1.4
Expected rates (controlling only age-composition)	25.4	25.5	29.0	27.8	29.5	32.5
Observed rates	25.7	25.5	26.9	27.4	29.2	33.4
Difference [2]	-0.3	0.0	2.1	0.4	0.3	-0.9
Expected rates (controlling only marital status-composition)	24.7	25.2	27.4	29.1	32.4	36.1
Observed rates	25.7	26.3	26.9	27.4	29.2	33.4
Difference [3]	-1.0	-1.1	0.5	1.7	3.2	2.7
'Interaction' effect [1-(2+3)]	0.0	-0.4	-0.8	-6.1	0.0	-0.4

Table 3.7   Normalised Ratios of Expected Numbers over Observed Numbers in the Labour Force for Various Demographic Groups in Great Britain — the Expected Numbers calculated by applying (a) 1931 and (b) 1951 Labour Force Participation Rates

Demographic Groups	Ratio			
	1931	*1951*	*1961*	*1971*
Total Males				
Ratio (1931 rates)	1.000	1.026	1.040	1.090
Ratio (1951 rates)	0.975	1.000	1.014	1.061
Difference	0.025	0.026	0.026	0.029
Total Females				
Ratio (1931 rates)	1.000	0.855	0.770	0.671
Ratio (1951 rates)	1.170	1.000	0.904	0.770
Difference	-0.170	-0.145	-0.134	-0.099
Single Females				
Ratio (1931 rates)	1.000	0.923	0.934	1.050
Ratio (1951 rates)	1.082	1.000	1.010	1.128
Difference	-0.082	-0.077	-0.076	-0.078
Married Females				
Ratio (1931 rates)	1.000	0.460	0.333	0.232
Ratio (1951 rates)	2.174	1.000	0.723	0.493
Difference	-1.174	-0.540	-0.390	-0.261
Widowed and Divorced Females				
Ratio (1931 rates)	1.000	0.890	0.732	0.695
Ratio (1951 rates)	1.124	1.000	0.795	0.742
Difference	-0.124	-0.110	-0.063	-0.047

Notes: The expected numbers in the labour force for each group were calculated by applying the age-specific participation rates of 1931 and 1951 to the population in the corresponding age-group and adding over all age-groups. The ratio of the expected numbers over observed numbers gave the normalised ratio. Normalised ratios were then calculated for various demographic groups using 1931 and 1951 age-specific labour force participation ratios.

patterns between the pre-war and post-war eras. For males the differences between the normalised ratios based on 1931 and 1951 ratios were small, positive and stable indicating little difference in participation patterns between 1931 and 1951. The absolute magnitude of the differences for married females fell by about half between 1931 and 1951, showing a significant transformation in labour force participation behaviour between the pre-war and post-war periods. A similar trend is noticeable in case of the widowed and divorced females. The stability of the 'differences' in the case of single females is also worthy of note.

So far we have investigated the effects of three demographic factors on the size and growth of the British labour force — namely, the size, age-composition and marital status of the population. There is another demographic factor which affects labour force participation of women, and that is the weight of domestic responsibilities that a woman may be called upon to bear, and this is partly determined by her marital status, but largely by the number and age of her children.[29]

We have taken account of the first factor; it is to the second that we now turn. Information on labour force activities of women by numbers and ages of dependent children is available only for the last three censuses.[30] An examination of the participation rates for this group and for these years, as shown in Table 3.1, shows that the rates:

(a) are negatively correlated with the number of dependent children;
(b) rise as the ages of dependent children rise; and
(c) have increased over time, with relatively greater increases being recorded among those with a large number of dependent children than among those with very young or very old dependent children.

A question that would then arise is to what extent was the increase in the participation of 'Wives and Mothers' due to changes in the number and age-composition of their children over time. Given the shortness of the period under review, any assessment is of limited value. However, using the same standardisation techniques as before, the results of studying the effects of family responsibilities on participation are shown in Table 3.9. Assuming that the distribution of dependent children by age and number remained at the level observed in the 1961 census, the expected overall labour force participation rates for 1966 and 1971 were compared to their corresponding actual figures. Table 3.9 shows that changes in the scale of family responsibilities had only a slight inhibiting effect on labour force growth of women with dependent children.[31]

The focus of the analysis now shifts from a consideration of the impact on labour force participation of long- and medium-term changes in compositional factors to an attempt to identify in greater detail various factors that may have contributed to the dramatic increases in labour force participation rates of married women and/ or females with family responsibilities since the Second World War. Unfortunately, as mentioned before, reliable data on economic activity of females by age, marital status and family characteristics have been available only since the 1961 census. So our analysis will be confined to the period between 1961 and 1971, a period during which participation rates increased by over 20% for a number of groups shown in Table 3.8. Other features brought out by this table include the recording of relatively higher increases among married women with large families (i.e., four or more dependent children), very old children (i.e. those aged over 16 years) and those with children of school-going age. The last group shows that it is important to consider the contribution of the expansion of part-time employment opportunities in explaining the labour force growth of females with young children — a point that will be taken up later in this chapter. For the 'Others' (i.e., widowed, divorced or single mothers), the increase in participation rates has been negligible among those with any children, and negative among those with very young children, possibly indicating an improvement in social security and other 'support' arrangements.[32]

Given the phenomenal increase in participation rates of married women with young children during the period 1961 to 1971, two questions arise. First, to what extent was this increase due to demographic factors such as changes in the age of the mother, age and number of dependent children? Second, what contributions did factors such as availability of part-time work, reduction in the numbers of hours spent in housework, educational and vocational attainment, and changes in economic circumstances, etc., make towards increasing the participation rates of young mothers? An attempt will be made to answer the first question immediately, but only a partial answer will be suggested with respect to the

Table 3.8 Labour Force Participation Rates of 'Wives and Mothers' by Numbers and Ages of Dependent Children in Britain: 1961–1971

No. of Children	Married Women				Others				All Wives and Mothers			
	1961	1966	1971	% change	1961	1966	1971	% change	1961	1966	1971	% change
With no child	33.2	41.4	44.7	34.7	26.2	28.4	28.4	8.4	32.6	40.4	43.5	33.3
With 1 child	30.1	39.8	42.8	42.3	60.4	62.3	59.9	−0.8	31.6	41.0	44.0	39.2
With 2 children	23.2	32.9	38.4	65.6	55.3	57.6	53.6	−3.2	23.9	33.5	38.9	62.6
With 3 children	18.1	27.7	34.8	92.2	40.4	44.3	42.2	4.5	18.3	28.1	35.0	91.9
With 4 children	14.9	23.8	30.8	107.1	30.9	35.9	32.3	4.7	15.2	24.0	30.9	103.3
With 5 or more	10.0	19.1	25.7	157.3	21.2	25.7	22.2	4.7	10.2	19.3	25.6	150.7
Age of Children												
0–4 years	11.5	17.8	19.9	72.1	39.6	38.3	32.7	−17.3	11.9	18.1	20.2	70.2
5–10 years	23.8	34.0	40.0	68.2	51.5	53.5	50.2	−2.6	24.5	34.5	40.4	65.1
11–15 years	33.5	46.1	52.2	56.0	58.1	60.4	59.6	2.7	34.6	46.7	52.6	52.1
16 and over	31.1	46.5	53.8	73.2	58.1	64.6	68.0	16.9	33.1	47.7	54.8	65.6

Sources: Derived from Household Composition Tables, 1961 and 1971 Censuses, England and Wales and Scotland, 1966 Sample Census, Great Britain.

contribution of part-time employment to labour force participation in this chapter.

In the period between 1961 and 1971, the overall participation rate of all married women increased from 29.7% to 42.9% — an increase of 13.2% compared to 8% in the previous decade. Over the same period, the labour force participation rate of married women under 45 years rose from 34.4% to 47.3% — an increase of 12.9%. Our analysis will be confined to this sub-group on the basis that by far the largest number of dependent children belong to women of this category. The question then arises as to how great a component of this increase is a result of a 'real' increase in the labour force participation rate, and how much of the increase can be attributed to compositional changes. Applying the 'Components of change' method described earlier to the data on married women workers by age and number of dependent children, the results summarised in Table 3.9 are generated. It should be noted that, due to the exigencies of the data, it was not possible to quantify the 'combined' effects of the compositional factors — age of mother, age of dependent children and the number of dependent children taken together. Instead, the 'joint' effects of age of mother/age of dependent children and age of mother/number of dependent children were considered separately.

Table 3.9 shows that if the participation rate of married women under 45 years (disaggregated by age, number of dependent children and age of these children) remained at the 1961 level, changes in compositional factors would have brought about a fall in the overall labour force participation rate of this group of women. Two possible reasons may be offered why changes in compositional factors may have worked towards reducing the labour force participation of these females. First, the inflated 1946–50 birth cohorts of the post-war baby boom had just reached or were reaching their age of maximal fertility by the latter half of the 60s. Second, for the reason just mentioned and for other reasons, the mid-60s saw the peak of the second post-war fertility cycle.[33] These two factors working together contributed to an increase in marriages and births, both of which in varying degrees inhibited married women's involvement with the labour force. A 'real' increase in the overall labour force participation rates of about 18% was needed among women of all child-bearing age-groups and family sizes to record a 'net' increase of 12.9% in the participation

Table 3.9 Components of Labour Force Participation Increase for Total Married Women Aged Under 45 Years in Britain: 1961–1971

Group	'Real Increase in Labour Force Participation Rate %	Contribution of:		Net Increase in Labour Force Participation Rates %
		Compositional Factors %	'Interaction' Between Compositional Factors %	
A. Married women by age and number of dependent children	15.7	−2.4	−0.4	12.9
B. Married women by age and age of dependent children	14.0	−0.3	0.3	14.0
C. Married women in part-time employment by age and number of dependent children	12.3	−2.2	0.1	10.2

rates over the period.

When the same exercise was performed in the case of married women cross-classified by their ages and the ages of their dependent children, the contribution of the compositional factors was insignificant, and the estimated 'net' increase of 14% was also the 'real' increase. However, data on labour force activity of married women by the ages of their children is not satisfactory since a married woman who has children in several age-groups is counted in all these groups, so that an analysis cannot discriminate between a woman who has several children in different age-groups and a woman whose child or children are confined to a particular age-group — a discrimination that is necessary to allow for important differences in the kinds of pressures faced by these two types of women in deciding whether they should join the labour force or not. More suitable data relating female labour force activity to the age of the youngest child is available as unpublished data only for the 1971 census.

Explaining Post-War Increases in Working Mothers: Some Concluding Remarks

In the previous chapter we have examined a whole series of factors 'explaining' both short-term and long-term changes in the labour force participation rates of married women. We now focus our attention on three main explanations for the dramatic increase in the participation rates of married women with young children in the post-war period. First, a combination of child rearing and paid employment has become easier either (a) because of changes in the type of work available, for example, part-time work, or (b) because women with young children find work at home less time-consuming — this may be as a result of the spread of labour-saving domestic appliances, or because of the growth of services such as child-care facilities outside the home. A third explanation may be sought not in terms of a reduction in the constraints imposed by young children, but in terms of the need to find paid employment — this may be desirable for life-fulfilment as the level of educational attainment has risen, and/or it may arise from changing income aspirations of younger wives compared to older wives.[34]

Given the necessary data, an empirical study could distinguish between the two explanations. In the first, the emphasis is on changes which may have reduced the constraint of children on mother's employment — notably availability of part-time work, reduction in time spent on housework, availability of outside agencies for child-care and home-based jobs. In the second, the emphasis is on age or generation factors affecting labour force participation — notably, higher income aspirations, improved fertility control and the consequent reduction in the number of unplanned children, and the postponement of the birth of the first child so as to improve the employability of a woman by raising her educational attainment and providing her with work experience.

The data requirements for such a detailed empirical study are formidable. Extensive profiles of individual women by age, number of children, age of youngest child, educational attainment, number of hours worked, family income excluding wife's earnings are needed. When this is available, as in the United States, where 1/20 or more commonly 1/100 and 1/1000 parts of population censuses can be purchased, multivariate analysis, especially multiple classification analysis, can be used to study the determinants of labour force activity of married women. A study by Sweet (1973) uses five main independent variables consisting of:

(i)   age of the youngest child,
(ii)   number of children under 18 years,
(iii)   educational attainment,
(iv)   age of woman,
(v)   income adequacy (measured by an indicator which has for its numerator family income less wife's earnings and the denominator is a measure of the minimum income needs of that family based on data derived from a 1959 budget study in New York to determine eligibility for public assistance).

Other family history and compositional variables including age at marriage, length of the first birth interval, and marital stability are added one at a time to assess their effects on employment, independent of their correlation with the main explanatory variables listed above. These family history variables are seen as providing an indication of the 'likelihood' that a woman will seek and find a job in the future on the basis that a woman who has had some work experience before or after a marriage is more likely to return, either because of a more favourable disposition to work and greater 'employability rating', *or* because family consumption has adjusted early in the marriage to joint earnings, *or* because of a different strategy of child-spacing which could adversely affect the fecundity of these women and provide more time for a downward revision in the desired family size.

The unavailability of such detailed census data (including income data which is not available from Population Censuses in this country) makes such an approach impossible here. There are, however, survey data of which, as we have seen in the last chapter, the most widely-used in recent studies are obtained from General Household Surveys. Given the size of the sample and the extent of the cross-classifications required, its use for studies similar to that of Sweet (1973) is impracticable. There have also been surveys of women in employment including Klein (1965), Jephcott *et al.* (1962) and Hunt (1968) which are valuable sources of information on the characteristics of women in employment. Even in these surveys the demographic profiles are not sufficiently defined, nor is detailed information on family income available. In the present study, where investigation concentrates on factors underlying temporal changes, information is confined to two sets of observations for 1961 and 1971 on the economic activity of married women in England, Wales and Scotland by age and number of dependent children, *or* by age and age of all dependent chidlren, *or* by the number of hours worked and number of dependent children, *or* the number of hours worked by age of dependent children.

A recent study by Joshi and Owen (1981) provides a detailed examination of the quantitative impact of family composition, age and marital status, as well as non-demographic variables, on female labour force participation decisions in post-war Britain. The dependent variable whose variations are being 'explained' is the proportion of women in insured employment by each year of age.[35] The 'explanatory' variables, grouped into three categories, consist of:

(a) *Life cycle variables,* such as those measuring fertility, family composition, marital status as well as female/male earnings ratio, whose values differ with age;

(b) *Cohort-specific variables,*[36] such as completed family size, education, experience of unemployment or war, whose values are specific to each cohort and do not change over time; and

(c) *'Period' variables,* consisting mainly of cyclical measures such as total vacancies, excess capacity, male registered unemployed rate whose values depend on the state of the economy.

Under ideal conditions, longitudinal data relating to individual women would provide the best basis for an empirical examination of the determinants of labour force participation decisions. In this study, the sources of data include census-derived statistics for demographic data and labour statistics collected for administrative purposes. The methodology consists of the familiar single equation econometric estimation procedure, with some modifications to allow for 'correct' estimation of fixed cohort effects. It involves regressing the proportion of women in insured employment (excluding students) in each cohort on the explanatory variables discussed above. The 'family formation' variables (defined by the age and number of children in the context of the life cycle position of different cohorts) is assumed to *determine* participation rates rather than *be determined* by it. Further, all exogenous variables are assumed to be exogenous to one another.[37]

Some of the interesting results from our point of view relate to the impact of demographic factors on the particpation decisions of married women. The cohort effect proved to be significant for almost all birth cohorts considered, highlighting the fact that different family formation patterns of different cohorts had a *qualitatively* different impact on participation decisions. The life cycle effects proved to be significant. The presence of a pre-school child per cohort member lowered participation rates on the average by 35%. The corresponding figures for each primary school child and secondary school child were 14% and 7% respectively. Yet the impact of number of children (after allowing for age) on female participation was surprisingly small. For example, between 1971 and 1981, the partial effect of the fall in fertility was a rise of 4% in the participation rate, with the effect expected to be even weaker during the 80s. There was also evidence of a weakening in the inhibitory effect of the presence of secondary school children on the participation of mothers during the period 1951 to 1974. Age of the women proved to have a negative effect on participation, with a fall of about 20% in the participation rates between the ages of 20 to 59. However, this age effect was of a smaller magnitude than the inhibitory effect of the presence of a pre-school child in the family. The impact on the length of working life of an average women arising from the presence of dependent children is less than normally assumed — being between 16 and 19 per cent of the time between ages 20 to 59. Finally, marriage as an independent factor from fertility proved to have little effect on participation rates.

An important limitation of the study by Joshi and Owen is the neglect of part-time work as one of the factors which has facilitiated the entry of married women into the labour force in post-war Britain. It is evident from even a cursory examination that the growth of part-time work has considerable significance for the rapid increase in participation rates among married women during the period from 1961 to 1971. Table 3.10 shows the percentage of women in part-time employment for the two census years 1961 and 1971, disaggregated by number and age of dependent children. Over the period, in almost all categories, an increase of over 15%

Table 3.10 Percentage of Married Women in Part-Time Employment in Britain by Number and Age of Dependent Children: 1961 and 1971

Year	Number of Dependent Children						Age of Dependent Children			
	0	1	2	3	4	5+	0–4	5–11	11–15	16+
1961	27.4	45.1	54.7	55.9	56.0	56.5	49.6	55.0	49.3	43.0
1971	38.5	57.1	68.3	69.2	68.0	67.2	69.4	69.0	61.7	57.1

Source: Population Census Household Composition Tables for England and Wales and Scotland: 1961 and 1971

Notes: (a) Post-enumeration Survey of the 1961 Census revealed a 5% under-enumeration of what was overwhelmingly part-time married women workers — an upward adjustment was made accordingly.

(b) An adjustment involving proportional allocation of those who did not state the number of hours worked was performed.

(c) The 1961 Census was ambiguous as to what constituted part-time employment, with part-time being defined as 'less than the normal hours in employment'. As a result there were persons working a 42 hour week who were included under the part-time employed. To conform with the more widely-accepted definition followed by the 1971 Census as well as the Department of Employment, only those working for 30 hours or less a week were included in estimating the proportions in part-time employment for various categories given in the table.

was recorded, suggesting that a crucial factor in the increase in the married women component of the labour force in recent years is the expansion in the opportunities for part-time employment. A quantitative assessment of the contribution of this factor to labour force growth is made particularly difficult by the unavailability of cross-classified data relating part-time employment to age, number of children and age of dependent children. A crude method of making up for the deficiencies in data is to estimate the expected numbers in each age/number of dependent children category from the data derived from the 1961 and 1971 Censuses and then apply multiple standardisation procedures mentioned previously. The results are summarised in Table 3.9. They show that, despite the inhibiting operation of compositional factors on growth of part-time employment, the 'real' increase in the proportion of total married women who had part-time jobs was about 12% over the decade between 1961 and 1971.

To sum up, the long-term changes in the size and composition of the British labour force have been due primarily to two opposing tendencies — a falling male participation rate and a rising female rate. When these changes have been particularly pronounced (after the Second World War) compositional factors such as changes in age/marital status and family composition have inhibited labour force growth of the female component, but this has been more than counterbalanced by dramatic increases in the labour force participation rates of married women, an important contributory factor for this increase being the rise in part-time employment opportunities for these women.

Trends in Labour Force Participation in the Seventies: A Postscript

During the seventies certain notable changes have occurred in the pattern of labour force participation of both men and women. These changes have been examined in a recent article entitled 'Labour Force Outlook to 1986' in the *Employment Gazette* (Department of Employment, April 1981, pp. 167–73). The article serves as the basis for much of the statistical data contained in this section. Table E in the Data Appendix is directly derived from Table 4 (p. 171) in this article.

During the period 1971–1980, the total labour force in Britain increased from 25 million to 26 million. This growth has not, however, been continuous, and masks certain important compositional changes. Between 1971 and 1976, an increase of one million occurred, but subsequently the trend appears to have been irregular, not showing much change overall. Certain changes in labour force shares of different groups also occurred. The male share fell from 64% in 1971 to 60% in 1980. The percentage of married women in the labour force rose from 23% in 1971 to 26% in 1980, while the share of the 'non-married' females remained fairly constant at 13–14 percent over the period.

Changes in the size of the labour force depend on three main factors. First, the size of the working-age population would clearly constrain the numbers entering the labour force.[38] Between 1971 and 1981, the total working-age population increased by about two million, of which 730,000 were added during the four years to 1981. It is estimated that this increase of 730,000 was a result of increases of 378,000 males and 552,000 'non-married' females and a *fall* of 200,000 married females.

These compositional changes in the working-age population during the four years were the result of the operation of two demographic forces. In the first instance, the low fertility which characterised the twenties and thirties of this century is reflected in a fall of 170,000 and 190,000 in the working-age populations of females aged 45–59 and males aged 45–64 respectively. Secondly, the post-war fertility boom resulted in an additional one million people aged 16–44, with numbers leaving school reaching record levels in 1980 reflecting the 'birth' peak in the mid-sixties. The combined effect of those two demographic forces is to raise the number of younger people (including single women) and reduce the number of older people (especially married women returning to the labour force after child bearing) who are available to participate in the labour force. The participation rates of the expanding group are among the highest of all groups.

A second factor determining changes in the size of the labour force is the participation rates. Two important changes have occurred in the participation rates during the seventies. Table E in the Data Appendix highlights the accelerating decline in the participation rates among the older age-groups i.e., 50–64 and 65–69 among males and 55–59 and 60–64 among females — with decline being particularly marked since 1975 when the rates for the two male groups fell from 85% and 26% in 1975 to 73% and 14% in

1980. A similar decline, more marked than that for previous years, was recorded in the participation rates of women aged 55–59 and 60–64. It may be conjectured that this accelerating decline is a temporary phenomenon reflecting the earlier exit of older workers brought about by the present-day economic climate.

The other change in labour force participation rates occurred among married women. Until 1977, labour force participation rates for married women rose steadily from 42% in 1971 to 50% in 1977. A convergence between the rates for married and 'not-married' females is clearly observable from the figures in Table E.[39] But since 1977, the increase stopped and there is even some evidence of a slight fall back in these rates.

Two main explanations have been suggested for this reversal in trends. First, the effect of the current recession with high unemployment had 'discouraged' women from participating in the labour force. Second, the lower participation is a reflection of the upturn in the birth rate which occurred around 1977.[40] It may be conjectured that the first explanation would imply a decline in participation rates in all age-groups, but especially in the older age-groups which represent to a large extent women returning to the labour force after a period of absence due to family commitments. The second explanation will be reflected in the fall in participation rates among women in the child-bearing age-groups. The data from Table E show that the decline in participation rates occurred in all age-groups, with the exception of the 45–54 age-group where a very slight increase was recorded. There is nothing in the data to indicate that the decline was more marked in the child-bearing age-groups, 20–24 and 25–34 years.

The third factor that determines the extent of the change in size of the labour force is the demand for labour. If we assume that a proxy for the demand for labour is the level of unemployment, it is possible to assess the importance of this factor.[41] There is evidence from regional labour statistics of the existence of a close inverse relationship between regional unemployment rates and the participation rates of age-groups at the margin of retirement (Department of Employment, April 1981, p. 17). There is also evidence, if one includes the *unregistered* unemployed, that the unemployment rate is now higher for women than men and the rate of increase in unemployment over the last decade is faster for women than for men. The effect of growing unemployment (or reducing demand for labour) could dissuade some women from entering or remaining in the labour force. And it is conjectured that this is in fact what is happening to married women whose loose attachment to the labour force, implied by the significant proportion of part-timers in the group, would make them more easily discouraged than any other group in the present economic climate.

In later chapters we shall examine the implications of the more recent trends in labour force participation for the type of jobs that women do, the efficacy of equal opportunity legislation passed in the seventies and the economic status of women generally.

Notes

1. Two notable American studies in this area are Bancroft (1958) and Durand (1948).
2. The earliest census whose coverage and classification make it possible to estimate the labour force was in 1881. The last census for which similar information is available was taken in 1971.
3. Total population rather than working-age population is used in this instance because of the uncertainty regarding the minimal age of entry into the labour force during the earlier years.
4. The role of immigrants in augmenting the British labour force should also be noted. During the period 1961 to 1971, the number of 'UK born' males in employment fell by 1.1 million. This was offset by an increase of 0.9 million 'UK born' females and 0.6 million immigrants of which 41% were females.
5. It is, of course, possible that a declining male labour force could have resulted in technical progress if there had not been a corresponding increase in the females.
6. See Table A, Data Appendix.
7. 1911 is chosen as the earliest year, because only from this census is reliable information available on the marital status of economically active females.
8. The raising of the school leaving age to 16 in 1972 has not affected our analysis since the 1971 Census provides the latest information on the labour force in this survey.
9. By the same token, the growing difficulties of school-leavers in finding jobs in recent times have led to a number postponing entry by staying on at school after 16.
10. Under certain restrictive assumptions with respect to the stability of age/sex/marital status-composition and measures of cohort economic activity rates, Joseph (1980) has constructed a matrix model to project the population and labour force of Britain simultaneously.
11. The *bimodal* pattern in female labour force participation replaced the

pre-war pattern of a *monotonic* decline in participation with age, as shown in Table C, in the Data Appendix to this chapter. This change in the age pattern of participation has also been observed in certain other developed countries, notably in North America and Scandinavia (Economic Commission for Europe, 1980).

12. After the detailed discussion of the determinants of labour force participation of married women in the previous chapter, the analysis contained in this paragraph is fairly simplistic. Its main purpose is to provide some statistical indication of the factors influencing the labour force participation behaviour of married women during the post-war period. The facts still remain; the principal characteristics that tend to increase the chances that a married woman will work or look for work are (a) need for money, (b) fewer competing responsibilities, and (c) employability.

13. Working mothers as a percentage of all mothers rose from about 15% in 1951 to 25% in 1961 to about 40% in 1971. Information from the General Household Survey, 1978, indicates that 52% of all mothers are in employment.

14. The data for Figures 3.5 (a)–(e) and for subsequent discussion of the age/sex specific labour force participation rates are given in Tables B and C in the Data Appendix.

15. The two sets of figures are for England and Wales only.

16. In a later chapter the post-war changes in occupational composition for both sexes will be discussed in some detail. The focus here is the 'contribution' of long-term changes in occupational composition to female labour force growth.

17. The technique of multiple standardisation which is applied in different parts of this book is a common procedure in demographic research. For a useful discussion of this and related techniques, see Kitagawa (1955).

18. Information from the 1951 Population Census is not comparable with that of subsequent censuses because there was no question on the number of hours worked by those who reported that they were in part-time employment.

19. Another illuminating breakdown would be female part-time employment by marital status and family responsibilities. This breakdown and the resulting discussion will be found in a subsequent section of this chapter.

20. The sex-ratios of the employees in 'Textiles' and 'Clothing and Footwear' were 46.5% and 73.7% respectively, according to the 1971 Population Census.

21. Yet another dimension to the character of the change in female participation is the growing importance of working mothers. Before the war, mothers with dependent children hardly participated in the labour force. But by the late seventies about half of all dependent children had working mothers and about 40% of the female work force consisted of working mothers.

22. The basic problem is that population census data relate to country of

birth rather than population by immigrant status. For Population Censuses prior to 1961, a multiple classification by country of birth and demographic characteristics was unavailable.

23. The family responsibilities of a woman depend on two inter-related factors — the number of children she has, and their ages — assuming that she is married in the first place.

24. The geographical distribution of a population would have an important bearing on the size and composition of its labour force if different areas showed marked variations in customs and attitudes associated with work, especially in the case of female workers.

25. The choice of 1881 as the base year was partly influenced by the availability of reliable data for similar age-groups from Population Censuses in England and Wales *and* Scotland, and partly because 1881 served as a useful starting point for any sequential examination of age-compositional changes over the subsequent census years and their effects on the labour force participation rates of different groups. There were also no apparent 'abnormalities' in the age/sex structure of the population in that year.

26. The average age of spinster marriages in Great Britain fell from 25.6 in 1901 to 22.5 years in 1970. The mean age of childbearing fell from about 28 years to 25 years over the same period.

27. The divorce rates increased from 4 per ten thousand married population in 1931 to 60 in 1971 in England and Wales.

28. The early 1950s were characterised by a levelling off of marital fertility and a subsequent decline but a sharp rise occurred in 1956, so that while the proportion of married women rose in the period preceding the census, with the 'baby boom' after the War the proportion of dependents also rose. The interaction factor may have caught the fertility effect which was on the whole conducive to the growth of the married women component of the labour force.

29. Children are more important in explaining the life cycle pattern of female labour force participation than marital status. But whether the presence of dependent children *inhibits* mothers from working less now than before is a different question. The *numbers* of young children and of mothers rose during the post-war period until the late sixties when dramatic increases in participation of wives and mothers took place. Changes in the *tempo* of childbearing recorded by Farid (1974b) contained contrasting tendencies insofar as their impact on the labour force participation of mothers was concerned. Of course, it is possible that the upward trend in participation occurred quite *independent* of the effect of children. Only a *longitudinal* study could provide some of the answers.

30. A 1% sample of the economic activities of 'Wives and Mothers' by age and number of dependent children is available for the 1951 Population Census. But this information was not used because of certain comparability problems with subsequent census data, as well as because of the reported existence of large non-response and sampling errors.

31. This weak conclusion is even further diluted if one takes account of the sampling errors and errors which may have arisen from disciplining the original census data to obtain meaningful categories.

32. It is difficult to speculate further unless data are available cross-classifying these women by age, family responsibilities, educational attainment, socio-economic class, number of hours worked, etc. Such data are available to some extent in the General Household Survey whose sample sizes for the level of disaggregation envisaged and the shortness of the series make their use still problematic. In the present analysis only the married women component of the labour force is considered. This is not, however, a serious drawback since the married component constitutes over 95% of the total 'Wives and Mothers' in England and Wales according to the 1971 Census. Moreover, this component constitutes the most dynamic element in the growth of the British labour force in recent years. Our present focus of interest is to quantify the relative contribution of factors such as changes in age-composition, family responsibilities and part-time employment to the growth in numbers of married women workers.

33. This is a highly condensed reference to the fertility boom which began in England and Wales in 1956 when the number of legitimate births rose by over 30,000 in one year, and continued to rise annually by 2–3% until it peaked in 1964, showing an increase of 23% over its 1956 level. Various explanations have been suggested. These include (a) a stronger tendency for childbearing to start earlier in a marriage (the average childbearing age of women in the 1945 birth cohort was about two years younger than that of women in the 1935 birth cohort); (b) a fall in the modal age at marriage and an increase in the proportion of women marrying (an increase of 27% in the proportion of women married once in the age range 15–44 was recorded between 1955 and 1977); and (c) an increase in the proportion of women marrying younger (the proportion of married women under 25 years increased from about 14% in 1955 to about 20% in 1970), consequently being exposed to the risk of child bearing when they were more fecund. For sources of statistics quoted in this footnote, see Farid (1974a).

34. Easterlin (1968) has argued that young adults have a desired income level determined by the experience of their earlier years. If their present income is high relative to the desired level, they would have more children and *vice versa*.

35. For the period 1949 to 1975, each employee was expected to make a social insurance contribution which was recorded on cards renewed annually. From a count of these cards, statistics on the numbers employed were obtained for each year.

36. A cohort is a group of people with a common characteristic referenced to a fixed point in time. Thus all women born in 1950 or all women married for the first time in 1975 when aged 20–24 are cohorts. The cohort method of analysis is concerned with a study of how a particular cohort compares with another with respect to some variable of interest. The basic advantage of this method of analysis is seen as

arising from the existence of unique cohort effects independent of both life cycle and 'period' effects. Its disadvantages arise from the need for long series of data for each cohort for the cohort effect to be identified *and* the fact that this method of analysis provides little indication of why different cohorts behave in the way they do. For example, a study of the participation decisions of different birth cohorts provided no explanation why the bimodal pattern of labour force participation has emerged in Britain since the War.

37. It is in the nature of regression analysis of this kind that a unidirectional causation spelt out by the relationship between family formation and participation is assumed. Similarly, for precise estimates of the partial effects of the explanatory variables included, it is assumed that all explanatory variables are unrelated to each other. In econometric jargon, the presence of simultaneity bias and multicollinearity raises serious reservations about the validity of single equation estimation procedures similar to the ones used in this study. And it is not merely a statistical problem of interpreting the results. For it is the basis on which endogenous *versus* exogenous classifications are made and the identifying restrictions imposed in the estimation procedures, that the value judgments implicit in the paradigm accepted, manifest themselves. The neoclassical paradigm dominates in empirical work of this kind.

38. The working-age population consists of the female population aged 16–59 and the male population aged 16–64.

39. 'Not-married' women is an unsatisfactory category, since it subsumes the difference between the participation behaviour of single women which is likely to be similar to that of males and that of widowed and divorced women.

40. Calot and Thompson (1981) have produced evidence to show a reversal in fertility trend in England and Wales which raised the Total Period Fertility Rate (i.e., the average number of children per woman that would result if women survived to the end of their child-bearing period subject to the age-specific fertility rates calculated for the year in question) from 1.68 in 1977 to 1.90 by the Spring of 1980 — a change of 15%, but with little change since.

41. It could be argued that 'Unfilled Vacancies' would be a better proxy for the demand for labour than 'Unemployment'.

Data Appendix

Table A   Percentage Share of Women in the British Labour Force by Age and Marital Status: 1911–1971

Census Year	Under 20		20–24		25–44		45–64		64 + over	
	MF	*SWDF*	*MF*	*SWDF*	*MF*	*SWDF*	*MF*	*SWDF*	*MF*	*SWDF*
1911	0.1	42.1	1.9	39.5	5.6	18.8	5.6	14.4	2.7	18.5
1921	0.1	43.5	2.3	40.6	5.5	19.9	5.0	13.7	2.5	16.0
1931	0.4[a]	45.3[a]	3.4[b]	38.1[b]	6.9	19.3	5.0	14.0	2.1	16.3
1951	1.0	48.2	11.0	31.1	15.4	12.1	11.8	14.0	3.5	16.1
1961	1.8	46.4	15.4	25.2	20.8	8.6	17.1	12.3	5.5	20.9
1966	2.5	45.2	16.4	23.6	25.2	7.2	23.1	11.3	9.0	22.8
1971	3.5	43.2	25.9	13.5	21.0	13.2	26.5	10.2	4.0	21.8

Sources: *British Labour Statistics Historical Abstracts 1886–1968*, Table 109; 1971 Census.
Notes: MF = Married Females; SWDF = Single, Widowed and Divorced Females
    (a) For ages 14–20 years.
    (b) For ages 21–24 years.

Table B Labour Force Participation Rates in Britain by Age, Sex and Marital Status: 1881–1971

	1881	1891	1901	1911	1921	1931	1951	1961	1966	1971
Total Males										
All ages (over 10 years)	82.2	83.9	83.7	83.7	87.1	90.5	87.6	86.0	84.0	81.6
under 20	—[a]	58.6	56.1	52.5	63.2	84.7[b]	83.8	74.6	70.6	66.4
20–24	97.3	98.1	97.4	97.3	97.0	97.2	94.9	91.9	92.6	90.1
25–44	98.1	97.9	98.1	98.5	97.9	98.3	98.3	98.2	98.2	97.5
45–64	95.1	93.7	93.5	94.1	94.9	94.3	95.2	97.6	95.1	93.0
65 and over	73.8	65.4	61.4	65.8	58.9	47.9	31.1	24.4	23.5	19.3
Total Females										
All ages (over 10 years)	33.9	35.0	31.8	32.3	32.3	34.2	34.7	37.4	42.2	43.6
under 20	—[a]	43.4	39.1	38.8	48.4	70.5	78.9	71.1	66.5	56.0
20–24	56.2	58.4	56.7	61.9	62.4	65.1	65.4	62.0	61.6	59.4
25–44	28.8	29.5	27.2	29.3	28.4	30.9	36.1	40.8	47.1	51.4
45–64	24.6	24.6	21.1	21.6	20.1	19.6	28.7	37.1	46.1	50.1
65 and over	18.2	15.9	13.4	11.5	10.0	8.2	5.3	5.4	6.7	6.8
Married Females										
All ages (over 10 years)	NA	NA	NA	9.6	8.7	10.0	21.7	29.7	38.1	42.9
under 20	NA	NA	NA	12.6	14.6	18.7	38.1	41.0	43.6	43.3
20–24				12.1	12.5	18.5	36.5	41.3	43.5	45.8
25–44				9.9	9.1	11.7	25.1	33.6	41.8	47.4
45–64				9.3	8.0	7.7	19.0	29.6	41.4	47.7
65 and over				4.9	4.2	2.9	2.7	3.3	5.5	6.9

'Other' Females										
All ages (over 10 years)	NA	NA	NA	56.9	53.8	60.2	55.0	50.6	49.2	44.7
under 20	—	—	—	38.9	48.8	72.1	80.7	73.2	68.4	62.8
20–24	—	—	—	77.6	80.5	84.0	91.0	89.4	86.7	81.7
25–44	—	—	—	70.3	69.3	74.5	81.2	84.2	84.2	80.5
45–64	—	—	—	44.7	44.3	43.9	50.5	57.4	60.0	57.7
65 and over	—	—	—	14.4	12.7	10.9	6.6	6.5	7.4	6.7
Total Labour Force										
All ages (over 10 years)	57.2	58.5	56.7	56.9	58.1	60.7	59.6	60.5	62.1	61.7
under 20	75.9[a]	51.0	47.6	45.6	55.8	77.6	81.3	72.9	68.6	63.5
20–24	62.1	77.2	76.0	78.7	78.3	80.7	79.7	76.8	77.1	74.8
25–44	58.1	62.3	61.1	62.4	60.4	62.5	66.7	69.4	72.6	74.7
45–64	43.0	57.1	55.5	56.2	56.0	54.7	59.5	66.0	69.6	74.7
65 and over		47.6	34.1	30.9	30.9	25.3	15.9	12.7	13.1	11.6

Sources: Derived from Censuses of Population including 1971 Census Estimates and *British Labour Statistics: Historical Abstracts 1886–1968.*

Notes: (a) Because of uncertainty as to the ages at which juveniles first entered the labour force for the years 1881, 1891, 1901 and 1911, the labour participation rates of the first age-group for these years must be treated with caution. It is assumed for calculation purposes that the relevant working-age population was 10 to 19 years.

(b) 1931 labour force participation rates for 'Under 20s' for all groups is really for 12 to 20 years. The next age-group is correctly 21–24 years.

Table C Labour Force Participation Rates in Britain by Age, Sex and Marital Condition (for Females): 1931, 1951, 1961, 1966 and 1971

Age-Groups	1931	1951	Census Years 1961[a]	1966	1971
A: Males					
Under 20	84.7[b]	83.8	74.6	70.6	66.4
20–24	97.2[b]	94.9	91.9	92.6	90.1
25–29	98.4	97.4[c]	97.8	97.5	96.6
30–34	98.5		98.7	98.4	97.7
35–44	98.2	99.3	98.8	98.4	98.0
45–54	98.5	97.7	98.6	97.7	97.2
55–59	94.1	95.8	97.1	95.4	94.3
60–64	87.6	88.5	91.0	88.7	82.4
65 & over	47.9	31.1	24.4	23.5	19.3
B: Total Females					
Under 20	70.5	78.9	71.1	66.5	60.7
20–24	65.1	65.4	62.0	61.6	59.4
25–29	42.9	36.9	39.5	40.4	43.0
30–34	29.7		36.6	41.5	46.4
35–44	24.4	34.5	42.4	52.7	58.5
45–54	21.0	34.1	43.3	54.8	60.9
55–59	18.8	27.7	36.9	46.2	50.5
60–64	16.3	14.3	20.4	27.0	27.7
65 & over	8.2	5.3	5.4	6.7	6.8
C: Married Females					
Under 20	18.7	38.1	41.0	43.6	43.3
20–24	18.5	36.5	41.3	43.5	45.8
25–29	14.7	24.4	29.5	32.2	36.3
30–34	12.0		29.4	36.3	42.5
35–44	10.1	25.1	36.4	48.6	55.7
45–54	8.5	23.6	35.3	49.8	57.5
55–59	7.0	15.6	26.0	38.4	45.2
60–64	5.6	6.6	12.7	21.3	24.8
65 & over	2.9	2.7	3.3	5.5	6.9

D: Single Females

Under 20	72.1	80.6	73.6	68.3	62.8
20–24	84.1	91.0	89.5	86.9	83.9
25–29	81.8	86.3	90.6	88.6	86.1
30–34	78.0		88.0		84.8
35–44	72.3	78.8	85.1	85.7	85.3
45–54	63.8	74.3	81.7	82.1	82.4
55–59	54.8	65.8	75.0	75.8	73.6
60–64	44.7	34.5	39.1	39.5	33.1
65 & over	20.2	12.4	10.9	10.4	8.5

E: Widowed and
   Divorced
   Females

Under 20	*(d)	*	*	*	40.0
20–24	37.5	78.9	62.8	58.6	90.9
25–29	56.5	64.2	68.6	65.7	56.9
30–34	54.0		68.2		61.9
35–44	45.2	67.1	71.7	74.3	71.4
45–54	35.6	52.0	66.6	72.4	73.5
55–59	28.8	38.4	51.8	58.3	60.2
60–64	22.0	18.6	28.2	34.7	32.5
65 & over	7.9	4.9	5.6	6.4	6.2

F: Total
   Population

Under 20	77.6	81.3	72.9	68.6	63.6
20–24	80.7	79.7	76.8	77.1	74.8
25–29	69.8	66.7	68.8	69.2	76.1
30–34	61.9		67.6	70.1	72.4
35–44	58.3	66.3	70.2	75.4	78.3
45–54	57.2	64.5	70.3	75.7	78.7
55–59	54.8	58.3	65.9	69.9	71.6
60–64	49.9	46.8	52.0	55.7	53.2
65 & over	25.3	15.9	12.7	13.1	11.6

Source: Derived from Censuses of Population Reports.

Notes: (a) 1961 estimates of 'Economically Active Populations' for various age-groups were corrected by two published bias factors before labour participation rates were calculated.
   (b) The first two age-groups for 1931 are 14–20 years and 21–24 years.
   (c) Age-groups 25–29 and 30–34 have been combined in some cases because of doubts about the accuracy of age-information on economic activity among certain female groups.
   (d) Data are either not available, or not reliable.

Table D Labour Force Participation Rates of Married Women by Age and Presence of Dependent Children in Britain: 1961 and 1971

	Participation Rates of Married Women with Dependent Children (%)		Participation Rates of Married Women With No Dependent Children (%)		Percentage of Married Women Who Have Dependent Children	
Age-Groups	*1961*	*1971*	*1961*	*1971*	*1961*	*1971*
Under 20	12	14	62	67	40	48
20–24	12	16	76	84	54	56
25–29	15	23	74	82	76	80
30–34	22	36	69	79	85	91
35–39	29	50	60	77	84	89
40–44	32	51	52	72	73	74
45–49	31	51	43	65	53	49
50–54	27	53	34	54	30	26
55–59	21	39	25	45	10	9
60–64	11	23	12	24	3	2
65 and over	4	9	3	6	1	0.5
All ages	24	39	33	45	50	49

Source: Population Censuses 1961 and 1971. *Household Composition* Tables.

Note: A dependent child is a child of pre-school age *or* undergoing full-time education. No upper age limit was established in the case of the 1961 Census. The 1971 Census considered a student under 25 living at home as a dependent child.

Table E   Labour Force Participation Rates in Britain by Age, Sex, Marital Condition (for Females): 1971–1980

percent

	1971	1972	1973	1974	1975	1976	1977	1978	1979	1980
A. Total Males										
16–19	69.7	67.4	67.1	64.6	65.8	72.6	71.3	70.7	70.7	70.7
20–24	89.9	89.4	89.1	89.3	88.9	89.0	88.4	88.2	88.2	79.3
25–34	97.5	97.5	97.5	97.4	97.4	97.2	97.6	97.2	97.1	96.9
35–44	98.3	98.2	98.3	98.1	98.0	98.1	98.1	97.5	97.8	97.5
45–54	97.6	97.6	97.5	97.5	97.5	97.5	97.2	96.9	96.7	96.1
55–59	95.3	95.0	95.3	94.9	94.8	94.1	93.5	92.9	92.4	91.2
60–64	86.6	85.7	86.6	84.6	85.1	83.0	81.5	79.5	75.8	72.9
65–69	30.6	28.5	30.6	24.5	25.6	23.8	22.0	20.8	16.7	14.3
70 +	11.0	9.5	11.0	7.5	8.0	7.8	7.5	7.1	5.9	5.5
All Ages	82.5	81.7	81.9	80.6	80.5	80.7	80.0	79.3	78.6	77.8
B. Total Females										
16–19	63.1	61.1	60.3	55.6	59.3	66.6	65.7	65.1	64.8	64.5
20–24	60.7	61.2	62.5	64.0	64.0	65.7	67.1	67.9	67.9	68.5
25–34	44.0	44.9	48.7	51.2	52.0	53.8	56.5	56.2	56.2	56.3
35–44	57.4	58.0	62.3	65.3	65.9	67.5	68.7	69.0	68.5	68.3
45–54	60.6	61.2	65.2	66.1	66.3	66.9	67.1	67.2	67.5	67.8
55–59	51.1	51.3	52.6	53.3	53.3	55.0	57.3	56.0	54.9	54.9
60–64	28.2	28.2	28.2	28.2	28.2	26.8	25.0	22.8	21.3	20.5
65 +	6.4	6.0	5.6	5.1	4.8	4.6	4.4	4.1	3.3	2.9
All Ages	43.0	43.0	44.8	45.5	45.7	46.9	47.4	47.4	47.0	46.9
C. Married Females										
16–19	42.4	44.4	48.0	51.0	51.9	52.5	54.7	52.8	50.9	51.1
20–24	46.7	48.3	51.3	53.5	54.3	57.6	59.0	59.5	57.8	57.7
25–34	38.4	39.3	43.6	46.5	47.2	49.1	52.2	51.6	51.5	51.3
35–44	54.5	55.2	60.1	63.5	64.2	66.0	67.4	67.8	67.1	66.8
45–54	57.0	57.8	62.6	63.8	64.1	64.8	65.1	65.3	65.6	66.0
55–59	45.5	45.8	47.6	48.5	48.8	51.2	54.9	53.3	52.1	52.1
60–64	25.2	25.4	25.6	25.8	26.0	24.6	24.6	22.1	21.5	21.0
65 +	6.5	6.0	5.7	5.4	5.2	5.1	5.0	4.5	4.1	3.7
All Ages	42.3	42.8	46.0	47.7	47.9	49.0	50.4	50.0	49.6	49.3

Table E *contd.*

D. 'Other' Females										
16–19	65.6	63.3	61.9	56.1	60.2	68.0	66.6	66.1	65.9	65.6
20–24	81.2	79.6	78.2	78.0	77.0	76.2	76.8	77.1	78.1	78.9
25–34	80.8	80.4	80.1	79.7	79.4	79.6	79.8	79.2	78.7	78.6
35–44	80.0	79.7	79.4	79.1	78.9	78.2	77.5	77.5	78.0	77.8
45–54	78.1	78.0	77.8	77.7	77.5	77.3	77.0	76.8	76.7	76.5
55–59	67.2	67.0	66.9	66.8	66.7	66.4	64.8	64.3	63.8	63.5
60–64	33.7	33.3	33.0	32.7	32.3	31.0	25.8	24.0	21.0	19.4
65 +	6.3	6.0	5.6	5.0	4.5	4.3	4.1	3.9	2.9	2.5
All Ages	44.4	43.4	42.7	41.4	41.8	43.1	42.6	42.8	42.8	42.9

Source: 'Labour Force Outlook to 1986', *Employment Gazette*, April 1981, Table 4, p. 171.

Notes: (a) Students are *excluded* in estimating labour force participation rates for age-groups 16–19 and 20–24 in all groups except 'married females'. Information is unavailable on female students by marital status, and so all female students are assumed to be unmarried, for all years other than 1971.
    (b) The labour force participation rates given in this table are not comparable with the census-based estimates for previous years given in Table C and elsewhere. The estimates of the numbers in the labour force for different groups in this table are obtained by adding total registered employed and unemployed to total unregistered unemployed (estimates of which from 1972 onwards are based on information from General Household and Labour Force Surveys) and Youth Opportunity Programme (YOP) participants. The population numbers in different groups were estimated from the 1971 Census figures.
    (c) The estimates for 1980 are projections based on provisional information on various aggregates.

4

Women at Work: A Survey of the Occupational and Industrial Patterns of Employment in Britain

Introduction

The occupation of a woman worker defines the type of work she does and the industry she works in, the final product of that work. It is her occupation which determines to a significant extent the remuneration she receives and also where she is located in the class spectrum. Variations in fertility, mortality, morbidity, political allegiance and social outlook may in part be associated with occupational differences,[1] so that any examination of the status of women in the labour force should provide an occupational dimension.

In the last chapter we examined briefly how changes in the occupational distribution during the period 1911 to 1971 in Great Britain had differential impacts on the growth of various components of the labour force. Forces that operated in increasing female entry into the labour force, such as the dramatic rise in demand for clerical workers and shop assistants over the period, more than made up for the fall in the relative number of females entering factories and domestic services. A statistical exercise aimed at measuring the *relative* impact of the 'occupational distribution effect' and the 'labour force growth effect' showed that the former had a greater positive impact on the growth of female clerical workers than on their male counterparts. But the reverse held in the case of professional, managerial, administrative and supervisory occupations. This was taken as an indication that the female share of the more responsible jobs was not growing as fast as the female share in total employment. In this chapter we propose to throw more light on the job characteristics of women workers in Britain, partly with a view to assessing whether the traditional distinctions between men's and women's jobs are being eroded by the increasing number of women entering the labour force. Such an examination of sex-related occupational differences could also serve as a backdrop to the discussions of occupational segregation, pay differentials and the probable impact of micro-chips on female employment contained later in this chapter, as well as illuminate the analysis of the nature and persistence of sexual divisions within the society as a whole, which will be continued in the next chapter.

Occupational and Industrial Composition of the British Work Force: The Sexual Dimensions of Past Trends

(a) The Nature and Sources of Statistical Data

The only sources of data covering a long time span of the occupational distribution of the British work force are the Population Censuses. Data for shorter periods have been collected from the employers on a monthly or annual basis by the Department of Employment which can be supplemented by those derived from the annual New Earnings Survey, first made in 1968, and from the biennial Labour Force Surveys conducted by all countries of the European Community from 1973. None of the supplementary survey data is as comprehensive or reliable as census data and there are problems of comparability which preclude them from being incorporated into the present trend analysis.

Occupational data from Population Censuses are based on answers given by heads of households on the 'kind of work done and the nature of operations performed' by those reported as economically active. The responses are then classified into occupational categories according to the current occupational classification scheme. Periodic revisions of these classification schemes rule out any meaningful comparisons over time from raw census data. Notable attempts at improving the level of comparability over time of occupational data derived from Population Censuses include work by Mitchell and Dean (1962), Gales and Marks (1974), Lee (1979) and Routh (1980). Their data serve as the basis for much of the empirical work contained in this chapter on long-term trends in the occupational distribution of the British work force.[2]

(b) Long-Term Changes in Employment Distribution: An Industrial Analysis

During this century the number of women in employment in Britain rose from 4.7 million in 1901 to 6.8 million in 1951 and to 8.7 million in 1971. This represents an increase of 5% in the female share of total employment between 1901 and 1951 and 6% during the next two decades, so that in 1971, for every 100 male workers there were 58 female workers. About one-third of the female work force and 4% of the male work force were part-timers in 1971.

An examination of long-term changes in employment distribution in this country can be undertaken only within broad industrial groupings. Table 4.1 presents the distribution of male and female workers in sixteen industrial groups and the relative number of females in each group for selected years from 1841 to 1971. There is evidence, in case of both male and female employment, of the declining importance of agriculture and related activities (i.e., the primary sector) and the growing importance of the service (or tertiary) sector. But over the whole period, a smaller proportion of women than men was employed in the primary and secondary sectors. For example, the primary and secondary sectors (i.e., Groups 1–10) employed between two-thirds (in 1971) and three-quarters (in 1841) of the total male workers and only about two-fifths of the female workers over the same period. The rest of the female work force was concentrated in the tertiary sector, and

Table 4.1 Percentage Distribution of Male and Female Workers in Britain by Industrial Groups: 1841–1971

Year	1841			1901			1931			1951			1961			1971		
Industrial Groups	Female	Male	% Female Workers	Female	Male	% Female Workers	Female	Male	% Female Workers	Female	Male	% Female Workers	Female	Male	% Female Workers	Female	Male	% Female Workers
1. Agriculture, Mining etc.	4.9	33.0	5.1	1.6	19.5	3.2	1.4	16.7	3.6	1.9	12.0	6.5	1.5	9.3	7.3	1.5	6.0	12.4
2. Food, drinks, tobacco	1.6	4.3	11.5	4.6	6.2	23.2	4.2	3.1	37.7	4.0	3.0	37.1	3.6	2.7	38.7	3.3	3.0	39.3
3. Chemicals, Metal Manufact., Engineering etc.	0.8	7.3	3.7	2.2	13.9	6.1	6.0	15.0	14.7	12.1	21.5	20.1	13.3	23.8	21.2	12.0	24.4	22.1
4. Textiles	19.1	10.3	39.8	16.8	4.8	58.8	11.3	3.5	58.8	8.0	2.9	55.6	5.6	2.6	53.9	3.2	2.1	46.5
5. Leather, leather products etc.	0.2	0.9	6.5	0.6	0.7	23.6	0.4	0.4	31.6	0.4	0.3	35.4	0.3	0.2	41.1	0.3	0.2	42.3
6. Clothing & Footwear	10.9	7.0	35.8	16.6	3.6	65.1	8.9	2.4	62.6	7.0	1.3	70.5	5.2	1.0	72.3	4.0	0.8	73.3
7. Other manufact. industries	1.2	4.1	9.7	4.1	5.8	22.5	5.2	6.4	26.4	6.0	6.5	28.9	5.7	6.9	28.6	5.0	7.4	28.3

8. Construction	0.1	7.3	0.4	0.1	10.9	0.2	0.2	7.1	1.4	0.6	8.8	2.9	0.9	9.7	4.3	1.1	10.5	5.8
9. Gas, electricity & water	0.0	0.0	2.0	0.0	0.7	0.2	0.1	1.7	3.3	0.4	2.1	8.8	0.5	2.1	11.0	0.7	2.0	16.9
10. Transport & Communication	0.2	3.3	1.7	0.6	11.3	2.0	1.8	10.8	7.0	3.1	9.7	12.6	3.0	9.2	13.5	3.0	8.6	17.0
11. Distributive trades	0.9	0.7	32.1	1.2	0.8	37.4	15.2	14.2	32.1	16.9	9.9	43.1	19.9	10.7	47.2	18.0	9.7	51.8
12. Banking and other financial services	0.0	0.1	0.7	0.0	1.0	1.6	1.5	2.3	22.7	2.2	1.9	34.4	3.1	2.1	41.2	5.3	3.2	50.1
13. Professional & Scientific Services	2.6	2.1	30.0	6.7	2.7	50.2	8.5	3.1	54.8	13.1	4.1	58.6	16.9	5.3	60.5	21.4	6.9	64.1
14. Miscellaneous Services	55.2	6.6	74.8	42.5	5.1	77.4	32.1	6.3	69.3	20.1	6.3	58.5	16.3	6.9	53.4	14.8	7.1	54.7
15. Public Administration	0.1	1.7	1.2	0.6	3.2	7.2	2.7	6.7	15.2	4.0	9.4	15.9	3.7	7.2	19.8	5.2	7.4	28.8
16. Not Classified	2.2	11.2	6.7	1.9	9.7	7.4	0.3	0.4	2.6	0.1	0.1	34.0	0.5	0.3	36.1	1.1	0.6	52.8
Total	100.0	100.0	–	100.0	100.0	–	100.0	100.0	–	100.0	100.0	–	100.0	100.0	–	100.0	100.0	–

Source: C.H. Lee, *British Regional Employment Statistics* (Cambridge University Press, 1979).

Note: To allow for higher degree of comparability between groups, Lee split-up the data series into Series A 1841–1901 and Series B 1901–1971. Hence the figures for 1841 and subsequent years are not strictly comparable.

especially in distributive trades and service industries (i.e. Groups 11–15). To the extent that economic development results in a relative shift of employment from the primary sector to predominantly the tertiary sector, this female concentration may be seen either as an 'explanation' for the relatively faster growth of the female labour force or a *raison d'être* for its increasing presence in the total labour force.[3]

Certain other changes in the historical pattern of female attachment to various industries are also discernible from Table 4.1. Traditional employers of female labour such as clothing and textile industries (which together contained 30% of the total female work force in 1841) were gradually replaced by the distributive trades and professional and scientific services whose share of total female employment rose to about 40% in 1971. The declining importance of 'Miscellaneous Services' (of which private domestic services constituted over three-quarters of the total female employment during the nineteenth and early twentieth centuries) as a source of employment is reflected in the fall in the relative numbers in this Group from about half the female work force in 1841 to about 15% in 1971.

An additional feature brought out by Table 4.1 which is of some relevance to the later discussion of trends in occupational segregation by sex, is the differences in the growth of the female share of total employment between various groups. The female share rose in all groups over the period, but the increases were particularly marked in those groups in which women had an important stake to begin with. For example, the female share of employment in the clothing and footwear industries rose from 36% in 1841 to 73% in 1971. A more modest rise from 40% to 45% was recorded in the textile industry over the same period.[4] On the other hand, the share of women in heavy industries (i.e., Group 3), construction, public utilities (i.e., Group 9) and transport and communication (i.e., Group 10) — which together accounted for about half the total male work force in 1971 — increased from about 1% in 1841 to 17% in 1971.

There is a limit, however, to the number of meaningful inferences that can be drawn from Table 4.1. Each industrial group is fairly heterogeneous both with respect to the skills represented and the type of operations performed by its workers. Consider the breakdown of the group, 'Professional, technical and artistic workers' given in the 1971 Census and presented in Table 4.2. This group contained about 10% of both the male and female work force. But this near-equal share for both sexes masks considerable compositional differences. About two-thirds of the female workers in this group were nurses and school teachers; only 13% of the males in this group were found in these occupations. An omission of nurses and school teachers from this group, would result in the female share of the total employed falling from 39% to 17%.

Table 4.2 also brings out the fact that the predominantly male occupations are those associated with 'higher professionals' such as engineers, medical practitioners, accountants and lawyers. The 'lower professionals', consisting of nurses, medical auxiliaries, teachers and social workers, have a larger share of women. It is also clear from Routh (1980, pp. 6–8) that while the number of women in the higher professional occupational class as a percentage of total women workers has remained around 1% between 1911 and 1971, the relative number of males in this class rose from 1.3% to 4.9% over the same period. However, the trends in the sex distribution among the occupations in the 'lower professional' class (consisting mainly of nurses, teachers, social workers and draughtsmen) indicate a greater degree of occupational integration than any other occupational class according to Routh's analysis. But the tendency for women to be over-represented in less-skilled, lower status and in all likelihood, lower paid jobs, is found in a wide range of occupational activities. A cursory inspection of the Occupation Tables of the 1971 Census would show that more men are found among 'Linesmen and cablejointers' than 'Assemblers' in the case of *Electric and electronic workers or* among 'Warehousemen, storekeepers and assistants' compared to 'Packers, labellers and related workers' in the case of *Warehousemen, storekeepers and bottlers or* 'Office managers' compared to 'Typists, shorthand writers and secretaries' in case of *Clerical workers*. It is to the facts regarding differences in the nature of and trends in the occupational distributions of the male and female workers that we turn next.

Table 4.2 Professional, Technical and Artistic Workers in Britain
1971

Professions	Number of Women	Percentage Distribution	Women as Percentage of Profession
Medical practitioners (qualified)	13140	1.2	20.0
Dental practitioners	1900	0.2	13.3
Nurses	401,030	37.6	91.3
Pharmacists	4360	0.4	23.6
Radiographers	6390	0.6	69.1
Other medical and paramedical workers	30500	2.9	56.4
School teachers	318,360	29.9	63.6
Other teachers	62170	5.8	33.1
Engineers and technologists	1960	0.2	0.4
Chemists, physical and biological scientists	7310	0.7	10.4
Authors, journalists and related workers	12680	1.2	24.6
Stage managers, actors, entertainers, musicians	11880	1.1	31.4
Painters, sculptors and related artists	16020	1.5	37.3
Accountants (professional), company secretaries and registrars	21230	2.0	16.8
Surveyors, architects and town planners	2160	0.2	0.2
Clergy, ministers, members of religious orders	5410	0.5	13.1
Judges, barristers, advocates, solicitors	2470	0.2	6.4
Social welfare and related workers	39690	3.7	64.8
Professional workers n.e.s.	24920	2.3	33.1

Table 4.2 *contd.*

Professions	Number of Women	Percentage Distribution	Women as Percentage of Profession
Draughtsmen	17380	1.6	10.9
Laboratory assistants, technicians	48210	4.5	38.9
Technical and related workers n.e.s.	18250	1.7	9.1
TOTAL	1,066,520	100.00	38.7

Source: Census 1971 Great Britain, Economic Activity.

(c) Occupational Concentration of Female Workers: Patterns and Trends

Table 4.3 shows the number of female workers in occupations with more than 60,000 workers where women constitute at least a quarter of the total work force. The figures are derived from the 1971 Census and are arranged according to size.[5] The table shows that about 70% of the country's female work force was concentrated in a narrow range of occupations, predominantly service and clerical, of which four million workers (constituting 40% of the total female work force) were from occupations in which 75% or more were women. Among these four million workers were to be found typists, secretaries, maids, nurses, canteen workers and sewing machinists, all of whom were in occupations with 90% or more women *and* charwomen and office cleaners, hairdressers, laundry workers, waitresses, kitchen hands, etc., all of whom belonged to occupations which had 75% to 90% women workers. An interesting feature of this list of occupations is the extent to which they coincide with tasks that are traditionally associated with women such as washing, cleaning, nursing, sewing, etc. We shall examine this link between tasks that women perform in their domestic role and what are sex-typed as women's jobs in the next chapter.

From our analysis so far, little evidence has emerged of any significant erosion in the traditional division of labour by sex. Within each occupational group, there is a tendency for women to

Table 4.3 Numbers in Occupations Exceeding 60,000 Employees with at least 25% Women Workers in Britain 1971

		Women workers (000's)			
		Percentage of total workers who were women			
SIC No.		25–49	50–74	75–89	90 & over
139	Clerks, cashiers		1542		
144	Shop assistants			779	
142	Typists, shorthand writers, secretaries				770
164	Maids and related workers				436
166	Charwomen, office cleaners			428	
183	Nurses				401
193	Primary and secondary school teachers		318		
161	Canteen assistants and counter hands				291
143	Hand and machine sewers etc.				229
076	Proprietors and managers, sales	228			
137	Packers, labellers and related workers		216		
140	Office machine operators			148	
167	Hairdressers, manicurists, beauticians			124	
162	Cooks		123		
163	Kitchen hands			103	
127	Telephone operators			93	
160	Waitresses		83		
155	Barmaids		76		
168	Launderers, drycleaners & pressers			68	
629	Assemblers (electrical & electronic)			67	
172	Service & related workers n.e.s.	66			
	TOTAL	294	2358	1810	2127
	Percentage of total women workers in each category	3.2	25.8	19.8	23.3

Source: *Census 1971 Great Britain*, Economic Activity.

be concentrated in a narrow spectrum of jobs. The question then arises as to whether this spectrum has changed over time.

Table 4.4 shows the percentage distribution of women workers in England and Wales in thirteen occupations during the period 1911 to 1971.[6] These occupations contained about 80% of all women

Table 4.4   Principal Occupations of the Female Work Force in England and Wales 1911–1971

Occupational Groups	Percentage of **all** employed					Percentage of women workers in each group for 1971
	1911	1931	1951	1961	1971	
Private domestic servants	26.1	20.7	5.7	3.8	2.2	83.8
Clothing workers	14.0	9.4	7.2	5.5	3.6	80.0
Textile workers	13.5	11.1	6.5	4.0	1.9	53.8
Laundry workers	3.5	2.0	1.5	1.0	0.7	77.4
Clerks, typists	3.0	10.2	20.3	25.4	27.3	71.1
Shop owners, managers and assistants	9.3	10.9	12.0	13.3	10.8	60.0
Waitresses, cooks and kitchen hands; maids and domestic staff in hotels & schools	3.2	4.5	7.8	7.1	7.0	82.9
Metal workers (including electrical & electronic)	2.2	3.2	6.0	5.5	4.4	11.0
Charwomen etc.	2.6	2.5	3.4	4.4	4.5	86.0
Nurses	1.7	2.5	3.3	3.7	4.3	91.4
Teachers (school)	3.8	3.2	2.9	3.7	4.1	63.6
Packers and bottlers	-	1.8	2.1	2.2	2.4	72.9
Hairdressers	0.1	0.6	0.7	1.4	1.4	78.3
Total for above occupations	82.9	82.6	79.4	81.0	74.6	53.7 (68.5)[*]

Sources: (1) Gales, K.C. and Marks, P.H., 'Twentieth Century Trends in the Work of Women in England and Wales', *Journal of the Royal Statistical Society*, Series A, 137, part 1 1974, Table 3.
(2) *Census 1971 Great Britain,* Economic Activity Part II (10% sample).

Note: * excluding metal workers.

workers over the whole period, though the total number of
occupations listed in different censuses ranged from 475 in 1911, to
584 in 1951, to 201 in 1961 and 223 categories in 1971. The relative
number of women workers in the first three occupations listed in
Table 4.4 declined from 60% of total females in employment in 1911
to about 10% in 1971. The practical extinction of domestic servants
(falling from 1.4 million in 1911 to 194,000 in 1971) and the marked
decline in employment in clothing and textiles saw the virtual end of
these traditional sources of employment for working-class females.
A rapid growth of clerical workers (previously a male preserve)
from 3% in 1911 to 27% in 1971 established these as the pre-
eminent female occupations of today. Female workers in the
distributive trades (of which shop assistants constituted 75% of the
work force in 1971) and catering, the second and third most popular
occupations, represented 11% and 7% of the total female work
force respectively in 1971.

A detailed consideration of the origins, causes and consequences
of the occupational concentration (or segregation) of female
workers will be found in subsequent sections of this book. But what
is again worthy of note is that in 1971 about 80% of all 'occupied'
women were concentrated in 6% of the listed census occupational
categories. If we now define, somewhat arbitrarily, as 'women's
jobs' those jobs in which at least two-thirds of all workers are
women, an inspection of Table 4.4 would show that nine out of
thirteen occupations listed were women's jobs. The persistence of
sex-typing of jobs over time is clearly evident from the table; its
prevalence is attested by the statistics contained both in Tables 4.3
and 4.4. It is these aspects of occupational segregation that have
attracted considerable interest in recent years mainly because it is
seen by many as a critical barrier to the attainment of economic
equality by women in the work-sphere.[7] Before examining the *facts*
behind the relationship between occupational segregation and the
low status of women workers, it would be useful to consider certain
summary measures of occupational segregation by sex which can be
used to make comparisons over time and space.

*(d) Measuring Occupational Segregation Over Time: Certain
Relevant Considerations*

Occupational segregation by sex occurs when there is a marked difference in the way that men and women are distributed over occupations. Now the ways in which men and women exercise occupational choice will be affected differently by marital status, family responsibilities, the availability of flexi-time work, among other factors. A comprehensive definition of occupational segregation should take account of the differential impact of these factors on the occupational choice of both men and women. And if data allow, it is possible to measure occupational segregation for different groups cross-classified by the factors mentioned above. But data rarely allow for such an eventuality; and it is not possible to do so in this study.

Another definition of occupational segregation, with the added advantage that it need not refer only to sex segregation, is one that identifies the existence of segregation in an occupation if the workers in that occupation are not distributed in proportion to the occurrence of certain pre-specified characteristics in the population as a whole, where such characteristics could encompass not only sex or race, but also those few occupations where sex is a crucial qualification, e.g., a fashion model for women's clothes or a wet nurse. However, as an operational definition to serve as the basis for constructing summary measures of occupational segregation, the definition leaves much to be desired.

If we confine our measure of occupational segregation to the degree to which workers of a particular sex are concentrated in a small number of occupations, Hakim (1978, pp. 1265–6) has suggested the following indices:

(i)   the proportion of the listed occupations in which no woman (or man) is employed;

(ii) the proportion of the listed occupations in which women (or men) make up over a specified percentage of the work force; and

(iii) the proportion of the listed occupations in which women (or men) form a higher proportion of the work force than they do in the population.

Hakim estimated these summary measures for England and Wales for the census years from 1901 to 1971. She found that the proportion of occupations with no women remained fairly constant at 9% up to 1961 and then dropped to 2% in 1971. The number of jobs with no male workers reached a maximum of 3 out of 475 listed occupations in 1911 (consisting of midwives, nursery nurses and charwomen), declined to 1 in 1951 (consisting of midwives) and none subsequently. A slight increase was recorded from 9% to 12% over the years in the proportion of occupations in which 70% or more were women — an indication that there is no evidence of a decline in the occupational concentration of women during the first seventy years of this century. Finally, it was found that about 75% of all occupations had a disproportionate number of male workers compared to only 25% for females.

Another interesting feature brought out by Hakim's study relates to differences in the change in the proportions of men and women working in occupations dominated by either sex. Hakim concludes that over the period the likelihood of working in jobs dominated by one's own sex was greater for men than women. And that 'male inroads into women's preserves has not been counterbalanced by women's entry into typically male spheres of work' (p. 1266).

The summary measures of occupational segregation discussed so far have used occupational categories as the point of reference. The relative numbers in each occupational category should be of some relevance in any overall measure of occupational segregation. Further, the summary measures described above are 'partial' in the sense that they do not take account of the dual dimension of occupational segregation, i.e., the simultaneous occurrence of male and female concentrations in different occupations.

A measure that gets over these problems is the widely used Index of Segregation (or Dissimilarity) developed by Duncan and Duncan (1965). This index is a measure of the *absolute* differences in the percentage distribution of males and females employed across occupations,[8] or more precisely,

$$S_t = \tfrac{1}{2}\sum_{i=1}^{n} |f_{it} - m_{it}|$$

where f_{it} and m_{it} are percentages of females and males employed in occupation i at time t respectively and $i = 1, 2, ..., n$ represent the occupational categories. Note that $f_{it} + m_{it} = 100$.

To take account of the relative numbers in each occupational category, a weighting scheme could be applied to the index (S_t) to obtain a weighted index of occupational segregation.

It can easily be shown that S_t lies between 0 and 100 where 0 represents a distribution of females across occupations which is exactly identical to the male distribution (i.e., there is no occupational segregation by sex); and 100 represents complete segregation with men and women being employed in strictly separate occupations. One way of interpreting S_t is to infer that its actual value represents the percentage of men (or women) who have to change occupations for the distributions to become identical. This presupposes that no segregation implies that all occupations have an equal *proportionate* share of males and females, so that, given women constituted about 40% of the British labour force in 1971, in each occupation for every six men there should be four women. Therefore a 'sex-fair' distribution in this context does not imply a sex ratio of 1:1. This, of course, begs a number of questions regarding distribution of talents, individual preferences and aspirations between the sexes which should all be relevant in determining what is a 'sex-fair' distribution of work. None of this can be captured by S_t, nor is the degree of attachment to the labour market indicated by sex differences in the proportion of part-timers in different occupations.

There is a further problem that arises in the use of S_t to make inferences about changes in occupational segregation over time. An observed change in S_t could either indicate a change in the proportion of women in one or more occupational categories (i.e., a sex-composition change) *and/or* a change in the occupational structure being studied (i.e., a structural change). For example, a decline in S_t may be a result of a fall in the relative numbers in predominantly male occupations with sex-composition within occupations remaining unchanged, *or* an increase in the relative number of females within one or more occupations with the occupational distribution remaining unchanged, *or* a simultaneous change in sex-composition and occupational structure. Using the same multiple standardisation technique as in the last chapter in examining the components of labour force participation changes, it is possible to *decompose* changes over time in S_t into (i) 'composition' effects, (ii) 'structural' effects and (iii) 'interaction' effects.

To examine the nature and components of long-term changes in the sex structure of occupations in Britain, the period 1841 to 1971 was split up into three sections: 1841–1901, 1901–1951 and 1951–1971. Periodic revisions of census occupational classifications precluded direct use of pre-war census data. Instead, a combination of occupational data from Lee (1979) for earlier years and census data for post-war years, with adjustments for comparability and relative numbers in occupations, provided the final data for estimating S_t. Subsequent estimation concentrated on decomposing changes in the values of S_t to the three effects identified in the previous paragraph.

Table 4.5 shows that the Index of Segregation (S_t) hardly changed between 1841 and 1911.[9] Subsequently, a fall of 16.4% (i.e., a decrease of 0.8% per annum) for the period 1911–1951 and a fall of 5.7% (i.e., a decrease of 0.7% per annum) for the period 1951–1971 were recorded in S_t. Despite this, even in 1971, occupational segregation remained a notable feature of the British labour force, for about 40% of the total females have to be reallocated to eliminate over-representation of women in occupations such as nursing and clerical work and under-representation in other occupations such as engineering, skilled blue-collar work, etc.

Table 4.5 also summarises the relative importance of the three effects in 'explaining' changes in occupational segregation over the period. An increase in S_t between the years 1841 and 1901 was primarily a result of changes in sex-composition within occupations, probably through the positive impact of higher growth in predominantly male industries such as metal manufactures, construction and transport and the declining importance of traditional employers of females such as the textile and clothing industries. Since 1901, S_t has been declining principally as a result of decreasing segregation within occupations (i.e., a negative 'composition' effect). Until 1951, the relative impact of the 'structural' effect was smaller than that of the 'composition' effect.

Table 4.5 Segregation Indices and their Sources of Change: 1841–1971 (Percentages)

Year	1841	1901	1911	1931	1951	1961	1971
S_t	62.0	67.2	60.1	48.4	43.7	40.6	38.0

Period	Actual Change	'Composition' Effect	'Structural' Effect	'Interaction' Effect
1841–1901	5.2	5.2	2.3	−2.3
1911–1931	−11.7	−8.9	−3.7	0.9
1931–1951	−4.7	−4.7	−0.3	0.3
1951–1971	−5.7	−4.5	−3.9	2.7

But the period 1951–1971, and particularly the second decade, was characterised by the growing importance of changes in occupational structure favouring a decline in S_t.

The impact of the 'interaction' effect on S_t was mixed over the period studied. The combined effect of changes in sex composition within occupations and of the occupational structure was to reduce S_t during the period 1841–1901, to have a negligible effect on S_t during the period 1911–1951, and finally to raise the value of S_t during the post-war period 1951–1971. It is interesting that the direction of the 'interaction' effect was opposite to the net impact of the other two factors over all sub-periods, possibly implying that the simultaneous effects of sex compositional changes and occupational structural changes were concentrated in occupational categories without any strong sex bias during both the periods 1841–1901 and 1951–1971.

An interesting question which may be asked is: What would have been the impact on S_t if a system of 'non-discriminatory' recruiting of workers had operated during the post-war years? Given the exigencies of data, one approach to answering this question is to assume that the *net* increase in numbers in each occupational category over the period 1951–1971 is allocated to each sex according to the sex ratio in that occupational category in 1971. The 'expected' number of males and females in all occupational categories can be used to make a conditional prediction of S_t for 1971. The difference between the actual S_t and the predicted S_t for 1971 gives a measure of random or 'sex-blind' hiring practices on occupational segregation.[10]

When this method was applied to occupational data derived from the 1951 and 1971 Censuses, it gave a predicted value for S_t of 31.7, compared to the actual values of 43.7 and 38.0 for 1951 and 1971 respectively. The implication, therefore, is that 'non discriminatory' hiring practices would have brought about *twice* the decline in S_t that occurred during the period 1951 and 1971.

There is still an important question that remains: Has the equal opportunities legislation passed in Britain during the seventies, notably the Sex Discrimination Act of 1975, had any significant impact on occupational segregation over the last few years? It is important to recognise that the question is not whether occupational segregation has declined over the seventies, since a long-term decline has already been observed, but whether the rate of decrease has quickened as a result of legislation. Using biennial occupational data for Great Britain from the European Community Labour Force Surveys, Hakim (1981) estimated a summary measure of occupational segregation for the period 1973 to 1979.[11] These estimates were supplemented by census-based values of the same measure for the years 1901 to 1971. A decline in this index from 2.49 in 1901 to 1.73 in 1971 was followed by a steeper fall to 1.57 in 1977, the trend being however reversed when the index rose to 1.71 in 1979. Hakim suggests two reasons for this reversal in the trend. First, it is possible that the rise in the index during the period 1977 to 1979 was more apparent than real, since the 1979 Labour Force Survey increased the number of occupational categories from 375 to 516. But this is not a totally convincing argument, since the index constructed on 223 occupational categories of the 1971 Census nevertheless recorded a higher value than the values for subsequent years.

The second explanation for the upward trend in occupational segregation focuses on changes in the climate of opinion about women working, engendered by the severe recession and growing unemployment in the late seventies. There is evidence, as noted in the postscript in Chapter 3, that certain important changes in the pattern of labour force participation have been making themselves felt from the mid-seventies. The participation rates of older men and women have showed a marked decline; the economic activity rates of women with young children have showed signs of stabilising and even falling back slightly; and an increasing shift towards part-time work by mothers after childbirth during a period of rising birth rate has been noted by Daniel (1980). All these factors would favour a movement towards 'female-type' jobs. And these factors, taken in conjunction with growing reluctance of employers to remove, and for women workers to press for the removal of, traditional barriers against female employment in certain occupations during a period of contracting jobs, could go some way towards explaining why the impact of anti-discriminatory legislation has been so short-lived.

(e) The Pattern and Prevalence of Sex Segregation within Occupations

In our analysis so far we have concentrated on the existence of segregation by sex in different occupations. But there is another kind of segregation where, though men and women work in the same occupation, men end up doing the more senior and responsible jobs. This intra-occupational segregation, sometimes referred to as vertical segregation, may be distinguished from inter-occupational segregation referred to as horizontal segregation.[12] For it is often the former that is more deeply entrenched and less susceptible to public pressure or legislative action and consequently more difficult to eradicate.

There are certain practical difficulties in evaluating empirically the magnitude of the problem of vertical segregation. Ideally, a longitudinal approach which involves examining over time the relative career advancement of two groups (one of each sex) who start with similar qualifications, job motivations and background, could provide the best indication of the nature and magnitude of segregation by sex in a particular job. The immense data required for this aproach precludes its use in most situations. Instead, we are left with the alternative of either examining sex-related differences in career structure at discrete points in time within a given occupation, or of using proxies such as class or socio-economic status of the men and women in the occupational ladder at discrete points in time. We shall examine both approaches briefly.

It was noted earlier that women tend to be under-represented in occupational categories such as higher professionals, employers, administrators, managers, supervisors and skilled manual workers and over-represented among lower professionals, sales and clerical workers. Bain and Price (1972) used census data for the period 1911 to 1961 to derive the number of women in the work force by ten occupational categories similar to the Registrar General's classification of socio-economic groups. Hakim (1978) updated their figures using the 1971 Census. A crude measure of under-or over-representation of women in any one of the ten occupational classes is the *ratio* of the percentage of women in a particular occupational class to the overall percentage of women in the 'occupied' population. Table 4.6 shows these ratios for the ten groups over the period 1911 to 1971, with values less than 1 indicating under-representation of women in those groups and values in excess of 1 showing over-representation. Lower-status groups among non-manual workers represented by lower professional, clerical and sales workers have values in excess of 1, while women were under-represented in categories (a) to (c) which

Table 4.6 Representation of Women Workers in Ten Occupational Classes in Britain: 1911–1971

Occupational Classes	1911	1921	1931	1951	1961	1971
1. All Non-Manual						
(a) Employers and proprietors	0.63	0.69	0.66	0.65	0.63	0.68
(b) Managers and administrators	0.67	0.58	0.44	0.49	0.48	0.59
(c) Higher professional workers	0.20	0.17	0.25	0.27	0.30	0.27
(d) Lower professional and technical workers	2.12	2.01	1.97	1.74	1.57	1.43
(e) Clerks	0.72	1.51	1.54	1.95	2.01	2.00
(f) Salesmen and shop assistants	1.29	1.48	1.25	1.67	1.69	1.64
White collar workers (excluding Employers and proprietors)	1.01	1.27	1.20	1.37	1.37	1.31
2. All Manual	1.03	0.95	0.97	0.85	0.80	0.80
(a) Foremen and supervisors	0.14	0.22	0.29	0.43	0.32	0.36
(b) Skilled	0.81	0.71	0.71	0.51	0.43	0.37
(c) Semi-skilled	1.36	1.37	1.44	1.24	1.21	1.27
(d) Unskilled	0.52	0.57	0.50	0.66	0.69	1.02
Total Occupied Population (%)	29.6	29.5	29.8	30.8	32.4	36.5

Source: C. Hakim, 'Sexual Divisions Within the Labour Force:
Occupational Segregation', *Department of Employment
Gazette*, November 1978, Table 6, p. 1267.

Note: The numbers above represent the ratio of the percentage of
women in each group to percentage of women in the total
'occupied' population. A ratio of greater than 1 indicates over-
representation of women in that group and less than 1 shows
under-representation.

were high status occupational classes.[13] Similarly, women were
over-represented in the semi-skilled manual categories and under-
represented in the higher-status manual categories consisting of
foremen, supervisors and skilled workers.

If we examine the trends in vertical segregation as shown by Table
4.6 over the period 1911 to 1971, it is clear that under-
representation of women in the managerial, administrative and
skilled manual work has become more pronounced over time, with

little change in their share among employers, proprietors and higher professionals. The female workers in clerical and sales occupations have been rising at a faster rate than the increasing overall share of women in the total work force. Hence the general trend exhibited by these figures is towards greater vertical segregation, with more women occupying lower-status jobs than men.

Hakim (1981) has examined trends in vertical segregation over the seventies and notes that women have made substantial gains in increasing their share of higher grade non-manual work. From 1911 to 1971, the index of female representation among higher professional workers rose from 0.20 to 0.27, representing a rise of 0.07 over 60 years, as shown in Table 4.6. But in the six years between 1973 and 1979, the index rose from 0.38 to 0.54, representing an increase of 0.16. Little change was recorded, however, in the index for those occupational classes in which women were over-represented, such as selling, assembling and packing, catering, cleaning, and clerical and related trades (Hakim, 1981, Table 7).

Finally, it would be useful to examine briefly how vertical segregation operates within a single occupation. School teaching has been for a long time one of the traditionally accepted female pursuits. When the Education Act of 1870 was passed, there were equal numbers of men and women employed as teachers in elementary schools. But by 1913, the proportion of women had risen to about three-quarters, and this was maintained until after the Second World War, when it fell to the present level of 60%. Equal pay for equal work has been accepted by this profession going back to the time when professional standards were established and articulated by bodies representing teachers. Yet a significant imbalance exists in the proportion of women and men who reach different scale levels up the promotion ladder, in spite of the operation of widely-accepted and uniformly based criteria for recruiting new teachers and a balanced intake of male and female probationers.

A National Union of Teachers Survey of promotion prospects for women teachers conducted in 1978, showed that there were four to five times more men than women in the most senior teaching posts (i.e., those on Scale 4 and Senior Teacher Grade). Women in the junior teaching positions (i.e., those on Scales 1 and 2) formed just over three-quarters of all women teachers in primary and secondary schools, compared to just about half of the total male teachers.[14] Further, women in senior positions were over-represented in what are traditionally considered women's 'areas', such as domestic science, commercial studies and social or pastoral care, and under-represented in subject areas such as mathematics, science and technology and in shouldering responsibilities for curriculum development, school administration and financial planning. Finally, the imbalance in promotional prospects was brought out by the fact that although women provided 77% of the full-time primary school teachers, they held only 43% of the headships. In secondary schools, women who provided 44% of the teachers held only 18% of the headships.

Explanations for the imbalance in the status of men and women in the teaching profession have been variously attributed to (i) a large proportion of part-time workers among women, (ii) a large concentration of women in the primary education sector, (iii) differences in the level of qualifications held by men and women teachers, (iv) discontinuity and instability in the work experience of women teachers and (v) low promotion orientation of women teachers. Certain relevant facts brought out by the NUT (1980) study would be helpful in assessing the validity of these explanations. The NUT report found that, while in 1976, 13% of women teachers and 2% of male teachers in England and Wales were part-timers, the removal of part-timers still did not alter the fact that women who formed 60% of the full-time teaching force held only 38% of the headships. The concentration of women in primary schools does work against them, since there are relatively fewer posts on Scale 3 or above in these schools. But even within the secondary school sector, only 57% of women compared to 71% of men achieve posts on Scale 3 or above. It is true that about 40% of men and 20% of women teachers are graduates, and this could be a partial explanation for the relative status of women teachers. But it is worthy of note that while 6% of the male graduates achieved headships, only 2% of female graduates held headships. The disparity is particularly striking in primary schools where proportionately six times as many male graduates as female graduates hold headships.

The effect of discontinuity of employment on the status of married women teachers has been examined, particularly in relation to male/female earnings differentials in the teaching profession. Turnbull and Williams (1974) found that the observed differentials in earnings of single men and women teachers could be in the main 'explained' by differences in their education and work experience. But even after adjustments for the 'lost' years arising from a break in their services, married women still earned less than single women with comparable qualifications. Further, an examination of salary levels of different groups for the period 1963–1971 led Turnbull and Williams to conclude that there has been some deterioration in the position of single women compared to men, but a greater deterioration in the position of married women *vis-à-vis* the single women.

Attempts to explain the lowly position of married women teachers, even after allowances have been made for breaks in service and part-time work, often take the form of suggesting that the lower wages at which married women teachers are willing to offer their services could be attributed to family constraints restricting their spatial mobility, their lack of desire for higher earnings and their low ambition. But this preconception of women teachers as consisting in the main of middle-aged married women, preoccupied by family concerns at the exclusion of other considerations, has been questioned by the recent NUT study, which found that there were as many 'not married' women teachers supporting children and aged dependents, as the archetypal married women, in the teaching force who would be as concerned as the men with the financial and other rewards of promotion. The NUT study concludes: 'Nonetheless, despite overall career orientation, women teachers do have difficulties in gaining promotion. Our analysis of the experience of the respondents in applying for promotion led us to the inescapable conclusion that a fair measure of discrimination exists' (p. 31).

(f) The Educational Dimensions of Occupational Segregation

It is sometimes argued that the lowly position of women workers in the occupational hierarchy is in part due to their inferior education and training. Such an inferiority results in their concentration into a narrow range of occupations, and thereby reduces their ability to enter higher status and better paid jobs and compete more effectively with their male counterparts. There are various views on how educational disadvantage is transmitted through occupational choice to determine the inferior status of women workers.[15] In this section we concentrate on some of the *facts* relating to the educational dimensions of the sexual divisions within the British labour force. We shall use the term 'education' in a broad sense to include both academic and vocational training.

The existing evidence clearly supports the view that male workers are in general more educated than women. The 1971 Census statistics of 'Qualified' manpower show that the proportion of male workers possessing a degree is about two and a half times that of women and the proportion of male workers is even higher if one considers those possessing at least one 'A' level. The Department of Employment reported in 1975 that only 8% of female school-leavers aged 15–17 entered apprenticeships, compared to 39% of boys in that age-group. A useful indication of an employer's commitment to the training of his workers is his willingness to release them to take part-time courses at further education institutions. The Department of Education and Science publishes annually statistics relating to students attending day-release classes by industry of their employer and the sex of the student.

If we now define as a measure of the sex-related differences in an employer's commitment to provide training for his young workers an Index of Female Avoidance (P_t), which is defined as a ratio of the *expected* number of female trainees corresponding to the sex composition of the work force in a particular industry to the actual number of female employees on day release in that industry at time t, this Index would provide us with a means of comparing the experiences of female avoidance or male preference in individual industries or over time.[16] If P_t is greater than 1, this would indicate that the actual number of females released for training is smaller than the number one would expect to be released, given the sex composition of the work force. On the other hand, if P_t is smaller than 1, this would indicate that there exists a preference on the part of employers to send their female employees on day-release training.

Data on male and female employees in 27 industries released for part-time study at further education institutions during working hours were combined with information on the sex composition in each one of the 27 industries to obtain estimates for P_t for two years 1971 and 1978.[17] These years were chosen so as to assess whether a change had occurred in employers' attitudes during a period when the climate of opinion and legislative action were conducive towards promoting equal opportunities for women. Over the period, P_t fell from 1.53 in 1971 to 1.40 in 1978. This would indicate that there still exists a marked tendency among employers to exclude women employees from a 'fair' share of day-release training facilities, but that this tendency has decreased slightly over the period.[18]

If we examine the ratio of the expected number of female trainees to the actual number in each industry for the two years as given in Table 4.7, certain interesting features may be noted. Between 1971 and 1978, these ratios fell in twenty out of twenty-seven industrial groups. Among the exceptions were Textiles, Clothing and Footwear and Professional and Scientific Services, all of which have a relatively high concentration of female workers (see Table 4.1). This may be interpreted as a slightly increasing tendency on part of employers to 'discriminate' against women in training in industries where female workers predominate. This conclusion was supported by the existence of a statistically significant positive association between the relative number of full-time female employees and the ratios given in Table 4.7. The Spearman Rank correlation coefficient increased slightly from 0.769 in 1971 to 0.783 in 1978, showing that the tardiness of industries employing large numbers of women in their work force in making 'fair' provisions for training their female employees was strongly persistent even at the end of the period. It is interesting that only in the group, 'Public Administration and Defence', was the expected number of female workers on training less than the actual number, showing that only the public sector seems to be carrying out policies to rectify the serious sex imbalance in training.

It is necessary to conclude this part of the analysis on a cautionary note regarding the suitability of the data on which the above statistical exercise hinges. Employment data collected on an 'industrial' basis fails to distinguish between a multitude of occupations followed in each industry. The nature and extent of in-service training needed would vary between occupations. So that it could be argued that differences in provision for in-service training is more a reflection of the particular occupational needs, rather than attempts at sex discrimination. But this does not answer the question why 'female' occupations are the ones which benefit less from in-service training compared to 'male' occupations. And further, how far does the absence of a 'training' element in female

Table 4.7 Female Workers in Twenty-Seven Industries on Part-Time Study at Further Education Institutions: 1971 and 1978

Industry	Actual Nos.		Expected Nos.*		Ratios*	
	1971	1978	1971	1978	1971	1978
Agriculture etc.	795	1176	1201	2620	1.51	2.22
Mining	314	356	596	552	1.90	1.55
Food, drink and tobacco	2518	2929	3510	3877	1.39	1.32
Coal & petroleum products	203	283	277	283	1.36	1.00
Chemicals and other industries	2777	3360	4071	4126	1.47	1.23
Metal manufacture	2367	1777	2421	1993	1.02	1.12
Mechanical engineering	3377	3589	9171	8813	2.70	2.45
Instrument engineering	360	592	1518	2110	4.22	3.56
Electrical engineering	1869	2559	12308	11925	6.58	4.66
Shipbuilding and marine engineering	146	279	379	569	2.66	2.64
Vehicles	1503	1746	3155	3035	2.10	1.74
Metal goods n.e.s.	1227	827	2656	2490	2.16	3.01
Textiles	1221	907	2416	2197	1.99	2.42
Leather, leather goods etc.	99	113	110	188	1.11	1.66
Clothing and footwear	1110	983	2195	2006	1.94	2.04
Bricks, pottery etc.	607	724	951	942	1.57	1.30
Timber, furniture etc.	227	320	954	1217	4.20	3.80
Paper, printing & publishing	1215	1471	4457	3396	3.66	2.31
Other manufacturing	829	1101	1946	2443	2.35	2.22
Construction	7420	1001	2039	3007	2.75	3.00
Gas, electricity & water	1694	2537	2589	2923	1.53	1.15
Transport & communications	2488	2332	4073	3725	1.64	1.60
Distributive trades	5576	6807	7578	7517	1.36	1.10
Insurance, banking etc.	1673	10690	3791	13037	2.27	1.22
Professional & scientific services	19765	19765	23302	27925	1.18	1.41
Miscellaneous services	17850	22917	23930	29029	1.34	1.27
Public administration	19078	31504	18834	30331	0.99	0.96

Sources: (1) Department of Education and Science, *Statistics of Education*, 1971 and 1978.
    (2) *Census 1971 Great Britain,* Economic Activity Tables.
    (3) 1978 Census of Employment.

Notes: * Expected Numbers in industry i = Total number of trainees from industry i × Proportion of total full-time employees who are full-time female workers in industry i
    **Ratio = $\dfrac{\text{Expected Numbers}}{\text{Actual Numbers}}$

occupations explain their low status and pay? In the next chapter, we shall consider theories which emphasise the sex-determined dualistic nature of the labour market where differential training provisions are an important feature of this dualism.

It is sometimes argued that the relative position of qualified women workers *vis-à-vis* their male counterparts rests on differences in their specialisation and skills. Table 4.8 shows the percentage distribution of qualified workers by sex and industrial activity in 1971.[19] Marked differences can be observed between the male and female distributions, with only 5% of total qualified women concentrated in manufacturing industries compared to 25% of males. About 80% of the qualified females are concentrated in educational and health services, but only 30% of qualified males. Female representation in 'Other Services' which include a number of professions such as engineering, architecture, law and accountancy was small compared to their male counterparts. This conclusion is further reinforced by studies of female membership of Professional Bodies carried out by the Department of Employment (1975) and UNESCO (1976). It must be remembered that membership of these bodies is often a requirement to follow the profession. The majority of the professions had less than 5% women members and these included bodies such as the Institute of Chartered Accountants, the Institute of Bankers, the Royal Institute of British Architects and the Institutes of Electrical, Mechanical and Civil Engineers. Just over 6% of the General Council of the Bar of England and Wales were women; and the professional bodies with the largest female membership were the British Medical Association (18%) and the British Dental Association (13%).

An Index of Segregation, constructed from more disaggregated data than those in Table 4.8, gave a value of 61.6 which indicates

Table 4.8 Percentage Distribution of Female and Male Qualified
Workers by Industry in Britain: 1971

SIC Number	Industrial Group	Female %	Male %
I, II	Agriculture, mining etc	0.5	1.6
IV–XII	Chemicals, metal manufacturing, engineering, etc.	2.6	19.5
XIII–XV	Textiles, leather & leather products, clothing and footwear	0.4	1.3
III, XVI–XIX	Other manufacturing industries	1.3	4.3
XX–XXII	Construction, public amenities, transport and communications	0.9	9.6
XXIII–XXIV	Distributive trades and financial services	3.9	11.3
XXV	*Professional & Scientific Services*		
–872	–Education Services	47.8	20.9
–874	–Health Services	32.3	8.3
–876	–Research Services	0.3	8.0
–871, 873 875, 879	–Other Services	1.8	4.0
XXVI	Miscellaneous Services	4.8	6.0
XXVII	Public Administration and Defence	3.4	4.0
	Total Workers (in 000's)	723	1337

Source: Census 1971 Great Britain, Qualified Manpower Tables, Table 7.

that about 60% of the qualified women have to be re-allocated
between industries for the distributions of male and female
qualified workers to become similar. Now if one compares this
value with the value of 38.0 obtained as a measure of segregation for
all women workers previously, it would be reasonable to infer that
the difference between the two values is some indication of the more
pronounced nature of occupational segregation among qualified
women compared to all women.[20] This conclusion is somewhat
surprising in the light of the neoclassical view that female
concentration in low-paid and low-status jobs can, to a significant

extent, be accounted for as a result of their inferior education and training. This point will be taken up in the next chapter.

It could be argued that a qualification *per se* is not the important factor, but it is what the qualification is in that determines to an important extent the distribution of qualified women between occupations. Table 4.9 shows the distribution of university degrees awarded by main subject areas for the years 1971 and 1979. Under-representation of women in Engineering and Technology and over-representation in areas of Arts and Education are the notable features brought out by the table. There is no evidence from the table of any significant shift in the distribution of female graduates between subject areas during the period 1971 to 1979. But a more detailed classification involving 80 subjects, used to construct an Index of Segregation, showed a fall in the Index from 40.5 in 1971 to 36.6 in 1979. A Component of Change analysis, similar to the one used in examining long-term changes in labour force participation and occupational concentration, showed that the relative impact of a larger proportion of women (men) specialising in subjects considered as male (female) preserves in the past was *less* important than that of changes in the 'subject specialisation' structure in explaining the reduction of female concentration in certain subject areas.[21]

Sex-related differences have also been found in the choice of school subjects. While girls on the average get more CSEs and 'O' levels and the same number of 'A' levels as the boys, the female passes are concentrated in arts, social studies and domestic craft at the expense of science, technology and economics. A more balanced distribution of subjects passed is evident among boys.[22]

To sum up, it is clear that in any examination of the type of work that women do, the qualifications and skills acquired before and during employment are crucial factors. There is some evidence that choice of subjects both at the school and post-school levels has some bearing on the nature of occupations that are generally followed by women. There is also evidence that employers on the whole prefer males to females in providing opportunities for their young employees to train and improve their career potential.[23] And the larger the concentration of women in certain industries, the greater the preference of employers for their male workers to be trained in these industries. Over the last decade, which has been marked by legislation aimed at improving the status of women generally, some

Table 4.9   Percentage Distribution of First Degrees Awarded by
Universities in the United Kingdom by Sex: 1971 and
1979

Subject Area	Male		Female		Percentage of Women
	1971	1979	1971	1979	1979
Education	2.3	1.2	7.2	3.3	62.5
Medicine and related subjects	7.9	8.4	6.7	8.8	38.0
Engineering and technology	22.1	21.0	0.8	2.0	5.0
Agriculture, forestry & science	2.1	2.0	1.0	1.5	29.4
Science	26.1	24.6	20.6	18.7	30.6
Social administration business studies	22.2	25.9	23.0	27.5	38.2
Architecture & other related professional and vocational studies	1.9	1.8	0.7	1.1	26.6
Language, Literature & area studies	8.3	7.4	24.0	22.4	63.7
Arts (other than language)	7.0	7.7	15.9	14.7	52.5
Total degrees awarded	36571	41396	16118	24061	36.8

Source: Department of Education & Science, *Statistics of Education,*
1971 and 1979.

amelioration in the differences of treatment of the sexes in
preparing for employment is discernible, though the facts presented
in this section provide no evidence of any significant improvement
in women's economic status through education. But recent work by
Greenhalgh and Stewart (1982) on the effect of work experience
and job training on the occupation and earnings of women shows
that the benefits of training on women's occupational status, if they
are employed on a full-time basis, are even greater than for men.
But family considerations and accessibility to full-time training

facilities are constraining factors. And accessibility is particularly important when women re-enter the labour force after the interruption for child-rearing activities.

An interesting implication of the last paragraph is that any substantive improvement in the status of women workers presupposes certain changes in the manner in which work is organised, so that a more explicit recognition is given to the following factors:

(i)   the non-peripheral nature of the female attachment to the labour force in recent times;

(ii)   the absence of the vast majority of women for a short period from the labour force for the purposes of childrearing;[24]

(iii)   a need to provide more flexible training programmes, particularly for those women who are re-entering the labour force in their mid-thirties or early forties; and

(iv)   a need to accept part-time work as being an integral part of an average woman's career structure.

A critical factor determining the status of women workers is how part-time work is perceived by the employers. In the last decade the number of part-time workers, almost all of whom were women, rose by over one million, while the number of full-time workers fell by about 800,000.[25] A question that arises is whether this move towards part-time work is merely a manifestation of how employers can adapt their recruiting policies, at times of uncertain demand, to take advantage of the sexual division of labour. It is to this question and the facts relating to the differences in the prevalence of part-time workers by sex, marital status and occupations that we next address ourselves.

Women Workers and the Changing Working Patterns: The Occupational Dimensions of Part-Time Employment in Post-War Britain

The Second World War represented a watershed in female participation in the labour force in more than one way. It was estimated that during the War up to 80% of all married women without children were economically active. Many mothers with young children also made significant contributions to the war effort by working on a part-time basis. The War saw the ending of restrictions on the employment of married women in professions such as teaching and nursing. Provision of daytime nurseries and location of factories in areas with untapped reserves of labour from young mothers with children were other features of the war-time efforts to mobilise labour. And the need to reconstruct a war ravaged economy, as well as the additional employment demands generated by the Korean War boom in the early 50s, may have prevented the repetition of the experience of married women after the First World War when the vast majority withdrew from the labour force.[26]

In an earlier chapter we discussed the trend in part-time employment of women workers and its contribution to female labour force growth. Here we begin with an examination of the demographic and occupational dimensions of part-time work. Table 4.10 gives the occupational distribution of female workers by marital status and part/full-time work categories. For comparitive purposes, the distribution of male workers by part/full-time work categories is also given. It is possible to examine two sets of related hypotheses using the information given in the table.

  (i) A strong positive association exists in the case of married women between the 'popularity' of occupations (measured by the relative numbers in occupations) and the availability of part-time work (measured by the relative number of part-timers).

 (ii) The occupational distributions of males and married female workers show a greater dissimilarity than those between the males and 'not-married' females (i.e., female workers who are single, widowed or divorced).[27]

The Kendall 'tau' coefficient of concordance of 0.53, statistically significant at the 5% level, established the validity of the first hypothesis.[28] Even a cursory inspection of Table 4.10 would bear out this result. Part-time work is particularly prevalent among bar-maids, charwomen and canteen assistants, the nature of whose work precludes full-time employment and among nurses and shop assistants whose work can be easily fitted into a part-time schedule. A preponderance of married women among part-time workers in these occupations reflects the need for most married women, especially those with young children, to have flexi-work schedules so as to enable them to meet their family commitments.

The testing of the second hypothesis involves estimating the 'tau coefficients' measuring concordance between the ranking of occupations of married women and men on one hand and between 'not-married' women and males on the other. The results proved surprising. The 'tau' coefficient relating to married women and males was estimated as 0.59; and the coefficient between 'not-married' females and males was 0.53. Both the coefficients are statistically significant at the 5% level. There are serious doubts about the legitimacy of using the information on the male workers' occupational structure as given in the table, since it covers less than 20% of the total male work force in 1971.

There is widespread agreement that certain important changes in the way that people work have been occurring during the last decade. Three aspects of these changes in working patterns continue to attract public interest. First, there has been a dramatic increase in the proportion of part-time workers in the total work force, particularly among married women. Second, in response to both growing unemployment and the increasing desire to extend the range of choices of both men and women in allocating their time between market work and other activities, different schemes of job-sharing have been mooted, though there are few indications that they will be implemented in the forseeable future.[29] Third, there is some evidence of the growing importance of self-employment — a trend helped by increasing redundancies among executives who make a new start as self-employed workers, the growing practice among some employers to sub-contract work to the self-employed and thereby save on various costs, and certain tax advantages enjoyed by the self-employed compared to employees.[30]

The dramatic increase in the demand for part-time female workers in the last ten years has an important occupational dimension. Increases in part-time workers during the 70s occurred mainly in the 'Professional and Scientific Services' and 'Miscellaneous Services'. Both sectors recorded an increase in total numbers of about 350,000, which constituted about half of the total employment increase in the first sector and about three-quarters of the second. In the first sector, the greatest increase was recorded in the health and educational services where part-time employment opportunities exist; and in the second sector the growth in employment in the catering trades was particularly notable. Except in case of the Distributive trades where a fall of about 40,000 full-

Table 4.10 Main Occupations of Female Workers by Marital
Status and Duration of Work (Males by Duration of
Work Only) in Britain: 1971

SIC No.	Occupations	Percentage of all employed			Proportion of Part-Timers		
		Married Women	Others*	Males	Married Women	Others*	Males
029	Assemblers (electrical and electronic)	0.8	0.6	0.1	35.1	5.5	–
039	Machine tool operators	0.9	0.6	1.4	27.1	5.2	–
064–081	Textile workers	1.9	1.8	0.9	29.4	8.7	2.3
076	Hand and machine sewers etc.	2.4	2.9	0.1	38.2	8.3	–
078–081	Bakers, pastry cooks and food preservers	1.1	0.9	0.8	49.1	11.9	–
127	Telephone operators	0.9	1.2	0.1	30.4	3.7	–
137	Packers, labellers and bottlers	2.6	2.1	0.5	44.2	11.5	6.0
139	Clerks, cashiers	15.9	20.1	6.0	35.1	6.6	3.7
140	Office machine operators	1.4	2.1	0.1	27.0	2.5	–
141	Typists, short-hand writers, secretaries	7.4	11.1	0.1	35.0	5.7	–
143	Proprietors and managers (sales)	3.0	1.8	3.1	19.8	11.7	3.8
144	Shop salesmen and assistants	9.2	8.0	1.2	60.0	19.2	7.1
155	Barmaids, barmen	1.1	0.4	0.2	59.8	46.6	11.3
160	Waiters and waitresses	1.0	0.8	0.2	64.0	26.1	–

Table 4.10   *contd.*

SIC No.	Occupations	Percentage of all employed			Proportion of Part-Timers		
		Married Women	Others*	Males	Married Women	Others*	Males
161	Canteen assistants, counter hands	4.2	1.9	0.1	73.2	52.4	–
162	Cooks	1.6	1.0	0.4	34.3	21.6	–
163	Kitchen hands	1.4	0.7	0.1	69.4	46.3	–
164	Maids, valets etc.	5.2	4.4	0.1	78.4	52.5	–
166	Charwomen, office cleaners etc.	6.2	2.5	0.4	89.1	82.3	32.3
167	Hairdressers, beauticians etc.	0.9	2.2	0.2	33.3	4.5	–
168	Launderers, drycleaners etc.	0.8	0.7	0.1	34.1	13.9	–
183	Nurses	4.0	5.5	0.2	41.9	6.6	–
193	School teachers	3.5	3.9	1.2	75.4	66.1	53.2
215	Social welfare and related workers	0.4	0.5	0.1	54.0	14.1	–
219	Laboratory assistants & technicians	0.4	0.7	0.5	28.7	3.8	–
Total for above occupations		78.2	78.4	18.2	–	–	–

Source: *Census 1971 Great Britain,* Economic Activity Part IV (10% sample).

Note: *'Others' consist of single, widowed and divorced women.

time workers coincided with an increase of about 210,000 part-time workers, there is no evidence that part-time work has grown at the expense of full-time employment.

There were certain financial and other advantages for the employers in recruiting part-time workers. The National Insurance regulations exempt an employer paying less than a specified threshold weekly wage (£27 in 1981–82) from making any contribution. This was estimated to have saved an equivalent of 13% of the total wage bill in 1981–82. Part-time employees, up to 16 hours per week, are not eligible for redundancy payments, maternity benefits, minimum period of notice or legal consideration against unfair dismissal. Leicester (1982) estimated that the numbers so excluded amounted to about 1 million workers in 1981–82. There is evidence from the New Earnings Survey that the proportion of part-time workers who fall into this unprotected category rose between 1975 and 1979 from 20% to 30% in case of women workers in manual occupations and from 18% to 23% in case of females in the non-manual occupations. Finally, there are advantages to employers, at times of uncertain demand and rapid diffusion of new technology, to have a flexible work force who are relatively unprotected by legislative provisions safeguarding their employment rights.

It is instructive that the same changes in working patterns that have allowed well over half of the married women under 45 to go out to work, have also made them increasingly vulnerable as workers. Hence the earlier question that we posed, whether part-time work is but a manifestation of how employers can adapt their recruiting policies to take advantage of the existing sexual division of labour, is not without some credence. But to many a more objective manifestation of the inequities in the present sexual division of labour is the peristence of sex-related differentials in the earnings of male and female workers. It is to the facts relating to the nature and trends in the male/female earnings difference that we turn next.

Occupational Concentration and Relative Female Earnings: An Empirical Survey[31]

It has been recognised for a long time that occupational 'crowding' could be an important cause of differences in the earnings between male and female workers. The argument, according to at least one of the neoclassical variants of the 'crowding' hypothesis, is that a large number of women crowding into a small number of occupations would lower the value of their marginal product and hence their earnings *vis-à-vis* their male counterparts. While we shall postpone our discussion of the assumptions underlying the suggested link between differentiation by pay and segregation by occupation (or more tenously industry) until the next chapter, the specification of the link does illuminate one aspect of the neoclassical work in this area. Both in the theoretical and empirical work, it is the monetary manifestation of sex inequalities in the labour market that holds the centre of the stage. Occupational concentration (or segregation) is generally considered as a subsidiary issue arising from an examination of earnings-related issues. It is hoped in this section, which contains a brief examination of the pattern and trends in relative female earnings in Great Britain, to provide a greater emphasis on the occupational dimensions where possible.[32]

Table 4.11 presents the ratio of average female to male earnings, expressed as percentages, for seven occupational classes for selected years between 1910 and 1980. The last two rows of the table show the *overall* ratios for these years *controlling* for (i) the relative sizes of the occupational classes (i.e., the current weighted average) and (ii) for both the size and occupational structure (i.e., the constant weighted average).[33] It is clear from the table that once these controls are imposed, the overall female/male earnings ratio had changed little before 1970, fluctuating between 50 to 60%. But at the same time the earnings gap narrowed in all classes with the exception of the semi-skilled manual worker category whose gap widened with the earnings ratio falling from 72% in 1913–14 to 50% in 1970. This class contained the largest number of workers for both sexes in all years.[34] Hence the widening of the earnings gap in this class to a large extent counterbalanced opposing trends in other classes to produce little change in the overall earnings ratio for the period until 1970. Since 1970, a considerable narrowing of the earnings gap has occurred in all occupational classes with the solitary exception of the small 'Higher Professional' group. In the case of three occupational classes (namely the skilled manual, the unskilled manual and the lower professional groups) the relative increase in female earnings between 1970 and 1978 exceeded the increase between 1913–14 and 1970. It would be useful to examine

Table 4.11 Female/Male Earnings Ratio by Occupational Class
for Selected Years Between 1910 and 1980

Occupational Class	1913–4	1922–4	1935–6	1955–6	1960	1970	1975
1A Higher Professional	-	-	-	(75)	(75)	84	81
1B Lower Professional	57	67	69	72	72	65	72
2B Managers & Administrators	(40)	33	38	54	54	55	63
3. Clerks	42	46	46	57	61	63	74
4. Foremen/women & supervisors	46	57	57	61	59	61	69
5. Skilled manual	42	48	44	51	50	47	52
6. Semi-skilled manual	72	78	75	57	58	50	62
7. Unskilled manual	44	57	57	52	53	53	67
All Classes							
Unweighted Average	49	55	55	58	58	60	67.5
Current Weighted Average*	53	57	56	50	54	48	56
Constant Weighted Average** (1911 weights)	53	58	56	52	54	51	49

Source: Routh (1980), Table 2.28, p. 123.

Notes: * Current weights consist of relative number of male and female
workers in each occupational class according to the Population
Census nearest to the year in question.

** Constant weights consist of the relative numbers according
to the 1911 Census.

in greater detail this trend towards equality between male and
female earnings during the last decade. But before doing so, a basic
shortcoming of the analysis so far should be noted.

A trend analysis based on such a small number of occupational
categories is bound to subsume earnings differentials existing in
particular occupations. For example, if we examined the trends in
the relative earnings of female shop assistants, who fall into the
semi-skilled manual worker category, we would find that the
earnings ratio rose from about 60% in 1906 to 70% in 1935 followed
by a fall back to 60% in 1960.[35] If we further subdivided shop

assistants according to the type of shops they worked in, then shops selling food, clothing, footwear and general stores, all of which have high female concentration, pay their workers lower wages than shops dealing in furniture, carpets and electrical goods which have a higher male concentration (Robinson and Wallace, 1977). Similarly, female teachers, who fall into the lower professional group, show a narrowing earnings gap from 68% of male earnings in 1913 to 90% in 1960, which however fell to 78% in 1973.[36] Hence the size of the earnings gap will be critically determined by the degree of detail in the occupational breakdown, and generally the finer the classification, the smaller the gap in the male/female earnings.

Figure 4.1 shows the annual female/male *median* earnings ratio of full-time workers for the period 1971 to 1981. Separate estimates have been made for manual and non-manual workers. The median gross weekly earnings were used to estimate the ratio since there is a considerable dispersion of earnings in all occupations with the coefficient of quartile deviation[37] lying between 20 to 25 per cent. The figure shows that the relative female earnings have been rising for all groups over the last decade, though the increases have not been uniform either with respect to years or groups. During 1971–3, a slight fall in the ratio for the three groups was followed by a dramatic increase of 5% in one year between 1974 and 1975, probably in anticipation of the implementation of the Equal Pay Act (1970) by the end of 1975. The rise continued more slowly until 1977, after which a decline set in with the possibility of a recovery to the 1977 level indicated by the figures for 1980 and 1981. Though it is possible to detect a broad similarity in the trend for all three groups, the pattern of change is less volatile for the non-manual workers compared to manual workers, particularly at the beginning and end of the period studied. The ratio for non-manual workers remained on the whole lower than that of the manual workers, and both were less than the ratio for all workers — a pattern symptomatic of certain contrasting trends in earnings in the manufacturing and non-manufacturing sectors, discussed by Chiplin *et al.* (1980, pp. 58–62).

It now remains to explore the alleged link between female occupational concentration and the relatively low earnings of female workers. Sloane and Siebert (1980, pp. 11–15, 24–26) have investigated the effect of female concentration in occupations and industrial groups on relative female earnings. This is a variant of the

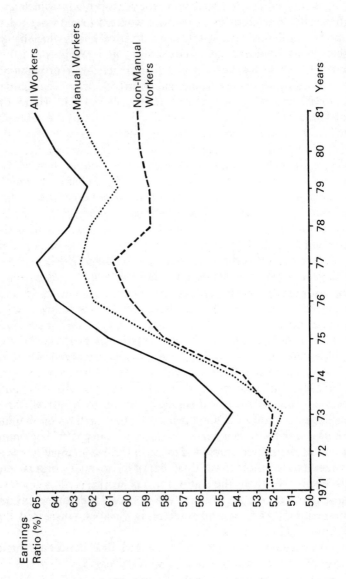

Fig. 4.1 *Female/Male Median Earnings Ratio (for the full-time employed): 1971–1981*

'crowding hypothesis' which, it may be remembered, infers that the low pay of women reflects their lower marginal productivity in those occupations into which they are crowded relative to other occupations. A distinction was made between part-time and full-time female workers for the purpose of this exercise.[38] A set of three interrelated hypotheses was tested using the New Earnings Survey data for 1976, where the dependent variable in a two variable regression model was some measure of female earnings.[39] The hypotheses were:

(i)   Female earnings fall as the proportion of women in the work force rises;

(ii) Male earnings rise as the proportion of women in the work force falls; and

(iii) The male/female earnings differential increases as the proportion of women in the work force rises.

For full-time female workers, Sloane and Siebert found no significant statistical association between female 'crowding' (measured by the relative number of females in each occupation or industrial group) and low female earnings (hourly or weekly), *or* high earnings of males (hourly or weekly), *or* high weekly male/female earnings differential ratio. For part-time female workers the results were different. A highly significant negative association was found between the proportion of female part-time workers in each occupational group and the male earnings in that group. This significant negative association persisted in the case of female weekly earnings, but proved insignificant when the explanatory variable was the male/female earnings differential ratio or female hourly earnings.

Other empirical work has produced conclusions different from those of Sloane and Siebert. Nickell (1977), using similar data but including more explanatory variables, found a significant negative association between female concentration and male *or* female earnings. For 1972, his results suggest that a 10% increase in the proportion of women in an industry would result in a fall in both male and female wages of between 1.5 to 2%. Woodward and McNabb (1978) established a significant positive association between female concentration and the presence of low-paid male manual workers in British manufacturing using the 1970 New Earnings Survey data. Hebden (1978) established a significant positive association between male and female pay by industry. However, in contrast to these studies, Wabe and Leech (1978) found that the sex composition of the work force was not a significant factor in determining relative earnings for their whole sample consisting of the 1968 data from manufacturing production.

In an attempt to update and extend Sloane and Siebert's empirical work, data on numbers and average earnings for 39 occupations from the New Earnings Survey, 1981, were used to estimate, from regression analysis, the relative contributions of female concentration and non-basic earnings components in explaining variations in the relative earnings of the female work force. The inclusion of a 'non-basic' component was to take account of considerable differences between the 'make-up' pay of male and female workers.[40] Payment by results, premium payments for shift work and overtime are likely to form a bigger component of male than female earnings in almost all occupations. This difference could have a significant influence on the male/female earnings differential, particularly among manual workers. It therefore becomes important that one controls for differences in the make-up of pay between the sexes in examining the relationship between female concentration and relative earnings. As a crude proxy for differences in the composition of earnings between male and female workers an index, measuring the ratio of the proportion of gross weekly earnings that consisted of non-basic earnings of female workers to that of male workers, was included as an additional explanatory variable. This variable proved to be highly significant and had the 'right' signs in all regressions involving the dependent variables, male/female earnings differential ratio, female weekly earnings and male weekly earnings. However, in all cases, with the exceptions of regressions of the relative number of part-time workers on male gross weekly earnings and on female gross weekly earnings, where significant negative relationships were established, the regression coefficients measuring the impact of female concentration on earnings were insignificant by the usual 't' test criterion.[41] Finally, an examination of the relationship between the earnings differential of part-time and full-time female workers and the difference in the average number of hours worked by the two groups, showed no significant association, possibly implying that part-time female workers constitute a separate disadvantaged group whose low pay is more a reflection of their lower status and powerlessness, rather than their sex and the number of hours they work.[42]

To sum up, the results from empirical work are inconclusive with respect to the precise effects of female overcrowding on relative female earnings. Limitations of the data used as well as certain methodological problems with respect to model specification should make one wary of accepting uncritically any of the empirical results discussed in this section. There is some justification for considering part-time workers as a separate and disadvantaged group whose low earnings are not merely a result of shorter working hours.

The Micro-Chips and Women's Jobs: Certain Pointers for the Future

A computer-on-a-chip, known as a microprocessor, which can be programmed to perform a multitude of tasks essentially involving storage, retrieval, manipulation and transmission of information lies at the heart of what many proclaim as the start of a new industrial revolution. There is virtually no field of human activity which will remain totally unaffected by this new technology. Microprocessors are already in use in the control of power stations, textile mills, printing presses, telephone-switching and in the gradual elimination of the human element from repetitive and mechanical tasks such as spraying, welding, lifting, etc. There are chips to extend the range and functions of domestic appliances such as cookers, washing machines, food mixers, motor vehicles, etc. A single micro-chip in an electronic sewing machine, for example, replaces 350 standard parts. It is the effects of this microelectronic technology on the employment of women in a whole range of occupations in the recent past and in the future that this section will examine. And the employment effects will be assessed both in terms of the effect on the numbers employed in different occupational or industrial categories (i.e., the 'quantitative' effect), as well as in terms of the possible changes in the type of work that women do (i.e., sometimes referred to as the 'de-skilling' effect).

Certain problems arise in assessing the quantitative impact of microelectronics on future female employment over and above the usual difficulties in predicting the future. For one thing, it is difficult to disentangle the impact of microelectronics on future employment of women from the combined effects of government policies, cultural and institutional constraints on women working, and the international competitiveness of British products *vis-à-vis* their foreign substitutes. But more specifically, any innovation in a particular industry is likely to affect not only the output, productivity and employment in that industry, but because of the interdependent nature of industries in developed economies, the 'linkage' effects could be substantial. For example, the introduction of word processors into offices could not only *directly displace* some of the typists in those offices, but could lead to *secondary displacement* of print workers who were supplying printed material to the offices before the arrival of word processors. The impact of this new technology is unlikely to stop here. There could be *compensating employment effects* arising from the increased output and real incomes brought about by this new technology, which could fuel additional demand for consumer or investment goods resulting in more being employed to meet this demand. It will become clear from our discussion of various forecasts of female employment that neither the secondary displacement nor the compensating employment effects are generally taken into account. It is the direct displacement of labour with an imperfectly specified rate of diffusion of microelectronic technology that forms the basis of almost all existing studies of employment effects.

Few studies have examined the effects of microelectronics on women's employment *per se*. A recent report by the Science Policy Research Unit's Women and Technology Studies Group (SPRU, 1982) contains a useful summary of previous work in this area and a detailed descriptive survey of the possible impact of microelectronics on women's employment in Britain. This report provides the factual basis for much of the discussion that follows.

Existing data on the occupational distribution and the industrial composition of the female work force could serve as the basis for making inferences on the impact of microelectronics on what are generally labelled as women's jobs. The manufacturing sector, which employs 20% of the economically active women in this country, has among its ranks 60% of females who are unskilled and semi-skilled operatives and a further 35% in offices and canteens. Two features emerge from these statistics. First, the relative paucity of women in skilled, technical and managerial jobs could mean that women as a group may have little influence on decisions made with regard to the nature and speed of the introduction of new technology. Second, female concentration in 'non-skilled' jobs could make them particularly vulnerable to displacement by less labour-intensive technology. As illustration of these and other aspects of the employment effects of microelectronic technology, consider the experience of female workers in different areas of manufacturing production.

A major decline in female employment in recent years has been among assemblers in the electrical and instrument engineering industries (Senker, 1980). Microelectronic technology would reduce labour requirements in those industries by rationalising the stages of production and encouraging automation. Sleigh *et al.* (1979, p. 19) estimated, for example, that total employment in television manufacture fell from 69,600 in 1973 to 45,800 in 1978, of which an overwhelming number of job losses occurred among female assemblers. Much of this fall could be directly or indirectly attributed to technological changes occurring in this industry. There was a significant increase in the number of imported components that went into the television sets. There was increased demand for Japanese sets which incorporated some of the more recent developments in microelectronic technology. Many multinational companies tended more and more to farm out the manufacture of components or even complete sets to low-wage Third World countries.[43] While it is difficult to disentangle the impact on jobs of the various factors mentioned above, it would be reasonable to infer from the experiences of the recent past that the direct displacement effect of the increasing use of microelectronics in this industry could be substantial losses of women's jobs in the future, with little prospect of these losses being curtailed by increased production or sales.

In an earlier section we noted that the important traditional sources of female employment in manufacturing had been the clothing and footwear, and textile industries in which 75% and 46% of the total employees respectively are women. Between June 1976 and September 1981, the number of female employees in clothing and footwear fell by 20%, while textiles recorded a fall from 216,600 to 175,300 (i.e., a decline of 27%). These two industries offer contrasting scope for introducing further microelectronic technology. The clothing industry has a preponderance of small firms (i.e., about 90% of all establishments employ less than 100 workers). This is likely to reduce the rate of diffusion of the new technology because of the high cost of investment. Again, the introduction of microelectronics in the clothing industry is more likely to affect areas which are male-dominated such as pattern design and cutting.[44] It could be argued that at least the short-run consequence would be to 'de-skill' these areas and thereby make it easier for women to enter.

The textile industry has had a long history of responding quickly to new technology, and the fierce competition from abroad in recent decades has made it fairly cost-conscious. Two main areas in which microelectronics are already affecting the production process are computer controlled Jacquard knitting machines and the electronic monitoring system. Both machines have already had a noticeable 'de-skilling' effect and a differential impact on the employment of men and women.[45]

In a study of the effects of microelectronics on Tameside (Greater Manchester) employment, Green and Coombs (1981, p. 49) found that the potential job losses would be particularly severe in three industries during the 80s — textiles, clothing and engineering industries. They estimated that direct displacement effects (based on estimates given by firms interviewed) of the numbers employed in these industries in the late seventies would be 0.8% for clothing and footwear (combined with the industrial category 'Fur and Leather') and 8.4% for textiles. They also allowed for structural displacement arising from 'secular trends in markets for certain types of products, changes in minimum efficient scale of production in some industries and changes in relative advantage of some geographical regions of production' (p. 48).[46] Job losses resulting from these effects were estimated to lie between 4.7% to 23.5% for clothing and related industries and 8.0% to 40.7% for textiles. While this study makes no attempt to separate job losses by sex and is based on the experience of a small area in the North West, an extrapolation nationally using the lower terminal value for structural displacement (i.e., what the authors describe as displacement from 'mild structural change') and assuming that the sex ratio within the two industries remains unchanged, the net job losses of the female work force during the 80s would amount to about 26,000 in the case of textiles and 9,000 in case of clothing, using the numbers employed in September 1981 as the bench mark. These numbers are to be compared to a fall of 59,300 in the textile industry and 41,200 in the clothing and footwear industry between 1976 and 1981.[47]

Female employment in the paper, printing and publishing industries fell by 23.4% between 1970 to 1980, compared to a fall of 18.5% in case of the male workers. In 1981, women comprised 31% of the workers with 101,700 employed in printing and 47,900 in paper and paper product manufacture (SPRU, 1982, p. 33). In printing and publishing, women were concentrated in the lower skilled non-craft jobs such as binding and collating and of course clerical services, all which are likely to be disproportionately affected by the introduction of microelectronic technology. If the present job segregation is maintained, which is quite likely given the strong exclusion tradition of craft unions, this would reduce the chances of women entering in any significant numbers expanding areas such as computer composition (i.e., the use of VDUs and computer controlled photo composers in place of linotype setting).[48] And this is in spite of what Cockburn (1979, p. 1) describes as the 'growing convergence between the traditional female work of typing and the male world of type-setting' (quoted in SPRU (1982), p. 36).

The main impact on female employment in the paper and paper product industries is likely to arise from the increasing use of microprocessor-based control equipment which could have disproportionate effects on the employment of machine minders in the processes involved in cutting, creasing and book-binding (Hirsch, 1980, p. 11). Applying the most conservative estimates of job losses of 8.7% from the Tameside study, would give a decline in female employment of 13,000 in these industries by the end of the 80s, compared to a recorded fall of 54,000 between 1970 to 1980.

Of the remaining manufacturing industries, 'Food, Drink and Tobacco' and 'Rubber and Plastic Process' industries are significant both in terms of the potential impact of microelectronic technology and as important employers of women. The scope for introducing microelectronics in food and related industries is immense and is likely to have a disproportionate effect on its 40% female work force who are mainly concentrated in areas such as packing, labelling and machine minding. In the case of rubber and plastic process industries which have about 30% women in their work force, the impact of the new technology is likely to be felt in the use of process control automation and in the handling and transportation of the products. While control of the production process may not have a substantive differential impact on male and female employment, the handling and carriage of goods being however men's jobs within the present pattern of sex-typing of jobs, if these jobs are replaced by the micro-chip it is unlikely to have much of an impact on female employment.

About 70% of all female workers are found in the service occupations and distribution trades. Of the service occupations, the largest in terms of female employment are office occupations, of which about 75% are in one occupational category — i.e., clerical and related workers. The potential impact of microelectronics on this occupational category could be enormous. For office work epitomises what the new technology is tailor-made for. It provides not only a means of automating what have been in the past separate tasks — such as recording, filing, processing, retrieving and transmitting information — but also integrating them by means of a microelectronic device known as a word processor. A word processor consists of a keyboard, a visual display unit (VDU), a storage memory unit and a printing facility. By linking it with a main frame computer, it becomes possible to transmit information over a wide geographical area. This has enabled the increasing adoption of electronic mail by business enterprises and the electronic fund transfer (EFT), the latter already having a considerable impact on banking operations.

There has been a spate of reports on the impact of microelectronic technology on office employment. Siemens (1978) estimated that up to 40% of office workers (i.e., two million typing and secretarial jobs) could be laid off within 10 years in West Germany. The Nora and Minc report (1978) warned that about 30% of the work force from the labour-intensive female dominated banking and insurance companies could lose their jobs in France by 1990. Forecasts in this country include one by APEX (1980) who forecast a loss of 250,000 jobs by 1983 in the typing, secretarial and clerical occupations; one by Barron and Curnov (1979) who predicted a fall between 10–20 per cent in the number of secretaries, clerks and office managers by 1995; one by Jenkins and Sherman (1979) who predicted an eventual decline of 30% in all information processing jobs, and one by Metra International (1980) who predicted that between 60 and 70 per cent of all clerical, typing and secretarial jobs would vanish eventually with the widespread adoption of microelectronics in offices.

Certain reservations need to be made about these forecasts, particularly with respect to the methodology relating to the area of technological impact on employment and similar aggregates in general. Almost all forecasts relate to the *potential* impact of new technology rather than a prediction of what will really happen. Certain technological, financial and human constraints could operate to slow down the rate of diffusion of the new technology. The technological constraints could arise from problems of inputting information into an automated office system. Encoding information has remained so far a laborious and highly labour-intensive process, acting as a serious impediment to the operation of subsequent tasks. Only with the development of an effective voice system can this bottleneck be overcome.

The financial constraint operates mainly through size. The small size of a firm may make the installation of a fully automated office system unnecessary. Often this is ignored in forecasting exercises. There are industries such as clothing where small firms predominate and which are unlikely to benefit, at least in the short run, from the widespread adoption of microelectronic technology.

Finally, the whole ethos of office work is not readily comprehensible purely in terms of any economic rationale. In the writings of Barker and Downing (1980), Benet (1972) and Vinnicombe (1980), the role of a secretary as an 'office wife' and 'gate keeper' is well highlighted within the patriarchal framework of a typical office.[49] The secretary is not only expected to perform certain 'wifely' tasks for her boss, but attains her status within the office hierarchy through her boss. As a 'gate keeper' she is expected to protect her boss from unwelcome distractions and act as a 'filter' of trivial and irrelevent information. Often the secretary serves as a status symbol for her boss where her looks or educational attainment help the location of the boss in the pecking order of an office hierarchy. A word processor, however justifiable on economic grounds, could hardly fulfil these functions! So that as long as secretarial work has these additional dimensions, it is unlikely to be threatened by the micro-chip in the forseeable future.

To complete our survey of how microelectronics affect employment in different industries, its impact on female employment in the distributive trades will be considered next. An area of considerable past growth of female employment, there were

1.4 million women workers out of 2.6 million total workers in 1981. The vast majority of the women are concentrated in retail trade; and it is on this area of activity that we shall concentrate. One of the most important developments in recent years has been the electronic cash register with laser screening devices. Such a register, in addition to its traditional functions, monitors sales of all lines and keeps tabs on stock levels by taking account of what has been sold at all terminals. A system of continuous inventory control would permit the holding of lower levels of stock and thereby reduce costs in terms of interest and storage charges. While this device may not have any discernible effect on employment in the short run, there are other developments such as PRESTEL, which involves remote mail ordering and Electronic Funds Transfer (EFT), which could have considerable repercussions on female employment even in the short run. However, a factor that could slow down the rate of diffusion of new technology is the preponderance of small establishments in the distributive trades. In 1980, 96% of the total establishments employed fewer than 10 workers.[50]

In most studies examining the future impact of microelectronics on different branches of industry, the primary emphasis has been on assessing the magnitude of direct displacement of employment. The Tameside study also attempted to allow for the second-round displacements by taking account of some of the factors that could slow down the rate of diffusion of the new technology, though the quantitative assessment was at best informed guesses on how different firms might be affected by structural changes. None of the studies attempted to incorporate possible employment generation resulting from greater productivity, higher output, and higher real income (or aggregate demand). It is possible to distinguish between different sources of this increased demand. It could be of a domestic nature arising from higher real income. It could result from an increase in foreign demand arising from the improvement in international competitiveness of British products. It could be the multiplier effect on real income and employment resulting from new investment in industries producing microelectronic products. And finally, the impact of the new technology on patterns of consumption could stimulate aggregate demand and employment.

One problem of incorporating these compensating employment effects into previous studies arises from their micro-character. Occupational or industrial categories or regions constitute their level of study and difficulties arise as to how to translate these results to the macro-level. Any method devised to quantify the indirect effects of microelectronic technology should take account of inter-industry linkages, separate its impact on final demand from that on intermediate demand, examine the price effect of changes in labour requirements per unit of output and evaluate the import requirements (or 'leakages') of adopting the new technology. Further, it should be possible to separate employment requirements by sex if the model is to be suitable for forecasting the impact of microelectronics on female employment. A dynamic input–output model incorporating technical change could be a useful vehicle for such a study.

Conclusion

In this chapter we have ranged widely over a whole host of issues relating to the type of jobs that women do and the industries in which they are employed. From a brief historical examination of the trends in the occupational and industrial distribution of women workers, we found that in spite of compositional changes and a long-term trend towards less female concentration, women workers are still confined to a narrow range of occupations, taking up positions in the lower echelons of the occupational hierarchy, with prospects for career advancement generally inferior to those of men. Some evidence exists that sex inequality in the labour market is associated with educational disparities between men and women arising from both differences in accessibility to vocational training and the job 'attractiveness' of the subject studied. Differences in occupational distribution were also to some extent reflected in sex-related earnings differentials, though a statistical attempt to relate female occupational overcrowding with low earnings proved inconclusive. The part-time status of a growing proportion of women workers, mostly consisting of married women, has an important bearing on the tendency for women to 'crowd' into certain occupations which are generally low-paid and low-status jobs. Their vulnerability has more than a sexual dimension. Finally, an additional dimension to the position of women in the labour market was provided by a discussion of the extent to which female employment and the type of work they do will be affected by the growing use of microelectronic technology in production, distribution and consumption processes.

There is evidence that women could be disproportionately affected in terms of job losses resulting from the new technology, though no conclusion can be drawn on whether the new technology is more 'de-skilling' for women than men.

In the next chapter we shall examine some of the broader theoretical issues raised by this chapter on women's status and role in the labour market, both in terms of the jobs they do and the remuneration they receive. The part played by institutions such as the family, the trade unions and the State in determining the economic status of women will form an important part of the discussion.

Notes

1. Studies relating to occupational differences in mortality, voting behaviour or social class are fairly well known. A recent study by Haines (1979) points to the existence of a remarkable degree of stability and international similarity in differential fertility among occupations. The average number of children ever born per woman aged 15–49 in England and Wales in 1951 varied from 2.25 for wives of agricultural, construction and building workers to 1.75 for textile workers, even after *controlling* for age at marriage and incidence of infertility. Generally, heavy industry workers and coal miners had larger families than light industry and service workers.
2. Unless the sources are specifically mentioned, data for subsequent analysis in this chapter were obtained from Population Censuses.
3. This theme will be taken up in a later chapter when we consider explanations of the impact of technology-induced economic growth on female workers.
4. A disproportionate concentration of Asian male immigrant workers (consisting of 10.5% of all Asian male workers in 1971) has been a significant feature of the textile industry since the mid-fifties. An interesting point is whether the relatively modest increase in female share in this industry is associated with occupational concentration of immigrants in the industry. Similarities between occupational distributions of immigrants and women merit further study.
5. The occupations considered are restricted in such a manner so as to avoid a large and unwieldy list. A reduction of the minimum number to 20,000 workers would add another 25 occupations to the list, but would have hardly any discernible effect on the total numbers in those occupations where more than half are women.
6. Problems of comparability between occupations for the earlier censuses have meant that the data used are from England and Wales only.
7. American studies focusing on the relationship between occupational

segregation and the status of women include Bergmann (1974), Blau and Jusenius (1976) and Blaxall *et al.* (1976). Attempts to measure the degree of occupational segregation include work by Blau and Hendricks (1979), Fuchs (1975) and Gross (1968). Notable studies by Hakim (1978, 1981) relate to the British experience and Hakim (1979) contains international comparisons.

8. In general, this index would tend to *under-estimate* the degree of occupational segregation for two reasons. First, the greater the degree of occupational disaggregation, the more likely would sex differentiation of jobs become detectable. Second, the differentiation of occupations tends to be less *precise* in service industries compared to other industries because of difficulties in distinguishing between people using the same sort of skills and working with similar materials in similar environments. For example, the 1971 Classification of Occupations includes under the third largest female occupational category typists, secretaries, shorthand writers, superintendents of typists, etc., producing a large undifferentiated occupational category where the numbers of men in the overall category mask their presence in overwhelming numbers in a few unimportant sub-categories.

9. S_l rose by about 5 points between 1841 and 1901.

10. The implicit assumption of this procedure is that 'replacement' recruitment does not affect the sex composition of an occupation — i.e., women are replaced by women and men by men.

11. The summary index of occupational segregation used represents the difference between measures of over- and under-representation of women in occupations, so that as this difference decreases in magnitude, it may be inferred that occupational segregation has declined over time. For a discussion of the derivation of this measure, see Hakim (1981, pp. 523–5).

12. A distinction between the two types of occupational segregation may be considered rather artificial. The neo-Marxist labour process theorists would argue that labour is distributed horizontally between different industries (or labour processes) and vertically within each labour process. Within this horizontal and vertical division of labour, a sexual division of labour exists and is maintained by an uneven concentration of men and women in different occupations. It is the difficulty of providing an empirical dimension to this dynamic concept of the sex division of labour that has led to this distinction being made in the first place. For a useful discussion of the role of sexual division of labour in the social labour process, see Gardiner (1977).

13. There seems to be a sexual dimension to the change in the status of certain jobs over time. In 1911, women were under-represented in the clerical occupations. But soon after the increasing entry of women into clerical work, a transformation took place both in the nature and status of such jobs. On the one hand, from a stepping stone for educated and ambitious young men, clerical or office work was downgraded gradually to become a low-paid and 'dead-end' job. The process of downgrading was helped by the 'de-skilling' of the job. Office work

was split up into typing, filing, shorthand writing and other tasks. The entry of women into offices was soon being justified as being particularly suited to their abilities — an analogy being drawn between playing a piano and typing!

14. The information on which these inferences are made is contained in Table 48 of NUT (1980). There were about 6 full-time women teachers to 4 full-time men teachers when the survey was made in England and Wales.

15. For a useful discussion, see Byrne (1978) and Deem (1978).

16. Or more precisely, the Index of Female Avoidance (P_t) may be defined as:

$$P_t = \sum_{i=1}^{n} T_{it} g_{it} \Big/ \sum_{i=1}^{n} F_{it} = \frac{\text{Expected number of Female Trainees}}{\text{Actual number of Female Trainees}}$$

where T_{it} is the total number of students from the ith industrial group at time t; g_{it} is the proportion of female employees in the ith industrial group at time t; and F_{it} is the number of female students in the ith industrial group at time t.

17. Statistics on day-release students by sex and industrial groups are obtainable from the annual publication, 'Education Statistics'. The sex-composition of full-time employees in each industrial group was obtained from the 1971 Population Census and the 1978 Sample Census of Employment.

18. If P_t is 1, this would indicate that the number of females released for part-time study is proportional to the relative number of females employed in the industrial groups. In that case, the employers are not operating a 'sex-blind' or random policy in offering day-release provisions, but are following a 'fair' policy of releasing numbers of each sex in proportion to the sex-composition of the work force.

19. The 1971 Population Census defined highly qualified manpower as those who hold educational qualifications beyond the level of the General Certificate of Education Advanced Level. They would, therefore, consist of those holding first degrees or equivalent qualification (i.e., Level b) or higher degree (i.e., Level a). Qualified manpower also includes those with at least one 'A' level or equivalent qualification (i.e., Level c) but not a degree. Qualified workers constituted 9% of the total British work force in 1971.

20. A direct comparison between these values is strictly invalid since the Index is sensitive to the number of industrial categories used. However, a repetition of the exercise for all women using the same industrial categories as for qualified women gave the former a value of 15 points less than that of the latter. The conclusion still holds.

21. A fall of 3.8 points in the Index between 1971 and 1979 was shared out between 'Compositional' (1.2), 'Structural' (2.5), and 'Interaction' (0.2) effects.

22. For a useful discussion of sex-related differences in the choice of school subjects and particularly the avoidance by girls of science subjects, see Kelly (1981).

23. There could be perfectly valid reasons, at least from the point of view of the employers, why they prefer to train men rather than women. We shall examine some of these reasons in the next chapter.

24. Joshi and Owen (1981, p. 81) estimated the working life of an average mother would be reduced by 7 to 8 years as a result of having children.

25. The source of this information is the annual Census of Employment reports, published in the *Department of Employment Gazette.*

26. A widely-held view of women's role in the First World War is of women being recruited by employers with considerable misgivings to replace men who had gone to the Front, growing confidence in women's performance in these jobs, and the willing surrender of these jobs by women once the men returned from the Front. This view ignores the considerable pressure exerted by the government, trade unions and male workers on women to conform to the existing 'ideology' regarding women and their domestic role. Braybon (1981) has an interesting discussion on demobilisation and its aftermath as it affected the women workers.

27. Data on single women workers would be more appropriate but was unavailable.

28. The Kendall 'tau' coefficient measures the degree of concordance or agreement between two variables expressed in ordinal terms (i.e., expressed as rank order). It may be interpreted the same way as correlation coefficients, with its value lying between −1 and 1. Kendall's 'tau' was preferred in this instance to the Spearman Rank correlation coefficient because of the presence of a number of near tied ranks in the data. The Spearman coefficient was also positive and statistically significant at the 5% level.

29. For a useful discussion of various schemes of job-sharing, see Equal Opportunities Commission (1981).

30. The growing importance of the self-employed is a predominantly male phenomenon. Clark (1982) has a useful discussion of why self-employment is gradually becoming one of the two main alternatives to full-time work as employees — the other being, of course, part-time employment. His article also forms the basis of the subsequent discussion contained in this section on the occupational dimensions of part-time female workers.

31. An extensive literature exists on this area relating to women's work on both sides of the Atlantic which mainly concentrates on the male/ female earnings gap and on the question of the low pay of women generally. A comprehensive survey of the growing literature in this area relating to this country is contained in Sloane (1981). Routh (1980) has discussed how earnings in different occupations have been changing during this century without any great emphasis on the sexual dimension of these changes.

32. A number of different measures of relative female earnings are scattered throughout this section. They are: (i) the male/female earnings differential — the difference between average male and female earnings, (ii) the male/female earnings differential ratio —

male/female earnings differential *divided* by average female earnings, and (iii) the female/male earnings ratio — the average female earnings *divided* by the average male earnings. The period of earnings may be hourly, weekly or monthly and the term 'pay' is used interchangeably with earnings.

33. The difference between the two weighted averages reflects the impact on the earnings differential of changes in occupational structure. A rise in the constant weighted average relative to the current weighted average would indicate a shift in the relative number of workers into occupational classes with a greater earnings gap.

34. See Table 3.1, Chapter 3.

35. For the data on earnings of shop assistants, see Routh (1980, pp. 106–12).

36. For the data on earnings of teachers for the years 1913 and 1960, see Routh (1980, pp. 70–73) and for 1973, see Department of Employment (1976)

37. The coefficient of quartile deviation is equal to

$$[(Q_3 - Q_1)/(Q_3 + Q_1)] \times 100$$

where Q_3 and Q_1 are the third and first quartiles respectively.

38. The participation of part-time and full-time female workers is fundamentally different both with respect to their relative numbers in different occupations and the way in which they are treated in terms of remuneration and career advancement. It is, therefore, more meaningful to consider the three hypotheses separately for the two groups.

39. The use of the New Earnings survey data presents certain difficulties. The data refer only to the month of April and to establishments with at least 100 employees. Since low-paid women workers are over-represented in smaller establishments, their exclusion would give an *upward* bias to the estimate of average weekly earnings of women. The Survey has different starting ages for adult males (aged 21 and over) and adult females (aged 18 and over) though this is not a serious problem, for its effect is to 'depress that female/male earnings ratio between 0 and 3 percentage points' (Sloane and Siebert, 1980, p. 10). Finally, exigencies of sampling constrain the degree of detail possible in occupational classification and thereby blur actual differences in jobs done by men and women in each occupational category.

40. There exists empirical work which examines sex differences in the composition of earnings and the differential impact of relative movement in wage rates and earnings (i.e., what is commonly referred to as the phenomenon of wage drift) for different occupational groups. For a brief summary of the differences in the 'make-up' pay of men and women workers and the differential impact of collective bargaining arrangements, see Sloane and Siebert (1980, pp. 34–43).

41. A tabulation of the numerical results of these regressions is not given here, since it adds little to the results obtained by Sloane and Siebert using the 1976 New Earnings Survey data.

42. This would suggest that the treatment of women workers as a homogeneous 'disadvantaged' group, implied in much of the feminist work in this area, is not very realistic. Another division of the female workers which is of some importance in this country is provided by the racial dimension. In an examination of job segregation in a meats product factory which included an abattoir, Liff (1981) found that the sexual division of work broke down with the introduction of the racial factor. For sharing with men in processing the carcases were a few West Indian women 'cleaning and preparing the guts which were then sold to other manufacturers' (p.9). She adds that the work done by the black women bears little resemblance to what is actually considered women's work in that factory. One is left with the suspicion that this failure to recognise the importance of the racial dimension in discussions of the labour force participation of women in this country could very well be in part a reflection of the ethnocentricity of researchers in this area.

43. Sivanandan (1979) has argued that it is in the assembly of the circuitry of the micro-chip in the 'toxic factories of Asia' by female (and juvenile) labour that multinationals make most of their profits. In search of cheap labour, these companies moved from Hongkong, Taiwan and South Korea where they established their factories in the sixties, to Malaysia in 1972, Thailand in 1973 and the Philippines and Indonesia in 1974. They go in search of fresh pastures where docile female and juvenile labour is available to work long hours for low pay and put up with toxic bounding chemicals used in assembly circuitry of the micro-chip. Sivanandan quotes a Malaysian publicity brochure extolling the virtues of indigenous female labour in the following words: 'The manual dexterity of the oriental female is famous the world over. Her hands are small and she works with extreme care. Who therefore could be better qualified by nature and inheritance to the efficiency of a bench assembly production than the oriental girl?' In two sentences this quotation encapsulates well both the sexist and the racist dimensions of the existing relationships of the rich and poor countries of the world.

44. About two-thirds of the craft tailors, pattern cutters and graders in 1980 were males (SPRU, 1982, Table 12.3, p. 27).

45. A new spinning mill, established by Carrington Viyella at Atherton, Greater Manchester, employs the electronic monitoring system operating 5 shifts, 24 hours a day and seven days a week. The new mill which employs 95 workers replaced three mills with a total work force of 435. Both the technical skill component and the operation of a shift system favours male employment (SPRU, 1982, p.32).

46. The measurement of the structural effects is based on a scale of vulnerability to structural change within each industry according to 'informed' judgments on how susceptible that industry is to structural changes during the period of prediction. For a discussion of the methodology, see Green et al. (1980), Chapter 6.

47. These comparisons are made purely for illustrative purposes. Both the

'heroic' assumptions underlying the extrapolation procedure, the methodogical limitations of the Tameside study, particularly with respect to the 'subjective' elements implicit in estimating the magnitude of structural displacements and the arbitrary choice of the lower terminal value of the structural displacement here, would combine to throw serious doubts on the validity of these forecasts.

48. The role of certain trade unions historically in restricting female participation in some occupations will be considered in the next chapter.

49. A distinction between a secretary and a typist is important in this context. A typist is an operative whose function derives from the work she performs. If her work can be done more cheaply by a machine she becomes redundant. A secretary, on the other hand, performs a range of duties which are not clearly defined and therefore not easily amenable to automation. She is a reference point in the office hierarchy and an example of how a patriarchal family structure is extended into the work sphere.

50. We have not discussed the impact of microelectronics on female employment in Professional and Miscellaneous Services which include education, health, police and the social services. In all these areas, at least in the forseeable future, demographic factors and public expenditure policies are likely to have a greater impact than microelectronics.

5

Work and the Status of Women: Theories and Institutional Realities

Introduction

The statistical survey of the occupational and industrial dimensions of women's work contained in the last chapter has brought out certain salient features which now need to be incorporated into a broad analysis of the status and role of women in the labour market. These features can be briefly summarised as follows:

(1) There has always existed a tendency for women to be concentrated into a narrow range of occupations which soon come to be considered as 'women's' work. While the actual occupations have changed over time, nevertheless they have always shared certain characteristics — a disproportionate number of them are in the service sector of the economy; a number of them involve tasks which are traditionally associated with women's work at home — such as washing, cleaning, nursing, sewing, etc.; many of them require little or no on-the-job training (which in any case employers are reluctant to provide because of the alleged intermittent nature of female participation in the labour force); and many require a fair amount of formal education (with the result that, in all occupations

which employ more women than men, the average number of years spent in full-time education is greater for a typical female worker than for a typical male worker — although, even in these occupations, supervisory and managerial jobs are normally held by men).

(2) From our detailed study of occupational segregation by sex, it is clear that, while there has been a gradual improvement during the 20th century (which accelerated in the early and mid-seventies before the recession began to bite from around 1977), job segregation still remains a fact of life. Female concentration is particularly noticeable among lower-grade blue-collar workers (such as assemblers and packers) and the lower levels of white-collar and professional jobs (such as clerical workers and nurses). Men are over-represented in the skilled manual categories and higher professions. Sex segregation *within* occupations shows no sign of improvement, with men holding relatively more of the senior and responsible posts (e.g., in school teaching). From an examination of subjects studied at universities, and from differences in the provision for day-release made by employers, it is clear that sex-typing of jobs starts early with education and training.

(3) There exist significant sex-related differences in what many consider the most objective criterion — earnings. While the earnings differential has narrowed, to varying degrees in different occupations, its actual existence seems quite impervious to the enormous increase in the number of women entering the labour market since the War, and to the climate of opinion that has produced legislation to promote equal opportunities for men and women.

(4) Given the present occupational structure of female workers, an attempt was made to assess the impact of microelectronic technology on the future employment of women. Here there is some evidence to suggest that relatively more women's jobs will be lost, partly because the nature of these jobs effectively restricts the influence that women can have on decisions made with respect to the use of new technology, and partly because it is expected that the rate of diffusion of microelectronics will be greater in those occupations where women are concentrated.

Given these features, can we knit together the different strands so as to create a coherent framework for a theoretical analysis of the status and role of women in and out of the labour force in terms of the jobs they do, the remuneration they receive and the institutions that affect their occupational choice and degree of attachment to the labour force? The approach we adopt in this chapter is to focus on a number of key questions raised by the survey and its features outlined above:

(i)   What are the different theoretical perspectives for examining the position of women workers in the context of the changes that have occurred in the British economy, especially since the War, and are likely to occur in the future?

(ii) Do women workers constitute a separate labour market?

(iii) Given the persistence and widespread occurrence of occupational segregation by sex, what explanations have been advanced for this phenomenon, and how is it related to the whole question of differences in pay between the sexes?

(iv) What part does sex discrimination play in explaining differences in pay in particular and the unequal status of women workers generally?

(v)   What roles have the State and trade unions played in promoting better opportunities for women workers and what scope exists in the future for legislation and affirmative action in improving the economic status of women?

It is clear that these questions are inter-related and fairly extensive both in terms of the issues raised and the vast literature that exists on them. In the discussion that follows, only a brief indication of some of the issues implied in the questions is possible.

Status of Women Workers in a Mature Society: Differing Perspectives on the Impact of Technology-Induced Growth

Broadly speaking, it is possible to distinguish between two paradigms for the impact of economic growth on the status of women workers. The first, which may be labelled as the liberal optimistic view, perceives economic growth, fuelled by technological developments, dimming eventually the existing inequalities between men and women. Reminiscent of Godwin's utopian view of the Golden Age established by scientific progress, technology is viewed as a factor which will eventually eliminate the need for physical strength and stamina, allow shorter and more flexible working hours and reduce the amount of time spent on housework and other chores — all of which would promote better integration of women workers into the labour force. The spectre of automation is glossed over, emphasis being placed on its role in eliminating repetitive and physically arduous work and on the additional employment generated by the higher incomes and lower prices resulting from automation in the first place. Within this paradigm, the existing sex inequalities at work are merely manifestations of the low career aspirations of women, the outdated prejudices of employers and the male domination of trade unions. In the context of a dynamic economy, the growing involvement of women in the labour force, backed by legislative action against discrimination on grounds of sex, and progressive job training provision for women both in the early years of their employment as well as on their return after childbearing, would lead to the gradual withering away of sex inequality at work. This view of the changing status of women, responding to a growing economy, need not be dependent on any significant alteration in the existing sexual division of labour within the family.

The second paradigm, which may be loosely described as the traditional Marxist position, sees the change in the status of women arising primarily with their removal from the confines of the capitalist family structure.[1] Once women go out to work, they are no longer exploited as women but as workers. And an improvement in the economic status of women workers has to await the coming of the revolution. In fact, Marx considered the entry of women into the labour force during the early period of industrialisation as a symptom of the unfortunate effects of capitalism. The benefits accruing to the capitalists from increasing mechanisation might induce them to re-organise labour processes in such a way as to facilitate employment of cheap labour (almost always spoken of as 'women and children'). Hence, the argument goes, opposition to technology by male workers and restrictive practices of trade unions aimed at women workers are but an expression of their perception of capitalist appropriation of even greater surplus product by their exploitation of women workers!

There are certain difficulties with both these viewpoints. If the liberal paradigm were valid, would not technical progress and economic growth, by facilitating the entry of women into the labour force and reducing skill differentials between the sexes, decrease occupational segregation and the earnings differential? If the traditional Marxist view prevailed, how is the link established between (a) re-organising the labour process for the purpose of exploiting women workers more effectively and (b) the eventual integration of women into the labour process (resulting in the elimination of sex inequality in the work place)?

Let us marshall some of the empirical evidence presented in the previous chapter to examine the relationships between women's economic status, growing female employment and economic growth since the War to see whether they could throw any light on the two paradigms discussed above. The following inferences may be made on the basis of the *facts* brought out in the last chapter:

(i)   Almost all additional female workers entering the labour market since the War must have gone into the service sector;

(ii) The net decrease in male employment occurred to a large extent in the manufacturing sector;

(iii) In terms of the numbers employed in different sectors, the growth in employment in the service sector more than compensated for decline in other sectors;

(iv) The divergence in the sectoral distribution of male and female workers has become even more pronounced during the last thirty years; and

(v)   There is a growing tendency for female workers, a tendency which has become even more marked in the last decade, to take up part-time employment.

The question arises: what are the implications of these trends for the two paradigms outlined above? It may be remembered that the liberal paradigm saw economic development (through technical progress) as leading to an improvement in the economic status of women by bringing about a more equitable balance between the sexes in different occupations and also between different levels within the same occupation. Technical progress — the generator of development and better integration of the sexes in the work place — was envisaged as first occurring in the more capital-intensive manufacturing sector. As we noted, post-war growth in female employment occurred in the services sector, and particularly in the relatively low-status occupations. Also, decline in male employment ocurred in the manufacturing sector where we should have expected it to rise. Sexually differentiated employment

patterns exist to a marked degree *between* and *within* occupations.
There is a growing tendency for married women to take up part-
time employment. The liberal paradigm has not prevailed, though it
could be argued reasonably that neither the empirical evidence
produced nor the pattern of post-war development in Britain offers
a suitable opportunity to test the viewpoint adequately.

The traditional Marxist position has also been found wanting. A
dramatic increase in the number of women entering the labour force
has not been accompanied by any significant reduction in the 'sex-
specific' exploitation of the work force. The persistence or even
aggravation of sexually differentiated employment patterns is
illustrated by a whole range of statistics produced in the last chapter,
and throws some doubt on the Marxist position that equality
between the sexes will be gradually established as the earnings
potential of women is first recognised and then realised. But in
fairness to the Marxist position, there has always been the
recognition that the pace at which women's emancipation will
develop depends on the success with which housework is socialised.
This has hardly occurred, either in the narrow sense of changes in
the sexual division of labour within the family to reduce the burden
of household work on women, or in the the broader sense of a
definite trend towards communalisation of food preparation, house
cleaning and child care.

A problem with both paradigms is the failure to come to terms
with domestic labour. Marx focused attention only on labour power
used in the production of goods for exchange — the rest of the
labour was 'unproductive'. Housework has not featured in
mainstream economics except recently as part of the household
choice theory discussed in a previous chapter. Goods and services
produced at home are not included in calculating the Gross National
Product, though with the growing interest in household production
there is interest both in calculating the value of household work and
in devising ways of including the value of non-market production in
the Gross National Product.[2]

Yet in recent years there has been a growing realisation of the role
of female labour in maintaining and reproducing labour power.
And it is the attempt to incorporate this 'reproductive' function of
women in the analysis of both domestic and paid female labour that
has contributed some of the recent developments in Marxian
feminist analysis.[3]

Female domestic labour is not 'productive' in the strict Marxian sense, since it is not directly a part of the capitalist mode of production. But such labour is engaged in the creation and maintenance of labour power. So it is a source of surplus labour in the capitalist mode of production and therefore makes a contribution to profits. Now the wage paid to a male worker, for example, also contributes to the maintenance and reproduction of labour power. Hence both wage labour and domestic labour contribute to surplus value, though the mode of appropriation is different in each case, and so are the locations of the two groups in the class struggle.

The question arises: Is it always in the interest of capital for the mode of appropriation to be based on a system where the capitalist mode of production co-exists with a family mode of production based on a primitive division of labour based on sex? The answer is that it is sometimes in the interest of capital for women to come out of their homes and serve the function of an industrial reserve army.[4] In post-war Britain there were factors which made the female industrial army become the primary source of additional labour for the expanding sector. Positive net emigration was a feature of much of the period. The pattern of fertility decline during the twenties and thirties left Britain with one of the lowest proportions of population in the working-age groups in the developed world. Later entry into the labour force (as a result of raising the school leaving-age first to 15 immediately after the war and then to 16 in the early seventies), coupled with the growing tendency for people to continue full-time post-school education, and earlier retirement among male workers were other factors.

An important characteristic of an industrial reserve army is that there exist limited possibilities for substitution between it and the existing workers. The fact that the additional two million female recruits since the War were mostly absorbed into new jobs in the services, rather than taking up employment in the well-established industries, lends some support to the view that women workers form an industrial reserve army. The existence and persistence of sex-related differences in occupational distribution and earnings differentials are other relevant factors. Further, this view of women workers is well within the mainstream of recent Western Marxian analysis, the work of labour process theorists of which Braverman (1974) is a notable example. According to this theoretical perspective, part of the capitalist strategy for controlling workers is the transfer of the labour process from labour to capital by breaking down craft skills (i.e., de-skilling) and replacing them with a highly specialised division of labour. This fragmentation of labour permits not only greater control, but also possibilities of greater standardisation of work and use of unskilled workers, both of which are conducive to the rapid introduction of capital-intensive technology. It is in the light of this development that one can view both the greater vulnerability of women workers to the introduction of microelectronic technology and yet at the same time the de-skilling character of modern technology diminishes any real skill differences between the sexes and thereby establishes a greater degree of sex equality in the market place.[5]

To sum up, we have examined two different viewpoints on how a woman's economic status, responding to her pattern of employment, will be affected by economic growth. An examination of the liberal and traditional Marxist paradigms in the light of certain post-war changes in the British economy offered little support for either of the viewpoints. Certain more recent Marxist theoretical perspectives were mentioned to highlight the relationships between domestic and wage labour, between capitalist control and the de-skilling process of modern technology and between a reserve pool of labour and capital accumulation. It is not our intention to spell out these relationships in any detail here. However, the brief discussion of the Marxian view of women and work does highlight one of its interesting features. It offers a framework to enable one to look behind the market relations and monetary transactions which seem to form so much of the preoccupation of non-Marxian economics. Yet by the same token, the Marxian viewpoint is not easily amenable to dealing with specific questions such as:

(i) Why does job segregation by sex exist to a greater or smaller degree in certain occupations rather than others?
(ii) What is the nature of the relationship between occupational segregation and sex-related differentials in pay?
(iii) Why is there a greater preponderance of women among the low-paid compared to men?

It is answers to such questions that could have an important bearing on the efficacy of legislation or 'affirmative' action on the part of government, employers and trade unions in dealing with the problem of sexual disadvantages in the area of employment and pay. Before discussing these questions and the track record of the government and trade unions in promoting equal opportunities for women workers, it would be useful to consider whether women workers constitute a group which is 'meaningfully' distinguishable from male workers. The persistence of what may be described as the 'secondary worker syndrome' is found both in popular and academic discussion of female participation in paid employment.

Female Workers as a Separate Labour Market: The Secondary Worker Syndrome

The question raised here is whether the female labour market exhibits a sufficient number of characteristics to distinguish it from its male counterpart. Or, taking a more narrow interpretation, is the demand and supply of female labour sufficiently distinguishable from the demand and supply of male labour for a sex differentiation to be introduced into the analysis in the first place? The type of answers given could explain the whole economic rationale of job segregation and earnings differentials that we shall discuss in subsequent sections.

Fairly early in neoclassical literature on female labour supply there arose terms such as 'women power' and 'secondary workers'.[6] In the early use of such terms, a whole amalgam of perceived differences in the patterns of male and female participation, social acceptability of men and women working, the relative number of men and women entering the labour force, and the nature and type of jobs held or considered suitable for men and women, were implied if not always stated. But behind these perceptions lay the influence of the traditional stereotypes of the male and the female. Men are the breadwinners; women are daughters, wives or widows. The male head of the household earns income to provide for the upkeep of the household; a female household member works to earn pin money or keep the household supplied with non-essentials. A woman, as a secondary worker, is often only a marginal participant whose other roles within the family are seen as more important and even more rewarding than outside work. If this implicit differentiation of sex roles is generally accepted, the subsequent stratification of the labour market into 'prime-age' males in stable, better-paid jobs with a well-defined career structure and most women into intermittent, low-paid and dead-end jobs would not be very surprising. A stratified or segmented labour market forms the reference point for the internal or dual labour market theories explaining occupational segregation and sex-related earnings differentials. The details of these theories will be examined in a later section. But here we are concerned with an examination of those characteristics that women possess which make them into secondary workers.

Barron and Norris (1976, pp. 45–69) suggested the following main attributes possessed by a secondary worker:

(i) *Dispensability:* This implies that a secondary worker can be got rid of without adversely affecting the efficient operation of an establishment. Since there is a 40% chance that she is a part-time worker, there will be little statutory or trade union pressure for her retention.[7] And finally, her apparently limited work aspirations, which could be affected both by the nature of the work she does and the priority she gives to her family role, would make her more readily aquiescent to her dismissal.

(ii) *Social Differentiability:* The existence of a visible social difference based on deeply entrenched beliefs emphasising sex roles, is the basis of attributing lower productivity to women workers in certain jobs, or the possession of certain qualities enhancing their suitability for other jobs. For example, work of a physically arduous nature requiring great stamina is often labelled men's work, while other jobs involving greater manual dexterity or requiring pastoral care of the young, the old or the sick are described as women's jobs. Often this sex categorisation of jobs takes the form of self-fulfilling prophecies. Large concentrations of women in certain jobs are taken as evidence of their special aptitudes for these jobs.

(iii) *Lower Job Commitment:* This is the familiar argument that a secondary worker shows a lower commitment to her job as evidenced by her alleged lack of interest in acquiring training, joining and actively participating in a trade union, or advancing her career. A difficulty with this argument is the familiar 'chicken or egg' problem. Is her alleged lower commitment a result of the way she is treated as a worker, or is she treated differently because of some 'observed' tendency among women to subordinate their commitment to work to their family and domestic responsibilities? It is difficult to give an unambiguous answer. Instead, some of the other factors that could affect work commitment and aspirations among women will now be reiterated.

It is clear from our discussion in the last chapter that women are under-represented in certain areas of higher education and in almost all areas of vocational training. This could be a reflection *either* of a deeply entrenched view in society that certain occupations, such as engineering, the law or accountancy, are more suited to male aptitudes, *or* of the fact that the time spent on vocational training may be seen as a waste by a number of women whose work commitment is essentially of a short-term character, *or* of a marked reluctance on the part of employers to expend resources on a group whose attachment, they feel, to the work force is intermittent or part-time. It was pointed out in an earlier chapter that the pattern of labour force attachment of the vast majority of female workers has become bi-modal in character since the War. This has replaced a previous pattern of most women withdrawing from the labour force for good after marriage.[8] There has also been a fall in the average duration of absence from the labour force among women who return after childbearing because of the long-run decline in completed family size and short-term trend towards closer birth spacing. Both these factors, together with the increase in female life expectancy, have combined to raise the average length of the period spent by women in the labour force.[9] But balancing this tendency towards an increased working life have been certain countervailing forces such as the increased tendency among women (especially married women) to take up part-time work and the rise in the mean age of women workers, both of which could serve to discourage employers from devoting considerable resources to training female workers. Greenhalgh and Stewart (1982, p. 333) have pointed to the importance of training as a means of alleviating some of the re-entry difficulties of married women who have interrupted their work experience to raise children.

Implicit in the notion of females as secondary workers is the relative paucity of their numbers and the marginal nature of their financial contribution to the upkeep of a typical family. Both these points need to be scrutinised in the light of the evidence today. In

1980, 42% of workers were women and about the same proportion of women in the working-age groups were in employment. Hence, women can hardly be described as a secondary component of the labour force. There is also growing evidence that an increasing number of women work either because their earnings are crucial to maintain their familes above the poverty line, or because they are the only source of income in a number of households. The Royal Commission on the Distribution of Income and Wealth (1978) estimated that one-half of all single-parent households compared to one-fifth of two-parent households were in the bottom of twenty-five per cent of the distribution of net family income. On the basis of this and other indicators, they concluded that low pay could have emerged as an important cause of poverty if women's earnings had not lifted the families out of the lower income bands.[10] There is also evidence that about 20% of all 'non-pensioner' households, the majority containing either children or adult dependents, were wholly or substantially dependent on a woman's earnings or social security benefits (Land, 1976, p. 116). The 1971 Population Census records 512,000 households with women as heads which constituted 3% of all British households. From these households, one in every three had a full-time working woman and one in seven had a part-timer. To view women as secondary workers because of the smallness of their numbers or their marginal contribution to the family income is no longer apposite.

The question remains: Are there sufficiently strong reasons for treating female labour as a separate entity compared to male labour? In narrow economic terms, the distinction between male and female labour may depend on how different the factors are which determine their respective demand and supply. The supply of female labour is strongly influenced by familial and cultural considerations peculiar to their sex, apart from age, education and the primary economic variables — price and income — discussed in an earlier chapter. These factors could have an impact of a qualitatively different kind on male labour supply. The demand for female labour, which we shall consider in some detail in a later section, is to a large extent restricted to a narrow range of jobs where lower relative earnings is a distinctive characteristic.

But the broader question of whether female labour experience is distinctive hinges on whether there exists a historically meaningful and homogeneous social category called *women*. We expressed some doubts earlier in the book about treating women workers as a homogeneous category, since that ignores the full-time/part-time dichotomy and the class and racial dimensions. Yet women do constitute a social category either on the basis of their biologically distinctive attributes or their social roles within the family, where the latter is often seen in terms of their life cycle states — i.e., as daughters, wives, mothers and grandmothers. Each of these socio-sexual reference points could be as important in the analysis of female work experience as their class positions or occupational status. The neoclassical viewpoint would see these reference points as being critical in exercising choice at the market place for labour. As we saw in an earlier chapter, some of the more recent innovations in the neclassical theory of labour supply place great emphasis on marriage (and the presence of children) in determining the nature and degree of female labour supply responses.

In a wider context, an understanding of the productive and reproductive functions of women as a group presupposes an examination of how these functions are shaped in the first place by the existing links between the mode of production and family structure.[11] Engels (1884) was one of the first to recognise the importance of these links. While it is not proposed here to review his historical account of the development of the family and the relationship between the sexes as they were affected by the way that production was organised in different societies, some of his conclusions have contemporary relevance. First, Engels recognised that the way a society organises its domestic labour (i.e., household work mainly done by women such as child care and family maintenance) is inextricably linked with the prevalent mode of production. Second, the institution of private property within a capitalist family structure was the primary instrument of female exploitation. Third, 'the first condition for liberation of the wife is to bring the whole female sex into public industry. This in turn demands that the characteristic of the monogamous family as the economic unit be abolished' (p. 60). The increasing entry of women into the labour force has not resulted in the liberation of the wife in any significant sense. Of course, the monogamous family has remained largely intact, though some have noted a movement towards a 'symmetrical' family where sex role changes have reduced male authoritarianism and increased joint family decisions (Young and Wilmott, 1973).[12] In socialist countries, a 'fundamentalist' interpretation of the writings of Engels (1884) and Bebel (1883) may have led to the belief that 'women would be "returned" to a position of equality by the destruction of the private property system, as part of a natural history process' (Scott, 1976, p. 42). But, in spite of a sizeable number of husbands and wives working and having similar occupational status, there is no evidence of any significant change in the status and authority of women in the USSR or East European countries.[13]

Unequal Pay and Job Segregation: Certain Theoretical Perspectives and their Empirical Assessment

(a) Introduction

To a number of economists the issue of inequality between the sexes may be reduced to what is its most visible symptom — the difference in earnings between men and women. Even job segregation by sex is seen as a byproduct of this gap in earnings. And it is the magnitude, persistence and prevalence of this gap that has attracted considerable interest on both sides of the Atlantic in recent years.[14]

It is possible to distinguish between three sets of explanations for the existence and persistence of a considerable gap between male and female earnings. The first set of explanations concentrates on certain characteristics, in some way peculiar to women, which result in lower productivity. These include lower physical strength and stamina, inferior education, lower levels of career aspirations and job commitment, looser attachment to the labour force and higher turnover in most jobs.

The second set of explanations concentrates on the negative effect of a woman's family role on her worth as a potential employee. Periods of absence from the labour force would reduce her chances of rising up to 'top' jobs in managerial and professional occupations. The possibility of her absence in the future would serve to discourage her employer from spending money on her training. Even when she returns to work, her continuing domestic commitments could restrict the distance that she is willing to travel to work and the amount of time she could work. The interruptions to her work experience resulting from child care could result in the depreciation of skills that are relevant for her future employment, and often the presence of children or unavailability of training could result in her taking up a job requiring lower skills and being paid less. Finally, her weaker attachment to trade unions and other organisations existing to protect the interest of the workers would disadvantage her both in terms of her conditions of employment and remuneration.

The third set of explanations for the lower valuation of women's work focuses on the 'imperfections' in the labour market from which the hiring takes place. Inadequate information on suitable jobs available may lead to some women entering inappropriate jobs.[15] More important, however, is the possibility that employers, faced with imperfect knowledge about potential recruits, might use sex as a 'filter' or 'screen' in their hiring or promotion practices. It may very well be that they perceive the costs of implementing hiring policies on the basis of complete and updated information on applicants could exceed the costs incurred as a result of following what are essentially inefficient hiring practices based on sex stereotypes or prejudice. Or again employers may avoid recruiting women for senior positions because they suspect possible antagonism on the part of their male work force.

All these explanations for the relatively low female earnings are at best partial explanations. They fail to recognise that the position of women in the labour market, as shown by their concentration in low-status and low-paid jobs, is a result of the interactions of a complex set of institutions, be they familial, legal or cultural, all of which serve to reinforce the existing sex inequality in home, work places and society. Explanations which ignore these institutional realities could be quite misleading.

The three sets of explanations are also partial in another sense. They consist apparently of a list of unconnected reasons for the lower valuation of female work, without a coherent framework for an examination of the mechanism by which these explanations are translated into the end phenomena, i.e., occupational segregation and earnings differences between men and women. In other words, we are in search of theoretical models incorporating occupational segregation and sex-related earnings differentials which are capable of empirical verification. It is within the neoclassical framework that such models have found their fullest development.

(b) The Crowding Hypothesis

One of the earliest explanations of pay differentiation by sex gives the centre of the stage to occupational crowding. Fawcett (1918), an early exponent, argued that restrictions on entry into skilled and lucrative jobs placed by trade unions, employers and social custom, had the result of crowding women into a narrow range of non-skilled jobs which had the effect of further depressing the wage levels in these jobs. Edgeworth (1922) reformulated this hypothesis into the language of the neoclassical theory of income distribution.[16] Given perfect competition and equal productivity of men and women in the same job, women would be substituted for men as long as women earned less than men. But such a substitution does not occur and women continue to earn less than men for the same job. The obvious inference is, therefore, that women are less productive than men.

Edgeworth was aware that the reality is more complicated than what the theory suggests. He suggested that the occupational world could be split up into well-paid male occupations, low-paid female occupations and a small number of 'mixed' occupations where equal pay was the rule as a result of equal productivity of male and female workers. The germ of an idea of a segmented labour market is apparent, though the neoclassical straitjacket imposed by the need to equate earnings with marginal product, prevented a consideration of different ground rules for income determination operating in different markets.

There was, however, another implication of Edgeworth's theory which went against hard realities . If perfect competition prevails, there is the clear implication that all workers (including women) are eligible to enter jobs given that they have the requisite skills and experience. But this ignores the existence of arbitrary restrictions on women entering certain jobs by trade unions and employers.

The answer to this difficulty was provided by Joan Robinson (1934) who argued that perfect competition did not operate as a rule in the labour market. Certain monopsony elements in the labour market resulted in differences in the way wages are determined for male and female workers doing the same job.[17] A female worker's wage is determined by the price at which she is prepared to sell her labour; a male worker on the other hand, with his trade union behind him, would obtain the maximum he can, which the neoclassical distribution theory would indicate is equal to the marginal revenue product of his labour. So that the effect of the monopsony elements is to cause a divergence between the wage and marginal revenue product of women workers.

Madden (1977) has examined the extent of this divergence of wage from marginal product by focusing on factors which could reduce the wage elasticity of female labour supply.[18] These include geographical immobility imposed by family considerations and restricted choice of jobs available as a consequence of occupational segregation. As a theory of wage differentials between men and women, it is also a particular version of the crowding hypothesis, since the villain of the piece here, as in the earlier versions of Fawcett and Edgeworth, is occupational concentration of female workers. But unlike the earlier versions, the relative wage elasticities of labour supply determine differences in earnings between the sexes, so that women earn less than men because female supply is less elastic in response to wage changes.[19] No substantive empirical evidence exists to adduce whether wage elasticity of women workers is less than that of their male counterparts in different occupations.

The works discussed so far relating to the crowding hypothesis have concentrated mostly on supply factors in explaining the relatively lower earnings of female workers. A simple extension of Bergmann's (1971) theory of race-related earnings differences to sex-related earnings differences would identify restrictions on demand for female labour in certain occupations as the main culprit. The result is to lower the marginal productivity of workers in those occupations characterised by overabundance of women workers and maintain marginal productivity at a high level in men's jobs. The differences in marginal productivity would be reflected in wage differences between the sexes as long as occupational segregation (or overcrowding of female labour in certain occupations) prevails. The persistence of occupational segregation is attributed to a 'taste' for discrimination on the part of employers against female workers.

There are certain difficulties with the different versions of the crowding hypothesis discussed here, apart from those mentioned already for specific theories. We saw in an earlier chapter that empirical work in this country examining the effect of female crowding in occupations on differences between male and female earnings has provided no definitive conclusions. However, studies by Fuchs (1971) and McNulty (1967), using American data from occupations and establishments respectively, found that the higher the percentage of women employed within an occupation (or establishment), the lower the wages for both males and females. A possible inference from these results is that if female concentration is a measure of the power of males to exclude females from the work sphere, then the extent of this power has a direct association with sex-related wage differentials. So that female crowding is but a manifestation of sex discrimination if there is no productivity difference between the sexes.

The crowding hypothesis presents certain theoretical difficulties as well. If competitive forces operate in an economy, it is difficult to see how sex-related differences in earnings can persist under conditions of equivalent productivity. Again, is the assumption of no sex-related productivity differences a valid one given that there exist considerable differences in investment in human capital between men and women, whether in terms of formal education, or in the the amount of job-specific training available to them, or the length and continuity of work experience? Finally, and this is more a criticism of Bergmann's theory, no explanation is given as to why employers develop such a strong 'aversion' to employing women that they are prepared to forego additional returns from recruiting women at lower pay. The critical question is: Is there any economic rationale for the actions of discriminating employers?

It is mainly in response to these difficulties that other approaches to the study of male/female earnings differences and job segregation by sex have been developed, primarily in the United States. The 'human capital' approach seeks an explanation for the earnings gap in terms of sex-related differences in investment in human capital resulting in differential returns on these investments (i.e., earnings). Economic theories of discrimination seek the rationale underlying what seems irrational behaviour on the part of employers. It is to these theories that we turn next.

(c) Economic Theories of Sex Discrimination in the Labour Market

Becker (1957), in a pioneering work on the economics of discrimination, showed that under conditions of perfect competition in the labour market, equivalent productivity of male and female labour and a given 'taste' for discrimination against women workers, a profit-maximising employer could discriminate against women on a 'rational' basis.[21] If discrimination can be treated like any other commodity with a price, then the utility function of a discriminating employer which needs to be maximised would include an additional *argument* that embodies a discrimination coefficient which is a measure of the employer's taste for discrimination. Becker suggested that the coefficient could be measured by the ratio of the difference between the equilibrium male and female wage rates to the female wage rate. The magnitude and the form of sex discrimination would be partly determined by the size of the discrimination coefficient and partly by the nature of female attachment to certain jobs and the even-handedness of trade union representation of the interests of male and female workers. The focus of the theory is on wage discrimination and the inference is that there are employers willing to sacrifice some profits so that they can enjoy the consumption of that intangible commodity–discrimination.

A theoretical difficulty with the model as it stands relates to the maintenance of wage discrimination between equally productive workers. If perfect competition prevails in the labour market, it is only a matter of time before the existing wage differentials are eroded gradually as more and more 'non-discriminating' employers enter the industry attracted by abnormal profits to be made out of employing women workers who are paid lower wages for equivalently productive work.

One way out of this difficulty is to drop the assumption of perfect competition while retaining the other two assumptions regarding equivalent productivity of male and female workers and the exogenously determined 'taste' for discrimination on the part of the employer. Market imperfections could take the form of *either* monopolistic firms controlling the productive process and indulging in their taste for discrimination without affecting the demand for their products, *or* restrictive practices of male-dominated trade unions resulting in women being 'crowded' into certain low-paid jobs. The effects of these market imperfections are to generate and sustain sex-related wage differentials in the labour market.

The introduction of market imperfections into Becker's original model, notably by Reynolds (1973) and Swinton (1978), begs a serious question implicit in the model. Why do monopolists indulge in discriminatory practices which are not clearly to their financial advantage? It is empirically an open question whether monopolists tend to be more or less discriminatory compared to competitive firms. Indeed, empirical work aimed at verifying different implications of Becker's theory have led to few definitive conclusions. Chiswick (1973) found a significant *positive* association between the proportion of the 'discriminated against group' in an occupational category and the dispersion of earnings of the 'not-discriminated against group' in that category, using data on whites and non-whites in the United States.[22] A repetition of the same test using the 1981 New Earnings Survey data showed no significant association in this country between proportion of women in occupational categories and the inter-quartile range of earnings of males in the same categories. Becker (1971, p. 48) found a greater ratio of black to white workers in competitive than in monopolistic industries, tending to support a long-term implication of his theory that discrimination would be less marked in competitive conditions than in monopolistic ones. Finally, Brown (1976) and Fuchs (1971) have produced evidence that sex discrimination by consumers is important. The inference is drawn from the facts that the female/male average hourly earnings ratio was lowest among self-employed workers, who as a group not only had a lower than average proportion of females but were more than likely to come into contact with consumers. None of the empirical work mentioned above can be considered as adequate tests of Becker's theory. It is doubtful whether an empirical test encompassing the substantive strands of Becker's theory of labour market discrimination can be constructed, given the existing data and methodological constraints.

An approach that has found favour in recent years is to relax an implicit assumption underlying the competitive models of labour discrimination, namely, the availability of complete or perfect information on which employers can base their recruiting and promotion policies. Sex discrimination is no longer seen as satisfying a certain exogenously determined 'taste' for male workers, but as actions by profit-maximising employers who find it cheaper to act on stereotypical judgments rather than seek full information in individuals available for employment. Such stereotypical judgments are based on beliefs that female workers are inferior to male workers, whether seen in terms of 'objective' measures such as qualifications, reliability and long-term work commitment, *or* on the basis of employers' records of past experiences of women workers, *or* on the inference that past disadvantages of women resulting from prejudice or inequality of opportunity could adversely affect their present and future work performance. It is the crux of this argument that even if employers are aware of the existence of exceptions to these stereotypes, the 'costs' of searching for these exceptions would outweigh the costs of using sex as a 'screening' or 'filtering' device.[23]

It is easily shown that this 'screening' theory of sex discrimination in the labour market is perfectly compatible with either wage or job discrimination in the short run. In an attempt to emphasise occupational segregation as an end product, Thurow (1975) has put forward a 'queuing' model. There exists at any moment in time a fixed number of jobs available requiring a different skill-technology mix, with their relative wages being determined mainly by social convention. A queue soon forms for these jobs, with the position in the queue being determined by what employers consider are desirable endowments or attributes for the jobs. If sex is such an attribute, females will soon be crowded into the low-paid occupations.

In our discussion so far on the use of sex as a screening device, the implication is that employers are engaged in what are essentially 'irrational' decisions which, however, have some economic rationale. The question remains: is there any rational basis for the belief that women are less 'productive' than men? Or, in what sense does the existing assumption of equal productivity of male and female workers hold? The more substantial discussion of these questions will be found in the next section when we consider the human capital approach to earnings differences and occupational concentration. But here we briefly review the implications of the assumption of equal productivity for the 'screening' theory of sex discrimination.

The 'screening' theory of sex discrimination (or what is more usually referred to as the statistical discrimination theory) is perfectly consistent with the assumption of the same average productivity of male and female workers. One version of the same theory sees female abilities as being more dispersed (i.e., having a larger variance) than male abilities, though both distributions have the same mean. Yet another version suggests that while both distributions are the same in all respects, women's performance in tests to measure their abilities shows a greater variance than that of men. Now employers prefer to recruit workers from the group which has a lower dispersion of abilities. So that whether the dispersion of female abilities is really or apparently greater than that of males, employers prefer male workers, and as a consequence women tend to be crowded into lower-paid occupations. The difficulty with the first version is that there is no empirical evidence of greater dispersion of female abilities compared to that of males. The problem with the second version is that in the perfectly competitive neoclassical world, it would be only a matter of time before more reliable tests were devised or better hiring criteria determined, if only to stave off the possibility that new firms waiting at the footlights would enter and earn high profits by employing women workers at lower wage rates.

It is possible to retain the essentials of the neoclassical model of sex-related pay differentials by dropping the assumption of equal productivity of male and female workers. Profit maximisation, perfect competition and taste for discrimination prevail, but the critical factor is seen as the differences in human capital endowments of male and female workers.[24] The market still remains the final arbitrator of the distribution of skills by sex, but differences in skills between the sexes emerge as a result of factors outside the market, and are seen in terms of the human capital embodied in the workers. The remuneration of the workers depends on their marginal product which is critically determined by the investment in human capital made by the workers. It is to the explanations why human capital embodied in male workers is greater than in female workers that we next turn.

(d) The Human Capital Approach to Sex Inequality in the Labour Market

Various explanations have been offered for differences in human capital endowments of men and women. Leaving aside empty speculations regarding inherent sex differences in natural abilities, these explanations have focused on:

(i) differences in educational attainment prior to labour market entry;

(ii) differences in opportunity to obtain job-specific training during early years of work; and

(iii) differences in the pattern of labour force participation.

We examined the facts behind the tendency for women to invest less in education prior to labour market entry and the sex differences in job-specific training in the last chapter. An inverse relationship between differences in male/female earnings and level of educational attainment has been found by Phelps Brown (1977) in Britain for industries, possibly indicating the importance of physical strength in determining the earnings differential in unskilled manual work. It is a moot point whether lower investment in education and training is a cause or result of sex-related earnings differences.

Of the differences specified above, it is the pattern of labour force participation of women that is often considered the crucial factor.[25] The argument may be expressed thus. Even if men and women were similarly endowed both in terms of intelligence and educational attainment, women accumulate less human capital through work experience, since they spend proportionately fewer years in the labour force than men. The reasons for this shorter period of labour force participation by women may be examined in the context of the household choice theory of labour supply described in an earlier chapter. To recapitulate, the household utility function includes not only leisure and goods derived from market work, but also goods derived from non-market work which is traditionally performed by women. So that within the perspective of a utility maximising household, a decision by a woman not to work continuously could be a rational decision. But the result is that she does not accumulate as much human capital as her male counterpart. Hence she ends up being paid a lower wage.[26]

To extend this explanation to the question of occupational segregation is a simple matter. Past discontinuities of work would discourage most women returning to the labour force from entering occupations where work experience could be important. Also the prospect of future interruption in their career would discourage many young women entering the labour force for the first time from taking up occupations which need long or expensive training. Further, employers aware of the risk of women leaving the labour force for a period of years are less likely to employ women in those occupations with an important on-the-job training component. The combined effect of these factors is to concentrate women into occupations in which continuity, vocational training and lengthy apprenticeships are not important considerations.[27]

It is worth noting that the human capital approach can easily lend itself to the notion that sex inequality in the labour market arises because of the possession of certain characteristics by women which make them unequal to men. By emphasising the supply factors at the expense of demand, it becomes easy to infer that the position of the woman worker can be explained by her inferior investment in human capital. A demand factor, the 'taste' for discrimination, could be a critical factor both as an explanation for occupational segregation and earnings differential and as a cause why women may invest less than men in education and training.[28]

The 'human capital' approach to explaining sex-related earnings differences has inspired a number of empirical studies whose main objective is to quantify the importance of the 'supply' factors and then measure the contribution of sex discrimination to these differences. It starts from the basic premise that differences in earnings between two individuals reflect differences in certain personal characteristics which affect the quality of labour they supply and the nature of the jobs they do. These characteristics include age, marital status, education and training, work experience, number of hours worked as well as job characteristics such as conditions of work, level of trade union activity and performance of firms in which the jobs occur. Once all these characteristics are taken into account, any remaining difference in earnings is attributed to sex discrimination. Age and marital status sometimes serve as proxies for human capital endowment and work effort respectively.[29]

There are certain difficulties with this approach from a statistical viewpoint. First, it is difficult to ensure that the influences which are excluded (or controlled for) from the earnings differential are not associated with sex or affected by the discriminatory practices. The number of hours worked is significantly associated with sex and marital status of the worker. The type of education received, we have seen in an earlier chapter, has a sexual dimension. Conditions of work and the level of trade union participation are both dependent on the sex of the worker. In general, the whole area of acquisition of skills, the nature of family role specialisation and the life cycle pattern of labour force participation are mainly sex-determined, so that the implied assumption of the residual being uncorrelated with the 'sex-free' explanatory variables is unrealistic.[30]

A second difficulty with the 'residual' approach is that certain productivity differences between men and women are not captured by one-dimensional measures such as the length of period of full-time education and training or the duration of work experience. In fact, the residual may well be in part a reflection of qualitative differences rather than sex discrimination in earnings.

Thirdly, there is some doubt as to what variables such as educational attainment or work experience are really measuring. It is assumed in this approach that these variables represent in a certain sense 'qualifications' which cause some people to be paid more than others. But an equally plausible inference is that these 'qualifications' reflect differences in opportunities available, which in turn are critically tied up with the different roles that society expects males and females to perform. In other words, the fact that women are expected, as part of their family role specialisation, to spend an important part of their lives outside the labour force, could discourage them from investing heavily in their career preparation. The question then is whether inferior qualification or work experience is anything more than a reflection of a generalised discrimination by society against women.

Finally, there is some doubt whether this approach emphasises sufficiently the importance of women's absence from the labour force to fulfil their 'reproductive' role during which there is a strong likelihood of a fall in their earning power, indicating a depreciation in their human capital component.[31] Mincer (1974) devised a 'segmented earnings function' approach to take account of life cycle changes in the familial role of most women. This involves splitting female labour force activity (or inactivity) into three separate life cycle segments. The first segment covers the period to the birth of the first child; the second comprises the period of childrearing when the attachment to the labour force is often partial or non-existent; and the third which defines the period from re-entry into the labour force on a full-time basis to retirement. The first period is characterised by some investment in training, followed by a period of disinvestment due to absence or partial attachment, and finally a period when new investment in training in preparation or following immediately after re-entry of the labour force may not be uncommon.

There has been a large number of American studies investigating both sexual and racial earnings differences found overall or in certain professional occupations.[32] Similar British studies have been notably lacking, principally because of the unavailability of suitable data. Unlike those of the United States, British Population Censuses lack information on income. But in recent years sample data on individuals from the annual General Household Survey are available on raw data tapes. They provide the information for the empirical studies by Greenhalgh (1980b), Layard et al. (1978a, 1978b) and Psacharopoulos and Layard (1979). All these studies are based on the human capital approach to earnings explored in the American studies. Greenhalgh's study is the only one to date which addresses itself to the question of male/female earnings differentials in Great Britain. The study also highlights the importance of marital status in any examination of the effect of family role specialisation on earnings differential and evaluates the impact of equal opportunities on sex discrimination in earnings. As an illustration of the methodology of empirical studies in this area and the pertinence of some of its conclusions, it would be worthwhile examining Greenhalgh's study in some detail.

Greenhalgh used sample data from Household Budget Surveys for 1971 and 1975 to estimate earnings functions for six demographic groups consisting of single and married males, single and married females and 'other' males and 'other' females. A number of 'control' variables measuring the effects on earnings of education, work experience, region of origin, age of eldest child,[33] skin colour, health, socio-economic status, job tenure, and industry, were incorporated into the model and earnings functions were estimated for each of the six groups. To obtain separate estimates of the effects of discrimination and family role specialisation, ratios were computed of the predicted and observed values of average hourly earnings for the two groups being compared. These ratios were used to estimate the 'unexplained' earnings differential (i.e., a measure of the residual) which could then be attributed to sex discrimination or disinvestment in human capital arising from prolonged absence from the labour force and/or family role specialisation, depending on the two groups being compared.[34]

Greenhalgh's results show that the 'unexplained' differential in the earnings ratio between married and single men fell slightly from 14% in 1971 to 10% in 1975, where these values were interpreted as a measure of differences in work effort and greater ambition to do well characteristic of married men compared to single men.

However, an increase in the 'unexplained' differential in earnings ratio between single women and married women from 3% in 1971 to 12% in 1975 showed that motivational differences arising from family role specialisation had become more important between the years. A measure of sex discrimination in earnings, which is independent of family role specialisation effects or decreases in the quality of human capital due to absence from the labour force, is the 'unexplained' differential in the ratio of earnings of single men to single women who are similar in respect of all characteristics which were controlled during estimation. This differential fell from 24% in 1971 to 10% in 1975, showing a significant move towards parity as a consequence of movements towards equal pay generated by legislative pressure and the social climate of opinion.[35]

A rough indication of the relative position of married women in the labour market can be obtained from estimating the 'unexplained' component of the overall differences in earnings between married men and married women, sharing similar characteristics. In 1971, the total 'disadvantages' of a married woman *vis-à-vis* a married man could be seen as the combination of disadvantages arising from her family role *vis-à-vis* a single woman (estimated as 3%), sex discrimination in earnings (24%) and the family role advantage of a married man *vis-à-vis* a single man (14%). By 1975, the relative components of the total 'disadvantages' of a married woman had changed with an increase in the family role as a wife component to 12%, a decrease in the discrimination component to 10% and a decrease in the family role advantage of a husband component to 10%. What these figures indicate is that, while the relative position of single women improved markedly between 1971 and 1975, there has hardly been any change in the relative position of married women. Married women, found in large numbers in part-time jobs in female-type occupations, remain a vulnerable group not adequately protected by equal pay and sex discrimination legislation.

We have already discussed some of the limitations of the 'residual' approach in estimating the magnitude of sex discrimination in earnings. A general criticism of this procedure is its *ad hoc* or inefficient methodology.[36] It is, as Zellner (1976) put it, 'like trying to discover whether you left your watch in the kitchen by looking for it everywhere else first (when) it would be more efficient to look in the kitchen' (quoted in Lloyd and Niemi, 1979, p. 215). To take this analogy further, the problem is even further compounded by the fact that once the watch is located, there is no certainty that it belongs to you.

There is also a conceptual problem arising from the use of the observed wage differential as a direct measure of discrimination. Gronau (1974) has argued that a 'selectivity' bias results from not using differences in wages offered to work, rather than the wages actually earned from working. Under certain restrictive assumptions, the size of this bias would vary directly with the difference in the labour force participation rates of the two groups compared and the direction of this bias is to *under-estimate* the true male/female earnings differential or the extent of sex discrimination in earnings. But, as Lewis (1974) pointed out, the direction of the bias would depend to a large extent on the life cycle patterns of labour force attachments of the two groups, as well as the specific factors determining their entry into or exit from the labour force. All that one could infer is that in making comparisons between two groups with different labour force participation rates, some of the observed differences in earnings do not reflect behavioural dissimilarities as much as statistical bias. And data requirements, particularly for estimating wage offer curves, would be so immense that it becomes impractical to make a true estimate of sex discrimination in earnings.

We have moved a long way from the simple model with which we started, where competition prevails, labour is homogeneous and mobile and individual choice has primacy. If these assumptions worked, then in the long run there would be a movement towards greater equality in earnings and a convergence in the distributions by sex of occupations and other related activities. But if these assumptions are relaxed, then there appears the possibility of labour market segmentation by sex or race or any other ascriptive characteristics. The theories that combine the way that labour market institutions operate with human capital theories of differences in labour productivity, form the basis of the labour market segmentation approach to sex inequality.

(e) Segmentation of the Labour Market and the Status of Women Workers: Different Perspectives

The earliest labour market segmentation approach is contained in the Internal Labour Market (ILM) analysis, of which Doeringer and Piore (1971) provide one of the better known expositions. An important application of the ILM analysis to sex-related pay and occupational differences is found in the Dual Labour Market (DLM) theory. What follows is a brief exposition of the ILM and DLM approaches, not with the purpose of providing a comprehensive or rigorous formulation, but to indicate their uses as potential modes of analysis in examining the position of women workers in the labour market.[37]

The ILM analysis starts by splitting up workers in an establishment into two groups. The first group, consisting of well-paid workers enjoying job security and recruited internally within well-defined promotional ladders, constitutes a primary group for whom an internal labour market operates within a bureaucratic structure allocating labour and determining wages in the establishment. The second group, consisting of low-paid workers with a high turnover rate and limited promotion prospects, constitutes a secondary group for whom an external labour market operates at the entry level. Within this two-tiered 'caste' system of occupations, movement up the tier is possible though unlikely. It involves navigating treacherous waters laden with minefields of customary and administrative rules and practices which determine upward mobility. Generally, however, mobility is determined by the entry level jobs (i.e., the 'ports' of entry) of individual workers.

In the context of this theoretical framework, the existence of occupational segregation by sex and its relationship with pay differentials is easy to establish. Sex is an obvious basis for group differentiation, since the preservation of intra-group homogeneity could become a critical element in decisions on how to allocate labour between groups. The resulting job segregation, however, does not preclude the possibility of further differentiation within the group of female workers on the basis of such ascriptive characteristics as education, marital status, work experience, etc. It would also follow logically that the earnings differential may be looked at as the monetary manifestation of the differentiation in job structure. But the scope for differentiation between individuals (or sex groups) varies markedly between different job assignments. It is greatest with respect to workers entering the establishment for the first time. For the secondary group who can be recruited through a number of ports of entry, job segregation and pay differentiation are notable features of employment, though the scope for differentiation decreases as the skill components of the jobs increase. But for workers recruited from internal sources, the wage differentiation between individuals within the same job category is limited to seniority and sometimes merit considerations.

The ILM approach can also provide certain useful insights into some of the difficulties implicit in the homogeneous labour market approaches to job segregation and earnings differentials discussed in previous sections.[38] First, there is the question of what the determinants of labour productivity actually are. The human capital theorists would point to characteristics such as education, training and work experience possessed by an individual worker as determining his or her productivity. A proponent of the 'crowding' hypothesis would probably highlight the amount and quality of equipment that a worker works with as an important determinant of her productivity. The ILM approach can encompass not only these and other factors, but would emphasise the extent to which an individual worker is allowed to deploy the human capital acquired through education and work experience in the actual work situation. The type of work situation faced by the worker is an amalgam of practices governing recruitment of workers, organisation and conditions of work, and remuneration and promotion prospects which could vary not only from primary group to secondary group within any single establishment, but also from firm to firm. So that an inferior work situation could have adverse effects on the productivity of a worker as great if not greater, than the much discussed deterioration in human capital resulting from interruption in work experience for child-rearing purposes.

In much of the neoclassical analysis of labour supply, a distinction is rarely made between occupational choice and occupational assignment. Occupational choice is mainly a matter of individual taste, formed as a result of education and training and social background of the person concerned. Only in a few jobs is a matching of training and individual preference with the job assigned possible. In most cases the employers assign workers to jobs within broad limits set by skills required and preferences expressed for the jobs. So that differences in the occupational distribution between two groups, the ILM approach would imply, reflect employers' decisions to assign one group of workers to a set of occupational categories from which the other group is restricted or even excluded. By operating different standards for promotion and upgrading one group more slowly than the other, the differences in occupational distribution created at the port of entry are further exacerbated. Hence, the ILM framework provides an explanation of sex segregation in jobs in terms of occupational assignment.

The ILM approach could also provide additional insights into the operation of statistical discrimination. Our discussion of statistical discrimination in a previous section focused on its explanation of the sex-related earnings difference, with job segregation by sex not being a necessary consequence.[39] But with the ILM approach, job segregation is an inevitable result of certain employers perceiving a particular group as indadequate in some respect, *independent* of whether that group is paid lower wages in response to higher fixed labour costs of the group.

The ILM approach was not initially formulated as a means of explaining sex- or race-related differences in remuneration or occupational distribution. The analysis was carried out in terms of the existence of a dichotomy between primary and secondary characteristics of workers. It is in the Dual Labour Market (DLM) analysis that the secondary and disadvantaged group is identified as blacks or women.[40] They share all the characteristics of the secondary group in the ILM approach — low earnings, poor career prospects, job insecurity and high turnover rate — irrespective of whether they have the same qualifications and attributes as those who form part of the primary group. On the other hand, the primary group, predominantly white men, are in well-paid, secure and stable jobs with good prospects of career advancement. Both in the way that their work is organised as well as in the way that they are remunerated, certain well-established criteria satisfying principles of equity and efficiency in production are adhered to, unlike the arbitrary and anarchic way that workers in the secondary group are treated.

The basic limitation with the DLM approach is its restrictive application.[41] The approach is not amenable to an examination of further job segregation by sex (or race) within each of the groups, nor does it provide a fuller elaboration of the characteristics that identify certain jobs as female-type jobs. It has, however, prompted research on how segmentation of the labour market and labour processes constitute a part of the redivision of labour in the latest stage of monopoly capitalism.[42]

It would be useful to end this brief discussion of the segmented labour market approach by examining the points of similarity and differences with the neoclassical approach to sex inequality in the labour market. The segmented labour market approach is hardly an alternative theory to the neoclassical view. It is best seen as a theory which provides an institutional context to the neoclassical approach discussed in previous sections. Both emphasise in varying degrees the importance of education and training explaining differences in earnings and occupational distribution, though the focus of the analysis in the case of the neoclassical approach is the earnings differential and it is job segregation in the case of the ILM model. Both assume profit maximisation and equalisation of productivities and earnings, though this equalisation occurs over time for a given group according to the neoclassical view and across individuals within each occupational category according to the ILM theory. Even the expected life cycle patterns of earnings differentials between the sexes would be similar for both theories though for different reasons. The ILM theory (or rather its DLM variant) would point to the exclusion of most women from the primary group and promotion ladders as the cause of the sex-related earnings gap, while the neoclassical view would emphasise the deterioration in human capital arising from the prolonged absence of women from the labour force at the time that men are accumulating human capital through work experience.

The major difference between the two approaches is one of emphasis about how significant is individual choice in decisions on what jobs to do and how much to earn. The factors constraining this choice and their differential impact on various groups are important in the ILM analysis while, even when they are recognised, they are rarely incorporated into the neoclassical analysis.[43] There are also marked differences in the potentialities of the two theories from the point of view of empirical verification. The neoclassical theories — the 'human capital' versions — have been particularly amenable to statistical testing. Not only have the contributions of education, work experience, family responsibilities, job tenure etc., to earnings been assessed, but attempts have been made to measure the effect of discrimination on the earnings of different disadvantaged groups.

The testing of the ILM theory is more problematic. It has to proceed in different stages. First, how widespread is the phenomenon of ILM? From a brief survey of recruiting and promotion practices in Britain, Bosanquet and Doeringer (1973) found some evidence of the existence of ILMs in Britain, though it is unlikely that they are as significant here as in the United States. Second, how influential is the ILM in determining who is to be promoted? There are reasons to believe that promotion procedures here tend to be more informal and relatively less well-developed than in the United States in the engineering industry (Mackay *et al.*, 1971). No evidence exists on the practices in other industries, though in the public sector and particularly in the Civil Service, there is a likelihood that well-developed ILMs operate. Third, how important a determinant of career ending is career origin? The ILM theory suggests that the port of entry could be a critical factor determining the extent of career advancement and pay increases that an individual receives over his or her working life. The problem for any empirical test in this instance arises from the difficulty of disentangling the characteristics possessed by the individual from the characteristics of the job itself, when career origin is included as a variable together with education, work experience and other attributes in estimating earnings functions.

Finally, is there any evidence of the existence of DLMs in this country? Sloane (1981, p. 31) lists three aspects which empirical work should concentrate on. They are: (a) the extent of mobility of women from secondary to primary sectors; (b) the extent to which investment in human capital increases the chances that a woman will be found in the primary rather than the secondary sector; and (c) the differences in the rate of return to education and training between the two sectors. Sloane adds that the existing General Household Survey data, which has been the major source of information for empirical work on labour supply and wage-related issues in recent years, contains much of the information for examining the three aspects listed above. But given the lack of any properly constructed test of the DLM hypothesis in Britain, we are left with certain observations on the pattern of British female employment.[44] There are certain aspects of women's employment such as part-time work and 'homeworking' which clearly fall into the secondary sector.[45] Yet at the same time, some areas of low-paid employment such as agriculture where men form the vast majority of workers and other areas of predominantly male employment such as construction where employment is highly insecure, show characteristics normally associated with the secondary sector. Further, employment of women in certain professional or semi-professional occupations, especially in public administration, has characteristics which one would associate with the primary sector.

To sum up, neoclassical explanations of the male/female earnings differential include human capital differences between the sexes, discrimination, discontinuity in work experience, monopsony in the labour market, the crowding of women into certain low-paid establishments or occupations and the exclusion of women from the higher-paid jobs in internal labour markets and the consequent concentration into the low-paid secondary sector. No single set of data exists in this country to ascertain the relative importance of the factors listed above in determining the observed earnings differential between men and women, even if the necessary empirical methodology exists to do so. There exists another factor, however, which could have an important bearing on whether work opportunities for women are fully exploited and expanded, and that is the attitude of trade unions to working women. It is to this subject that we turn next.

Women and Trade Unions: Certain Relevant Considerations

There are two related issues to be examined here. First, what is the nature and extent of female participation in trade unions in Britain? This would involve considering both the role of women as members and office holders in trade unions, as well as the differential impact of female workers on trade union activities in various occupations and industries. Second, what has been the contribution of British trade unions to promoting fuller opportunities for women in the field of employment? These questions are related in the sense that trade union policies aimed at improving opportunities for women could partly depend on the influence that women workers can bring to bear on unions through participation at both local and national level.

Lewenhak (1977) has shown that, historically, trade unions in this country have exerted their influence mainly towards excluding women from jobs and membership. For example, the campaign in the 1840s for shorter working-days by the early trade unionists went hand in hand with demands that women should withdraw from factories. Though a growing number of women continued to work in factories, trade unions in general did little to curb the tendency towards increasing job segregation by sex and the emergence of the pattern whereby women were predominantly concentrated in low-paid occupations. Women continued to be excluded from a number of trade unions until the Second World War.

Partly in response to the indifference — and in some cases the hostility — on the part of male trade unions, the Women's Protective and Provident League was formed in 1874. The League was not a trade union, but a national association serving as a benevolent institution providing help to its sick and unemployed members, acting as an employment agency and as an arbitrator in disputes between its members and their employers.[46] The League has as one of its aims the active promotion of unionisation of its members. This resulted during the last two decades of the nineteenth century in the establishment of between 80 and 90 societies for women workers in a wide range of activities including clothing and tailoring trades, office work, ropemaking, laundry services, and industries such as glass making and tobacco processing. Women workers began to be admitted into male trade unions beginning with textile workers and gradually spreading to tailors, shoemakers, pottery workers, etc.[47] As a result, female membership of trade unions rose from 37,000 in 1886 to 118,000 in 1896 to 167,000 in 1906.

In 1906 the first general women's union, the National Federation of Women Workers, was established, providing further impetus to the unionisation of women workers. However, up to the 1960s, female membership of trade unions remained around 15% of the total membership, with a phenomenal growth occurring subsequently, so that the female share rose to 29% in 1978. This represented an increase from 1.4 million female members in 1960 to 3.4 million in 1978.

The principal factor behind this growth was the dramatic increase in the number and proportion of women in the labour force, particularly with the increase in married women taking up both full-time and part-time work, which was discussed earlier in this book. But there were also far-reaching changes in the industrial and occupational distribution of the working population which determined the pattern of the increases in female membership of different trade unions.

Table 5.1 records increases since 1950 in women joining the 'top'

Table 5.1   Female Membership in 'Top' Ten Unions in Britain: 1950–1978 (in 000's)

Union	1950	1958	1966	1974	1978	Women as % of total 1978
NUPE	40.0	68.3	124.4	294.6	457.4	66.0
NALGO	–	–	130.8	200.5	318.8	44.9
NUGMW	152.0	160.9	195.9	269.3	318.2	33.6
TGWU	129.4	154.8	199.6	266.3	317.9	15.7
USDAW	136.0	164.6	171.0	184.2	270.5	61.3
NUT	–	–	–	186.1	212.7	73.6
COHSE	20.1	24.8	36.4	80.7	159.4	75.4
CPSA	73.5	75.2	87.8	147.5	158.8	70.1
AUEW (E)	34.8	65.1	98.8	154.2	148.3	12.8
NUTGW	103.9	97.0	91.8	101.2	106.0	89.9
Total as Percentage of Women Members in Trade Unions affiliated to TUC	56.7	58.4	65.0	72.4	72.4	–

Source: TUC.

Note: NALGO and NUT were affiliated to the TUC in 1964 and 1970 respectively.

Key for Tables 5.1 and 5.2:

NUPE	National Union of Public Employees
NALGO	National and Local Government Officers Association
NUGMW	National Union of General and Municipal Workers
TGWU	Transport and General Workers' Union
USDAW	Union of Shop, Distributive and Allied Workers
NUT	National Union of Teachers
COHSE	Confederation of Health Service Employees
CPSA	Civil and Public Services Association
AUEW (E)	Amalgamated Union of Engineering Workers (Engineering Section)
NUTGW	National Union of Tailors and Garment Workers
APEX	Association of Professional, Executive, Clerical and Computer Staff

ten trade unions arranged according to the relative numbers in 1978. Areas of traditional employment such as clothing (shown by the numbers in the National Union of Tailors and Garment Workers (NUTGW)) and distributive trades (shown by the numbers in the Union of Shop Distribution and Allied Workers (USDAW)) recorded relatively modest increases over the period, falling from the positions of fourth and second highest number of female members in 1950 to the tenth and fourth positions respectively in 1978. This could partly be a reflection of the decline or small growth of these industries and partly the existence of a high degree of unionisation allowing limited scope for further growth.

The areas of significant growth in female membership were the newer areas of female employment such as public administration (represented by the Civil and Public Services Association (CPSA)), engineering (represented by the Amalgamated Union of Engineering Workers (AUEW)) and Services generally. It is the last category that offers outstanding examples of expansion of female membership of trade unions. The National Union of Public Employees (NUPE), which represents unskilled and semi-skilled ancillary workers in local government, health and education, increased its female membership by about 11 times between 1950 and 1978. During the same period the Confederation of Health Service Employees (COHSE) increased its female memership by about 8 times. The National Association of Local Government Officers (NALGO), which may be considered as representing workers in public administration, more than doubled its female membership between 1966 and 1978. With the exceptions of NALGO and AUEW(E), all other unions mentioned as expanding their female membership are unions which have majorities of female members and operate in industries and occupations which have experienced considerable expansion in employment during the period under review. Hence the principal reason for the growth of union membership is the expansion of employment in these areas.

There are other reasons suggested for growth in female membership in areas of large concentration of female workers. Bain (1970), in his study of white-collar unionisation, has indicated three main factors. First, there has been a growing tendency towards physical concentration of production in the public sector with the consequent bureaucratisation often associated with large-scale enterprises. This is exemplified in the centralisation of amenities such as laundries or kitchens following the re-organisation of National Health Service. The resulting employment concentration is conducive to collective action expressed in the form of unionisation. Second, there has been a growing recognition of unions as representatives for negotiating agreements, so that employment legislation, such as the Trade Union and Labour Relations Acts (1974 and 1976) and the Employment Protection Act (1975), has given impetus to the growth of trade unions. Finally, the areas recording considerable growth of female membership have waged vigorous recruiting campaigns aimed at female workers, such as NUPE's attempts to attract part-time workers by concentrating on issues of relevance to women workers like low pay, maternity provisions, etc.

Table 5.1 also brings out an additional feature of the growth in female membership and that is the increasing concentration of women in a few unions – a phenomenon analagous to that of occupational concentration of women workers which we discussed earlier. It is clear from the last row of the table that the percentage of female members of trade unions contained in the top ten unions rose from 57% in 1950 to 72% in 1978.[48] Attempts at establishing a statistical relationship between occupational concentration and the extent of union concentration of females are fraught with methodological and data problems. Complete data on trade union membership are available only for trade unions that are affiliated to the TUC. Trade unions rarely organise along lines which correspond to the standard industrial classification which is the basis of recording employment statistics. Ellis (1981, Table 3, p. 60) provides data on the proportion of women workers and union density (i.e., proportion of workers who are trade union members) for 18 industrial groups. No significant association was established between the level of female concentration and the degree of unionisation in different industries, as shown by a Spearman Rank Correlation Coefficient of -0.05. Yet the degree of unionisation varies markedly between male and female workers, with the proportion of male and female workers who were members of trade unions in 1979 being 63% and 40% respectively (Ellis, 1981, p.11).

On the basis of this rather limited statistical evidence, a possible inference is that sex is not the main determinant of difference in the degree of unionisation between male and female workers.

Lockwood (1958), in an examination of the membership of white-collar unions, found that the type of job rather than its sex composition was more important in determining union density. For example, the degree of unionisation in the distributive trades or professional and related services, which have a majority of women workers, is much lower than in the case of public administration and defence or mining and quarrying which are predominantly male industries. On the other hand, construction and agriculture have a low proportion of women employed and a low degree of unionisation. Further, the clothing and footwear industries, which have relatively large numbers of female workers, are also highly unionised.[49]

Bain (1970) provides a further dimension. The degree of unionisation varies directly with the size of the establishment. So that the concentration of women into smaller establishments, characteristic of services such as catering, hairdressing, and cleaning would explain at least in part sex differences in unionisation.

The membership of a union is only a very partial indicator of the influence that women workers can have on the policies of that union with respect to improving their status in the labour market. It is the extent to which women participate in the running of the union that could be an important factor. Three indicators of participation suggest themselves. An obvious measure of participation is the number of meetings attended at the branch level. Harrison (1979), from a study of one branch of the Association of Scientific, Technical and Managerial Staff (which has a national female membership of 17.5% in 1978), showed that the proportion of women who attended no branch meetings in 1977 was 75% compared to 63% for men. A survey by the Association of Cinematograph and Television Technicians of a sample of its own membership in 1973–74 showed substantial differences in the pattern of attendance by sex between different branches of the union. The proportion of members in the film production unit who said they 'usually' or 'always' attended meetings were 76% and 77% for men and women respectively. Corresponding figures for the laboratory branch were 68% and 31% for men and women respectively. Given the paucity of information at a national level, it would be difficult to make any definitive inference, except that one would expect a larger proportion of men than women to attend meetings, but considerable variation in the pattern of attendance would exist between different branches (or unions) and between different women depending on their personal and family circumstances, including whether they are part-time or full-time workers. Stageman (1980) studied a group of female trade union members and representatives from six union branches of four trade unions located in Hull. Her conclusion is that priority should be given as part of collective agreements for members to attend branch meetings during working hours, so as to encourage women with home and family responsibilities to attend. She also suggests that, if the provision within the Employment Protection (Consolidation) Act of 1978 permitting shop stewards working over 16 hours per week to have time off with pay for the purpose of carrying out their duties or undertaking relevant education and training could be extended to part-time workers who attend union meetings, this could provide an added impetus for women workers to participate in trade union affairs.

Another indicator of participation in trade union activities is the extent to which women hold office in various capacities within the unions. Table 5.2 shows the representation of women in various official posts in eleven top unions in September 1976. Three types of official positions are recognised here. It is clear from the table that women are under-represented in all unions and at all levels. Irrespective of female membership, in all unions the actual number of office bearers falls short of the expected numbers based on the sex-composition of the union membership. The result is a handful of full-time officials within the trade unions, few members in the National Executive Councils of the unions and delegations to the TUC dominated by men. What the table does not show is how pervasive male dominance is at the branch level. A survey of shop stewards by NUPE over the period 1973–77, in a union which has the largest number of women members among all trade unions, showed certain interesting statistics. Female membership in the education sector, which constitutes 90% of all members, contributed 37% of the shop stewards. The corresponding figures for the other sectors were: 64% of the NHS 'ancillaries' contributed 37% of the shop stewards and 38% of the 'Other local government' sector contributed 12% of the shop stewards. It follows that under-representation of women begins at the branch level and continues to the highest national level.

Table 5.2 Representation of Women in 'Top' Trade Unions in Britain: September 1976

Union	Percentage of Women Members	Full-Time Women Officials (Nos.)	Women Executive Committee Members (Nos.)	TUC Women Delegates (Nos.)
NUPE	65	2(79)*	6(17)	4(21)
NALGO	43	17(82)	5(28)	5(32)
NUGMW	33	10(93)	0(10)	4(22)
TGWU	16	3(77)	0(6)	2(12)
USDAW	59	4(78)	1(10)	5(15)
NUT	75	2(19)	4(36)	1(23)
COHSE	70	5(28)	1(19)	0(5)
CPSA	68	4(19)	8(17)	8(20)
NUTGW	88	6(35)	5(13)	5(13)
APEX	55	1(3)	4(8)	3(7)
AUEW(E)	14	1(26)	0(1)	0(5)

Source: *Equal Pay and Opportunities Campaign: Survey of Unions and Equal Pay Act*

Note: * Figures in brackets show the *expected* numbers in each category that reflect the proportion of female membership in the Union.

Various reasons have been advanced for the low participation of women in the running of trade unions. Ellis (1981, pp. 19–29) suggests that the main reasons are:

(i) A tendency for women to be dispersed among industries in which the work places are small and scattered which makes it difficult for collective action;

(ii) A tendency for women to change jobs more often, making it less likely for them to maintain continuity of membership in a particular branch or union;

(iii) In both manual and white-collar occupations, there is evidence that interest in trade union activities, including office holding, tends to be greater in the higher echelons of the occupational hierarchy. The concentration of women in the lower echelons could be an important cause of their under-representation at the higher levels of trade union management;

(iv) The dual role of a working woman, with time-intensive family responsibilities, would restrict her activities, including trade union participation, more than that of her male counterpart;

(v) Many working women see their jobs and trade union activities in *instrumental* terms, and not as something that provides intrinsic satisfaction; and

(vi) Finally, there are obstacles to female trade union participation which, just as obstacles to female labour force participation, have their roots in the patriarchal system operating both at the economic and ideological levels of the society, and which tend to replicate the hierarchical position of the sexes found in many other areas of human activity.[50]

It is clear that the reasons adduced for the low participation of women in trade unions bear considerable similarity to those responsible for female under-achievement in employment. Where women occupy official positions in trade unions, it is either because of the lack of men to take up union offices, or they take up some junior positions or fulfil roles which are sex-typed as appropriate ones, e.g., secretaries at branch level.

The question then arises as to the nature and scope of policies that trade unions can follow to improve the position of their female members. The TUC record during the inter-war years and the immediate post-war years was not impressive. The campaign for equal pay during this period, as Lewenhak (1977, p. 254) points out, was led by white-collar unions such as NALGO and NUT, which were not affiliated to the TUC. But the achievement of equal pay in public services in 1961, followed by Britain's desire to enter the European Economic Community, led to a TUC commitment to equal pay embodied in a TUC Women's Charter in 1963.[51] But this did not include any strong pressure by the TUC on its individual members, nor any attempt to influence the government or employers through its membership of various committees with these groups during the sixties.

During the seventies there were certain pressures building up to bring about a change in trade union attitudes to women's pay and employment opportunities. A number of unions became aware of the implications of the growth potential of female membership. There was growing recognition of the industrial muscle of women workers, when organised as groups, on the part of both trade unions and the government. Strikes by women sewing machinists at Fords Dagenham in 1968 over a demand to upgrade the skill component of of their work, Leeds clothing workers' strike over equal pay increments for men and women and the more recent highly publicised strikes at Trico and Grunwick are notable examples of collective action by women which have had a considerable impact on trade unions. Equal Opportunities legislation embodied in the Equal Pay Act of 1970 and Sex Discrimination Act of 1975 have also helped to create a climate of opinion in the trade union movement favourable to improving the status of women workers. The general approach among trade unions is to oppose legislation that deals with issues of collective bargaining and trade union activity, though there is a growing recognition that certain legislation may be needed to modify entrenched practices and attitudes which negotiations are unable to resolve.

Certain serious reservations exist about the scope of the equal opportunities legislation already on the statute book. A Special TUC Conference in 1977 proposed amendments to the Equal Pay Act including acceptance of the ILO definition of equal pay as being pay for *work of equal value*, where pay includes not only the basic pay but any additional emoluments arising out of employment, and a job evaluation system based on the same criterion for men and women. The ineffectiveness of the Sex Discrimination Act prompted another Special TUC Conference in 1979, which raised the following issues. There was a need to place the burden of proof on the employer to show that he is not discriminating, and thereby hasten investigation of complaints by the Equal Opportunities Commission. There was also a need to reassess the 'genuine occupational qualification' clauses which permit employment of a particular sex under certain circumstances.[52]

The responses of different unions to the TUC initiative have varied enormously. Almost all unions have followed the TUC lead by passing resolutions in support of equal opportunities at their conferences. Special working parties or committees have been established to advise on matters affecting women by unions such as NALGO, COHSE, the NUJ and the NUT. Other unions such as TGWU, and GMWU have appointed union officials with main responsibility for women. Yet other unions, such as AUEW (E), TGWU and COHSE have held special conferences to discuss matters of particular concern to women. Special courses have been run for women about union work. Publicity and information on problems of women have been provided in union journals, pamphlets and newspapers. Changes in structure, re-allocation of resources and increasing female participation have been proceeding apace, though it is premature to speculate on their effectiveness in improving the status of women in trade unions generally.[53]

The Impact of Equal Opportunities Legislation on the Status of Women Workers: Some Concluding Remarks

British legislation relating to female employment has, until quite recently, concentrated on conditions of employment. An elaborate superstructure of statutes dating back about a hundred and fifty years, of which the Employment of Women and Young Persons Act (1963) and the Factories Act (1961) are but recent examples, have laid down the maximum number of hours that women (and young persons) may be employed in factories and other work places. Limits operate on maximum daily and weekly working hours, maximum continuous spell of work, earliest starting and latest finishing times, and the length and timing of overtime work. Similar controls on working hours of those aged 18 or over have been the exception rather than the rule. Restrictions on female employment in factories at nights, on Sundays and other public holidays apply, with certain exceptions being made for some religious groups and in the case of certain types of employment. Other laws which aim to protect women from health or physical hazards have been instrumental in separating them from the male labour force, with a further wedge being driven by the eligibility for state pensions at different ages for men and women.[54]

There has been a widespread view in the past that issues relating to women's pay and occupational status should be a matter of negotiation between workers and management with little government involvement — a view also shared by the trade union movement which, in spite of resolutions brought up and passed regularly at the annual TUC Conference on improving the status of women workers, did little to promote equal opportunities for women in collective bargaining negotiation. But from the sixties onwards an important change occurred. The government began to intervene in regulating wages and promoting industrial awareness. There was a growing awareness of the need for legislative action to improve opportunities for the fast-growing female work force in the face of the impotence of existing institutions and practices. The Equal Pay Act (1970), which did not become effective until the end of 1975, and the Sex Discrimination Act passed in November 1975 were the result.[55] The first Act was aimed at ensuring equality of treatment in terms of remuneration for men and women engaged in similar work; the second Act had as its primary purpose the promotion of equal access to jobs and covered the areas of hiring, training and promotion. Both Acts aimed at eliminating discrimination, with the Equal Pay Act dealing with wage discrimination and the Sex Discrimination Act prohibiting job discrimination on the grounds of sex or marital status.[56]

It is not proposed here to consider the contents of the two Acts in detail. Instead, we concentrate on certain features of these Acts which have an important bearing on their effectiveness in promoting equal opportunities for women in employment. The Equal Pay Act stipulates equal pay for the same or similar work. The legislation is not explicit on what constitutes the same or broadly similar work. The focus is on the *type* of work done, rather than the *value* of the work in determining similarity in work.[57] A reliable system of job evaluation would be absolutely essential, though there is no legal requirement within the terms of the Act for employers to undertake such an evaluation.

There are other problems in interpreting the Act. First, there is the question of what 'pay' does the Act refer to. Should it refer to basic pay or should it include all non-basic elements, such as premium payment for overtime or shift work and fringe benefits in money and in kind? Second, as the fourth Annual Report of the Equal Opportunities Commission points out: 'The constraints imposed by the rigidity of this (i.e., Equal Pay) act which insists on the existence of a definite male comparison, does not allow comparisons of equal value in the absence of job evaluation schemes, and does not recognise the concept of indirect discrimination' (p. 11). In other words, traditionally female jobs such as nursery nurses or charwomen do not fall within the province of the Act since direct male comparisons with men's pay are not possible, given that there are difficulties in evaluating such jobs.

The Sex Discrimination Act makes it unlawful to treat a worker, on the grounds of sex or marital status, less favourably than any other worker of the opposite sex. The Act distinguishes between two types of discrimination, namely, direct and indirect discrimination. Direct discrimination arises, for example, if young men rather than young women are preferred for in-service training on the grounds of sex *or* not promoting a person who is next in line because she is a woman (or married woman). Indirect discrimination arises if unreasonable conditions are applied to a job which would favour one sex or marital group. For example, if an employer recruits only people aged 20–35 years as a sales person, this would indirectly discriminate against women, since a large proportion of women within this age-group are likely to be engaged on a full-time basis in looking after dependent children at home.

It is the exemptions from the Sex Discrimination Act that raise some doubts about the general effectiveness of legislation in dealing with sex discrimination in the labour market. Firms employing fewer than five persons or households hiring outside paid labour are not covered by the Act. The Act exempts those occupations where sex is a genuine occupational qualification (e.g., acting or fashion modelling), *or* where for reasons of decency only one sex is employed, *or* where jobs involve work abroad in countries which operate a sex-bar, *or* where provisions for care of supervision require one sex (e.g., prisons). Again, certain specific occupations in the Armed Services, the Church or in competitive sports, underground mining, shift or night work are also exempted from the provisions of the Act. Given the wide area of exemption, the possibilities for both direct and indirect discrimination are considerable. Glucklich *et al.* (1978) who have monitored the effects of the equal pay and sex discrimination legislation in 26 organisations, found 16 cases of possible indirect discrimination arising mainly from: (a) the requirement that employees should be geographically mobile; (b) the requirement that employees should be willing to undertake lengthy residential training before being promoted; and (c) the tendency for promotion to take place along a strictly defined path, reminiscent of the internal market structure discussed in an earlier section, from which women are generally excluded because of their absence at particular points in the promotion ladder.

It is in the implementation of the two Acts that further doubts about their efficacy arise. The implementation of the Equal Pay Act is based on a complainant taking her case to an industrial tribunal composed of a chairman who is a legal personage, a trade union representative, a member nominated by the TUC and a member nominated by the Employers' Organisation. If the tribunal, whose decisions are based on the guidelines established by the Employment Appeals Tribunal (EAT), decides that there is a case to answer, the matter is then referred to either the Central Arbitration Committee (CAC), or the employer, or the Secretary of State for Employment for redress. Only a small number of cases have been referred to the CAC whose record has been in general to uphold the spirit rather than the letter of the law. The procedure is slow and cumbersome, and the dependence of the industrial tribunals on precedents established by the EAT has resulted in great emphasis on the legal niceties of the Act. So that, unlike the United States which has broadly similar equal opportunities legislation to Britain, the primary objective of the British legislation is to prevent discrimination rather than to encourage the acquisition of a fairer or more equal share of the remuneration for a given job.

Certain recommendations were made by the 1978 Women's TUC Conference for making the Equal Pay Act more effective. These include:

(i) The adoption of the *ILO Convention 100* definition of equal pay;

(ii) The burden of proof that a worker is *not* entitled to equal pay should be shifted to the employer;

(iii) Trade unions should be permitted to submit equal pay claims on behalf of their members;

(iv) The powers of the CACs should be extended so as to enable them to deal with a larger proportion of the complaints and make awards of back pay, in successful cases, for longer periods than from the date of submission of claims as at present; and

(v) The Act should address itself to the question of occupational pension schemes, and make it unlawful for different schemes to be applied on the grounds of sex or marital status only.

There exists a more elaborate machinery for implementing the Sex Discrimination Act. Two different procedures are envisaged. An individual may take a complaint against her employer to an industrial tribunal where she has to prove that she was discriminated against by the employer. Or, the Equal Opportunities Commission is empowered to institute legal proceedings in respect of persistent discrimination.[58] In the case of an individual complaint, the Commission could assist in formulating and presenting the case in an effective manner. A Conciliation Officer, provided by the Advisory, Conciliation and Arbitration Services (ACAS), may, if there is a reasonable chance of success, bring together the two parties before a tribunal hearing to resolve the complaint. Where a tribunal decides in favour of the complainant, orders to discontinue the discriminatory practices and/or payment of compensation to the complainant may be made.

In recent years there has been a growing awareness of the limitations of this Act. Recommendations to improve its effectiveness have included the following:

  (i) The burden of proof of discrimination should be shifted to the employers;
 (ii) The Act should not restrict its coverage to only certain areas of employment;
(iii) The 'gateway', genuine occupational qualification, should be carefully scrutinised to ensure that it is not used as a means of evading legislation; and
(iv) The Equal Opportunities Commission should initiate more actions and deal with them more quickly.

A further recommendation is that the two Acts should be amalgamated into one. The Acts should be seen as complementary and there are dangers in treating them in isolation. A standard economic argument would lead us to conclude that, at least in the short run, an inverse relationship exists between equal pay and equal opportunity since, given equal pay for men and women, there would be a tendency to prefer men. Implied in this view is the assumption that, if wage discrimination is not permitted, fewer women would be employed. But it could equally well be argued that as a result of equal pay legislation, the costs of indulging in the 'taste' for discrimination may become so high as to bring about a change in the attitudes of employers.[59] However, if discrimination were initiated by male employees (or trade unions), the effect of equal pay legislation would be to aggravate occupational segregation, though this need not necessarily have an adverse effect on total female employment (Chiplin and Sloane, 1976).

The simultaneous operation of the equal pay and sex discrimination legislation could have unexpected consequences on employee remuneration and on the economy in general. To evade the provisions of equal pay legislation, fringe payments and premium payments not covered by the Act may be introduced. If such payments are not possible, employers may resort to hiring practices which favour male workers though they may not offend the letter of the law. If the government responds by imposing minimum female quotas to be hired or implementing positive discrimination measures in favour of women in those jobs at their disposal, this could have an adverse effect on productive efficiency within the economy.

A fundamental problem with equal opportunity legislation is that it implies a form of statistical parity between the sexes which may not exist. There is evidence scattered throughout this book to show that the labour force participation behaviour of the sexes shows some striking differences both in terms of occupational choice and the degree of life cycle attachment to the labour force. Of course the choice is constrained and the participation behaviour is determined by the existing sexual division of labour within and without the family. Legislation aimed at improving the economic status of women should be aware of these constraints and take cognisance of the fact that the occupational aspirations of a large number of women today do not support statistical parity in the work sphere, however much it aims to modify or eliminate the existing situation.

Notes

1. There has been some controversy among early Marxists as to how the abolition of the capitalist family structure would liberate women. Engels (1884), who was the first to recognise the link between the economic status of a woman and the capitalist family structure, saw the institution of private property within such a structure as the primary means of female oppression. Bebel (1883) saw the liberation of women from the capitalist-patriarchal family structure mainly in terms of the relaxation of sexual mores which Lenin (1934) dissented from. But all saw female emancipation arising from socialisation of household work by establishing communal cleaning, catering and child-care facilities which would then free women for 'productive' work.

2. For a useful survey of research on estimating the value of household production, see Hawrylyshyn (1976) and Murphy (1978). For a discussion of the limitations of conventional Gross National Product estimation, see Scitovsky (1976).

3. Gardiner (1976, pp. 109–20) has an interesting discussion on the role of female domestic labour in a capitalist society.

4. The industrial reserve army or surplus working population is seen as an important mechanism for capital accumulation and perpetuation of the capitalist mode of production. It serves both as a pool of new labour to be brought into production so as to facilitate capital accumulation and at the same time acts as a means of ensuring that the existing workers are kept under control.

5. Braverman's prediction that, in the new industrial revolution, thought itself will be eliminated from the labour process is particularly apposite.

6. 'Women power' was the title of an American publication by the National Manpower Council in 1957 which examined trends in female participation and the determinants of female labour supply in the United States.

7. The proportion of women in part-time work in the United Kingdom in 1977 was 41 percent. This was considerably higher than 28 percent, the next highest proportion recorded for the EEC countries in West Germany and the Netherlands, according to the 1977 EEC Labour Force Surveys.

8. The established pattern now, emerging first among birth cohorts entering the labour force during the late twenties and the thirties of this century first recorded in the 1951 Population Census, is for most women to continue to work until the first child and then return in increasing numbers, even if only on a part-time basis, once the children start school.

9. In an earlier chapter, some of the relevant statistics were quoted to support these assertions. What is being argued here is that with female life expectancy in Britain rising from 50 at the turn of this century to 75 years today, with the maternal role being largely concluded by age 40, women are available for continuous employment for a period of at least 20 years.

10. The Royal Commission on the Distribution of Income and Wealth defined 'low' pay as that level of pay equal to or below the lowest decile (i.e., the bottom 10%) of the distribution of the full-time weekly earnings of manual workers. This worked out to be approximately two-thirds of the average earnings, or at least equal to the supplementary benefit entitlements of a married couple with two children (Sloane, 1980, p. 1).

11. It is not intended here to provide more than a bare outline of the issues raised by these links. There is a growing literature dealing with these issues of which Barker and Allen (1976) would serve as an example.

12. It is interesting in this context that the Parsonian model of the linkage between the family and the outside world, while allowing for the wife to have a link with world of jobs, saw family status in terms of income and prestige existing only through the husband's job.

13. For a useful discussion of the labour force activity of Soviet women and its impact on their family role, see McAuley (1981).

14. There exists a comprehensive literature on wage-related issues and sex

discrimination in labour markets. A notable work for this country is Sloane (1980) which is a collection of papers specially prepared for the Royal Commission on the Distribution of Income and Wealth (1979) examining the facts and theories underlying the relative pay position of women. A recent publication by Sloane (1981) provides a useful review of empirical work done in this country on the earnings gap between men and women. The survey of theories and evidence contained in this section provides only a bare outline of the issues that have been exercising the minds of economists on both sides of the Atlantic over a considerable period of time.

15. Most married women in this country are not entitled to unemployment benefits, and would therefore have little incentive to register with job centres.

16. This theory states that the income accruing to labour, capital and natural resources would be determined by the marginal productivity of these factors if perfect competition prevailed in the factor markets.

17. Monopsony arises when an employer, acting as a sole buyer of labour, is able to affect the wage paid to the workers, which need not necessarily be equivalent to their marginal product. Given fewer alternative sources of employment available and the existence of widespread unemployment, the monopsony power of employers could become important.

18. An inverse relationship exists between the deviation of wage from marginal revenue product *and* the wage elasticity of labour supply (i.e., the sensitivity of labour supply to wage change).

19. It is worth noting that we are referring here to wage elasticity of labour supply in individual firms rather than that of total female labour supply. It could be argued that women workers as a whole would be more sensitive to wage changes than their male counterparts.

20. Sex discrimination in the labour market mainly takes the form of wage or job discrimination. Wage discrimination operates when men and women, similar in all other respects, are paid different wages for doing the same job. Job discrimination occurs when women are denied access to certain jobs despite having similar qualifications to men. A 'taste' for discrimination could originate with employers, male employees or consumers. Most theories of discrimination relate to discrimination by employers and sometimes, by implication, discrimination by male workers. But consumers refusing to buy the services of women doctors or lawyers unless they are cheaper than their male counterparts could also be important.

21. Becker's theory is aimed at explaining racial wage differences though it can be easily extended to the cases of sex and religious discrimination. The 'taste' for discrimination, shown by an employer having a clear preference for hiring and working with men, is assumed to be exogenously determined and 'given' as in the case of all other neoclassical economic theories.

22. The rationale of this test rests on an implication of discrimination by white workers. If the discriminating group is willing to work alongside the 'discriminated against group' only when they are compensated by a

higher wage, then white workers in 'integrated' work situations could expect to earn higher wages than the equally productive white workers in segregated work situations. This test could as validly be applied to examine sex discrimination.

23. This 'informational' approach which has achieved considerable mathematical elegance was pioneered by Arrow (1972a, 1972b), Phelps (1972) and Spence (1973). For a useful survey of work using this approach, see Aigner and Cain (1977).

24. Human capital consists of those attributes that a person acquires or possesses which create income. Through a gradual process of self-investment acquired at home, school or work place, every individual increases his or her human capital endowment at different stages in life. By the same token, a depreciation in human capital can arise as a result of discontinuity of work experience.

25. Differences in earnings arising from hours worked, premium payments for overtime and shift work, age and experience have been observed between men and women workers but are ignored in subsequent discussion.

26. It is interesting in this context that the roots of sex inequality which, in the view of many feminists, lie in women's role in the family, have hardly been discussed by 'human capital' theorists. The female domestic role is considered as part of institutional reality and is taken as 'given'.

27. Hebden (1978, p.58) noted that in Britain in 1972 the proportions of boys and girls entering apprenticeships in the manufacturing sector out of the total numbers in each group employed in that sector were 43% and 1% respectively. A considerable disparity was also found in the non-manufacturing sectors, where 22% of the girls as opposed to 54% of the boys received training.

28. The problem here is to devise appropriate tests which could identify the direction of causation.

29. The traditional sexual division of labour sees marriage and career as complementary for males and competitive for females. The presence of children makes the father work hard, while the mother sacrifices her career for her family.

30. The most common statistical technique in empirical studies involves estimating single equation models where the dependent variable is some measure of the earnings differential and the explanatory variables consist of characteristics affecting human capital endowment. For the technique to be appropriate, the following assumptions need to be satisfied. First, the explanatory variables must be pair-wise uncorrelated. Second, the residual (which measures the extent of sex discrimination) must be independently distributed from the explanatory variables. A violation of these assumptions would throw doubts on any statistical inferences drawn from the estimated regression equation.

31. Mincer and Polachek (1974) estimated a depreciation in the earnings power of 1.2% per annum among American white women aged 30–44 during their period of absence from the labour force (which was

estimated on the average to be 10.4 years).
32. For a useful survey of American studies, see Lloyd and Niemi (1979).
33. The age of the eldest child is used to 'correct' for over-estimation of the period of work experience for married women, since this period could only be indirectly estimated from the sample data as the age of the individual *minus* the normal qualifying age for the highest qualification that the individual obtained.
34. For a more precise expression of the computation procedure, see Greenhalgh (1980b, p. 770).
35. A replication of the same exercise using data for more recent years would provide some indication whether the trend towards parity in earnings has continued after 1975. It is interesting that discrimination may be one of the reasons for the overall differences in earnings between single and married women and between single and married men. Marital status has contrasting implications for discrimination, with single women being preferred to married women and married men being preferred to single men. Marital status discrimination in relation to men has attracted little interest in empirical work where the practice is to include a dummy variable for marital status in male earnings functions.
36. Most empirical work in this area involves the incorporation of a large number of dummy variables to represent explanatory variables. There are certain problems raised by the excessive use of dummy variables. The regression coefficient associated with a dummy variable can indicate only whether that variable is statistically significant in its effect on the dependent variable and whether this effect is positive or negative. The dummy variable itself seldom 'explains' the behaviour of the dependent variable. The incorporation of dummy variables is often seen as a means of eliminating the 'nuisance' influences before examining the 'real' relationships between economic variables. Therefore, a large number of dummy variables on the right side of a regression equation raises questions about model specification and interpretation.
37. There is neither the consensus nor the analytical rigour characteristic of the neoclassical approach to be found in the various labour market segmentation theories discussed in this section. As a consequence, the brief exposition that follows has even a stronger interpretative character. For a detailed survey of the theoretical and empirical issues relating to labour market segmentation and low pay for women, see Sloane (1980, pp. 127–63).
38. The applications of ILM theory discussed below are derived from the analysis contained in Blau and Jusenius (1976).
39. In neoclassical analysis, statistical discrimination would lead to a pay differential reflecting higher fixed costs of one group who may be prone to absence from or shorter stay in employment. But given flexible wage rates, these labour cost differences need not necessarily lead to job segregation, since different wage rates could prevail within each occupational category.
40. The DLM analysis arose in response to the 'disadvantaged' position of

black workers in the United States. For notable expositions of the DLM approach, see Gordon (1972) and Piore (1971).

41. For a detailed critique of the DLM approach, see Wachter (1975).

42. It is not proposed to discuss here why at this particular stage in the development of monopoly capitalism, a redivision of labour has occurred leading to a segmentation of both the labour process and the labour market. For a detailed discussion, see Edwards *et al.* (1975).

43. It is interesting in this context that the unit of analysis in the neoclassical paradigm has remained for a long time the individual. Where the unit becomes a household, it remains a 'surrogate' for the individual, so that any discussion of tensions within the household or between the household and the wider world is delegated to the sociologist, psychologist or anthropologist. Since these disciplines, in their state of underdevelopment, cannot provide any systematic usable knowledge on how these tensions affect patterns of work and earnings, they are ignored in any model building exercise.

44. There is a useful survey of American and British empirical work on labour market segmentation in Sloane (1980, pp. 143–51).

45. The existence of homeworkers as a component of female employment has not been discussed before. The TUC estimated that there are at least 250,000 homeworkers in a range of manufacturing and service trades including clothing, toy making, packaging and clerical work such as typing and addressing envelopes. In addition, a conservative estimate puts the number of childminders as approximately 130,000. Hakim (1980) studied a sample of 50 homeworkers and found that they consisted of women (a) who failed to find flexible part-time work; (b) who were almost all aged 25–44 years of age with dependent children of pre-school or school age; and (c) who considered themselves as being a separate category from other low-paid workers with the stark choice of accepting what they were paid or no work at all. Crine (1979) found that one-third of the homeworkers in the Low Pay Unit survey earned less than 20 pence per hour.

46. The League was also the first of the women's organisations to recognise that indirect barriers to female employment, embedded in various Factory Acts, had to be eliminated if the future status and employment prospects of women were to be improved.

47. A number of these unions opening up membership to women also operated systems of differential benefits for their male and female members.

48. The corresponding figure for male trade union members in 1978 was 36%.

49. These comparisons are based on the data contained in Ellis (1981, Table 3, p.60). A useful comparison would be between male and female unionisation rates controlling for sex differences in occupational and industrial composition, based on the method of multiple standardisation used elsewhere in this book. But appropriate data are unavailable for such an exercise.

50. For a useful discussion of this point, see Stageman (1980, pp. 37–9, 120–22).

51. The 1963 Charter, updated in 1968 as a *Six Point Charter for Women at Work*, contained recommendations on equal pay and promotion opportunities for women, improved provisions for apprenticeship and training for younger women, retraining for older women and special care for the health and welfare of women workers. Article 119 of the Treaty of Rome laid down the principle that men and women should receive 'equal pay for equal work.'

52. The provisions of this legislation and their effectiveness in promoting equal opportunities for women will be discussed in the next section. Here we are concerned with the response of trade unions to this legislation.

53. For useful discussion of the responses of trade unions to the growing demand for equal opportunities for women workers both at work and in trade unions, see Ellis (1981, pp. 45–55) and Stageman (1980, pp. 6–26).

54. The Mining and Quarries Act (1954) prohibits employment of women as underground workers. The legal barriers towards female employment have long been recognised as major obstacles to women achieving similar status to men in the labour market.

55. Employers were given a period of five-and-a-half years to begin the implementation of the Act, so as to avoid possible disruption that could arise from sudden changes in wage structure. An examination of trends in relative female earnings shows evidence that some firms began to implement the Act even before it became law.

56. The Sex Discrimination Act also has provisions to deal with discrimination in education, sale of goods, service facilities and advertising.

57. The ILO Convention 100 on *Equal Pay for Equal Work of Equal Value* raises certain difficulties in measuring value of work. Should it take account of differences in the equipment available for work, or differences in life-time productivities of workers affected by depreciation of human capital?

58. The Equal Opportunities Commission was set up as part of the Sex Discrimination Act with powers to monitor the legislation and initiate investigations. It has produced a number of useful reports on the pay and position of women workers and made submissions to Commissions of Enquiry. For a useful discussion of some its initial difficulties and limitations, see Coote (1978).

59. In economic jargon, the effect of equal pay legislation is to change the relative price of labour between the sexes which could lead to a substitution away from the 'good' whose relative price has risen. This must be balanced against the rise in the expected cost of discrimination to the employer which will equal the *product* of the cost of violating equal opportunity laws and the probability of being found out.

6

Conclusion:
Work and Home in the
Future

In this book we have highlighted the growing importance of women workers in Britain, both in terms of their numerical impact in different industries and occupations and as regards their contribution towards breaking down the traditional assumptions about the division of labour between the sexes. No longer is it valid to consider the man as the sole breadwinner when in 1979 only 8% of the male labour force consisted of sole providers for the archetypal family containing a non-working wife and two children (Rimmer and Popay, 1982, p. 259). Nor is it reasonable to suppose that most women work for pin-money, when a recent survey of Lambeth showed that the likelihood of women, with husbands and dependent children present, raising their family above the poverty line increased by about 25% when they took up full-time employment. One consequence of the substantial increase in women workers is the growing realisation of the need to modify deeply-held views of what constitute work and production in the economic sphere, given the dual role of women at home and in the market place. It will be argued that it is the failure to recognise the dual nature of women's role, and especially the central role of the family, that underlines the limited theoretical perspectives of different paradigms of women's work, as well as the ineffectiveness of legislation in improving women's status in general. The discussion will conclude with a brief examination of the future of the family as an institution as it affects women's work and the development of working patterns consistent with the family needs and work aspirations of its female members.

There has been a tendency in both the neoclassical and Marxian paradigms for the concept of work and the analysis of the production process to be confined within the narrow boundaries imposed by the market. Even the production of services has been considered as part of the production process only because of the payment element involved and because services often consist of the application of labour to facilitate consumption of goods produced. The growing female presence in the labour force has brought into focus the fundamental importance of 'non-market' production on labour supply decisions. Within the framework of a family, the 'non-market' production, overwhelmingly performed by women, consists of the production of both people and goods upon which a substantial amount of domestic labour is expended.[1] Two main questions arise in any attempt to incorporate domestic labour into the production process. First, what is the role of domestic labour in the production process? Second, what are the implications for the status of women workers of the fact that the overwhelming part of domestic labour is still supplied by women?

The role of domestic labour in production within a capitalist economy aroused considerable controversy in Marxist circles during the early seventies.[2] The argument centred on whether domestic labour could be considered as 'productive' in the Marxian sense of producing value. Since *value* was defined by Marx only in terms of market production of goods, and since there was no recognition of how labour power expended in the production of labour power could have any bearing on the social relations of production, domestic labour remained outside the realm of Marx's analysis of the production process within capitalist society. As a consequence, sexual division of labour and power relationships within the family have generally been ignored in Marxian analysis. An area of continuing interest is the possibility of incorporating domestic production into the analysis of the production process, while recognising differences in the social relations and the organisation of production in the realms of the home and the market. In no sense is this incorporation complete or widely accepted (Sargent, 1981; Smith, 1978).

The neoclassical paradigm sees the role of female domestic labour mainly in terms of an 'allocation of time' problem. The availability of female labour for market work is determined by the opportunity cost of the time spent in household work. The need to estimate the value of such work becomes important, and some of the more interesting methodological innovations have been directed towards that end.[3] So that even within this paradigm, discussion of the supply of female domestic labour takes place as an adjunct to market work and independent of the structure of power relationships within the family and society in general.

Yet in both the approaches mentioned above, there is a move, however reluctant, towards a recognition of the importance of gender in the labour market, based on the existence of certain perceived differences between the situation of male and female workers.[4] These differences have already been explored in some detail in this book. Lower pay, occupational segregation, greater vulnerability to technological unemployment, relative inaccessibility to training before and after taking up work, lesser protection afforded by trade unions mainly concerned with the interests of their male members, and overprotectiveness on the part of the State of the conditions of employment pertaining to women, are all manifestations of the relative status of women workers in general. And the pattern of female labour force attachment predicated on a system of dual responsibility to the family and the market is yet another barrier to the achievement of sex equality in the labour market.

The existence of these differences in the economic situation of male and female workers has been attributed to a number of reasons considered in some detail in this book. The human capital theorists emphasise how the differences in characteristics brought by men and women to the labour market directly or indirectly affect their productivity. Market discrimination on the part of employers wishing to indulge their 'taste' for discrimination could be an important explanation for the sex-related earnings differential. No explanation is, however, offered as to how or why this 'taste' develops in the first place. Instead, there is a tendency to pass the buck to sociologists and psychologists and then lament the fact that these 'disciplines have not developed much in the way of systematic useable knowledge about tastes' (Becker, 1975, p. 817). Other explanations of market discrimination see such acts as perfectly consistent with the objective of profit maximisation, either because of the lower wage rates that could be paid by employers to women who have an inelastic supply response, *or* because informational considerations made it less expensive at the time for employers to work on unreliable stereotypes rather than complete information on potential recruits.

There is another type of discrimination which could be important in explaining differences in the situation of male and female workers. This is a form of discrimination which arises from institutionalising the role stereotyping of women within society. At the heart of this 'institutional' discrimination lies the family, a conservative and durable institution, which has historically determined the roles of both sexes. While there has always been a tradition in Marxist thought, starting with Engels, to establish links between the status of women and their role within the family, little attempt has been made until recently to show how the sex inequality established within the family is transmitted into the wider world, including the labour market. In other words, 'institutional' discrimination is recognised but not incorporated in any meaningful way into the analysis of sex-related differences in earnings and occupational distribution. It might be worthwhile to supply two examples illustrating the consequence of this failure of theory. The first has been discussed earlier, but the other has only been referred to in different parts of this book.

The equal opportunity legislation passed in the seventies is based on the premise that sex inequality at work is primarily due to market discrimination, so that elimination of discrimination would restore equality between the sexes in the market place. While it is undoubtedly true that such legislation could reinforce or even hasten the process of bringing about equality of opportunity, it can do little to reduce those differences between men and women which are firmly rooted in sex stereotyping and patterns of life cycle attachment to the labour force permitted by the family circumstances. Indeed, there could be a danger that legislation may be counterproductive. This could arise from the fact that the *raison d'être* of this legislation is some form of statistical parity between men and women. A system of 'proportional representation' applied to men and women over the whole occupational and industrial spectrum does presuppose a similarity in job preferences, pattern of life cycle attachment to the labour force and career motivation. There is no evidence to suggest that this is so. Hence a policy which imposes an arbitrary rigidity in the division of work between men and women could have *in toto* a deleterious effect on social welfare.

The other illustration of the failure of theory to take full account of familial constraints in examining the perceived differences between male and female workers considers the effect of recession on women's employment. There is evidence that women's employment tends to be cyclically more volatile than that of men in most advanced industrial countries (Niemi, 1974; OECD, 1976; Rubery and Tarling, 1982). Further, a common neoclassical view sees female labour force participation as pro-cyclical, because of the greater strength of the 'discouraged' worker effect among women, leading to many women leaving the labour force during a recession. Alternative 'radical' views vary depending on how women workers are viewed in relation to the labour market. If women workers are viewed as a reserve pool of labour who are hired or fired according to the state of the economy, this would be quite consistent with the neoclassical view. But the evidence in the 70s does not substantiate this view, for expansion in female employment went hand in hand with contraction in male employment. A second view sees men and women constituting separate labour markets whose segregation implies no substitution between the groups at least in the short run. A third view sees the recession bringing about an expansion in female employment as a result of employers substituting expensive full-time male labour with cheap part-time female labour. It is possible, as Rubery and Tarling (1982, pp. 47–75) point out, that over the whole recession all three possibilities can apply at different times depending on the type of jobs that women do, the rate at which jobs are shed in different sectors and the extent and timing of redundancy policies which apply mostly to male workers. But a critical factor affecting women's employment is the access to jobs. Given the patterns of labour force withdrawal and eventual re-entry characteristics of the participation behaviour of most women trying to fit in child-bearing and rearing activities, the availability of suitable jobs becomes an important factor. A period of recession is characterised by reduced access to employment. Therefore any examination of the impact of recession on female employment should take account of the familial constraints affecting re-entry into the labour force. A recession could impose different kinds of social and financial constraints on women who may wish to take up employment. It may be financially advantageous for some women whose husbands are receiving social security benefits to remain outside the labour force rather than take up low-paid or part-time jobs. A recession could make it more likely for women to give up their present jobs and follow their unemployed husbands to new places in search of jobs. If a decline in child-care provision in the form of nurseries is a byproduct of recession, this could adversely affect female employment. If a recession results in firms employing more women as part-time, casual, or home workers so as to reduce their fixed labour costs or total wage bill, then female employment would expand.[5] And some women may prefer such working arrangements because they are easier to fit in with their child-care responsibilities. Finally, various obstacles to women re-entering the labour force could affect their family building and spacing plans which in turn could make it difficult for them to enter the labour market once the state of the economy improves.

If there is a central theme running through this book it is the impact of the changing employment/family nexus on female labour force participation behaviour. A woman's membership of her family could be seen in terms of her link to a 'caring' cycle over her life time which has important implications for her employment. In her twenties and early thirties, the likelihood of her not working, the number of hours that she can afford to spend outside her house and the type of job she takes up are all conditioned by the nature and extent of her responsibility to her young (and particularly pre-school) children.[6] But as her children grow up, the effect on her employment is reduced, to be replaced in some cases by the need to look after elderly parents or other relatives, a responsibility that is most likely to affect her when she is between 45 and 54 years of age. But after that, and during the last phase of the 'caring' cycle, she may increasingly have to devote her time to looking after her older husband.[7]

There are certain trends which make it likely that the care for the old could become even more important in the future. There is a trend towards an ageing population, though the proportion of the population aged 65 and over is expected to fall over the next two

decades. But it is estimated that by the year 2000, the proportion of
the retired population aged 75 and over will rise to 40%. Further, an
important change in the pattern of marriages could increase the age
disparity between husband and wife. A tendency for the age
disparity between a man and his second wife to be greater than the
disparity at the first marriage has already been noted by Leete and
Anthony (1979). The combined effect could be that the care of the
old could become an even more important responsibility in the
future than in 1965 when Hunt (1968) found that one in every five
housewives in her survey had a disabled or elderly person (i.e. a
person aged 65 or over) living with them. It is obvious that the effect
of this increasing burden of care is to inhibit the labour force
participation of women.

While dramatic increases in female participation have been
recorded in recent decades, certain far-reaching changes in the
family as an institution may be discerned. The family remains a
thriving institution, though its character is being altered by an
increasing number of people cohabiting and a growing proportion
of marriages ending in divorce.[8] But this increasing divorce rate
does not spell the end of marriage as an institution, but the
emergence of a pattern of serial monogamy within the framework of
a more liberal legal and social regime. The family is becoming more
home-centred and symmetrical with a growing degree of role-
sharing. The primary emphasis of the modern family is on
consumption rather than production activities. Alternatives to the
standard nuclear family emerge or are increasingly sought. The
number of one-parent families, with the vast majority headed by
women, has increased dramatically over the last two decades.[9] To a
much smaller extent, attempts — particularly on the part of
professionals — to combat the social isolation of the nuclear family,
have resulted in the creation of 'communes' which bring together a
few couples to try to reproduce some of the benefits of the three-
generation extended family without having to surrender all the
privacy and independence found within the nuclear family.

The impact of these changes in the family on female employment
is difficult to fathom. There is evidence that lone mothers are less
likely to work than other mothers, though a higher proportion of
lone mothers work full-time (Rimmer and Popay, 1982, p. 257).
The diminishing importance of the traditional sex roles within the
family, the family-centred activities of a growing number of

couples, and the increasing use of microelectronics at home could eventually lead to some degree of reversal of roles — with more husbands staying at home and more wives going out to work. Now an important aspect of family-centred activities is that they involve consumption of goods and services, such as holidays, cars, colour television, etc., the financing of which would require more women to work. Finally, the growing instability of marriage may have induced more women to seek careers, both as a means of developing interest outside the home as well as ensuring some degree of current or potential economic independence.

Whereas far-reaching changes are occurring in both the family and employment, the possibility of a woman fitting into the changing employment/family nexus is to a large extent going to be determined by future developments in working patterns. A decline in full-time employment is likely to continue with some increase in part-time work. Job-sharing could be a means of both improving the utilisation of part-time workers and accommodating the dual calls of home and work place. There may be a case for some income maintenance scheme to be operated if people are to be induced to stay at home and look after dependents, assuming of course that family or community care is preferable to institutional care. There are, however, difficult questions regarding the level of support necessary to influence people's decisions on labour force participation and the method of financing such a support scheme that need to be resolved. In the ultimate analysis, the real question is whether the family as an institution needs to be supported. In spite of its oppressive aspects which have been examined in some detail throughout this book, the family remains an important focal point of loyalty for most individuals, upholding largely non-material values often based on altruism, providing a refuge and support for the insecure, the incapable and the inadequate, *and* protecting individuals against the excesses of the two other major institutions in Western society — the State, and, to a greatly diminished degree, the Church. Many believe that it is to the diminution of the family that some of the social evils of our time can be attributed.

Notes

1. The term 'production of people (or labour power)' is used broadly to describe all such activities as procreation, feeding, clothing, caring and teaching carried out within the confines of a family.

2. For a useful survey of the domestic labour debate, see Kaluzyuska (1980).
3. For a useful survey of research on estimating household production, see Hawrylyshyn (1976) and Murphy (1978).
4. This reluctance in the case of socialist political economy is due to a fear that by pointing out divisions based on sexual or racial grounds, the fundamental unity that is believed to exist in the working class will be threatened. Neoclassical political economy sees the world as populated by individuals (or households) harmoniously pursuing their own self-interest.
5. It could be argued that during a boom firms may employ women on similar working arrangements so as to meet the excess demand in their order books. If women merely serve the function of a reserve pool of labour, it would follow that they would no longer be employed once the economy takes a downturn.
6. In contrast, the presence of dependent children raises the participation rates of the fathers and make them more likely to take up shift or overtime work.
7. For a useful discussion of the nature and prevalence of the 'caring' cycle, see Equal Opportunities Commission (1980).
8. It is estimated that well over 90% of all women marry before the end of their child-bearing age. But an increasing number of the marriages end in divorce. So that of all marriages that took place in 1921, one in 200 ended in divorce within ten years. The comparable figure for marriages contracted in 1961 was 1 in 17. It is expected that if the present trends continue one in every three marriages will eventually end in divorce (Haskey, 1982).
9. In the early 80s, one in every eight children is brought up by a lone parent (Rimmer and Popay, 1982, p. 257).

Bibliography

This bibliography contains both items referred to in the text, as well as those consulted in the course of writing this book. The list given below is hardly exhaustive in its coverage, though it encompasses a reasonably broad spectrum of literature relating to 'women and work'. Almost all the studies mentioned below emanate from Britain or the United States, between whom, in any case, there is a great traffic in research ideas. Both in the construction of subject divisions and in the allocation of individual items to different areas, there can be reasonable grounds for disagreement. But in any case, given the large number of items in the bibliography, some form of subject classification is preferable to a simple alphabetical listing.

A. Changing Size and Composition of the Labour Force: An Examination of the Demographic, Occupational and Industrial Aspects of the Historical Growth of Female Employment

Alexander, S. (1976) 'Women's Work in Nineteenth Century London: A Study of the Years 1820–1850', in A. Oakley and J. Mitchell (eds), *The Rights and Wrongs of Women*, Penguin Books, Harmondsworth.

Blau, F.D. and Hendericks, W.E. (1979) 'Occupational Segregation by Sex: Trends and Prospects', *Journal of Human Resources*, 14.

Braybon, G. (1981) *Women Workers in the First World War*, Croom Helm, London.

Department of Employment (1981) 'Labour Force Outlook to 1986', *Employment Gazette*, April.

Durand, J. (1948) *The Labor Force in the United States: 1890–1960*, Social Science Research Council, New York.

Easterlin, R.A. (1968) *Population, Labor Force and Long Swings in Economic Growth: The American Experience*, National Bureau of Economic Research (NBER), New York.

Gales, K. and Marks, P. (1974) 'Twentieth Century Trends in the Work of Women in England and Wales', *Journal of the Royal Statistical Society*, Series A, 137.

Garfinkle, N. 'Job Tenure of Workers', *Special Labor Force Report*, No. 77, US Department of Labor, Washington DC.

Gross, E. (1968) 'Plus ça Change ...? The Sexual Structure of Occupations over Time', *Social Problems*, 16.

Hakim, C. (1978) 'Sexual Divisions within the Labour Force: Occupational Segregation', *Department of Employment Gazette*, November.

Hakim, C. (1979) 'Occupational Segregation' Research Paper No. 9, Department of Employment.

Hakim, C. (1981) 'Job Segregation: Trends in the 1970s', *Employment Gazette*, December.

Hunt, A. (1968) *A Survey of Women's Employment*, Government Social Survey Division, London.

James, E. (1962) 'Women at Work in Twentieth Century Britain', *Manchester School*, 20.

Jephcott, A.P. *et al.* (1962) *Married Women Working*, Routledge and Kegan Paul, London.

Joseph, G. (1978) 'A Statistical Analysis of Changes in the Size and Composition of the British Labour Force during the Twentieth Century', unpublished PhD dissertation, University of Manchester.

Joseph, G. (1980) 'Future Changes in the Size and Composition of the British Labour Force: A Regional Projection Exercise', *Regional Studies*, 14.

Kelsall, R.K. and Mitchell, S. (1959) 'Married Women and Employment in England and Wales', *Population Studies*, 13.

Klein, V. (1965) *Britain's Married Women Workers*, Routledge and Kegan Paul, London.

Knight, R. (1967) 'Changes in the Occupational Structure of the Working Population', *Journal of the Royal Statistical Society*, Series A, 130.

Oppenheimer, V.K. (1970) *The Female Labor Force in the United States: Demographic and Economic Factors Governing its Growth and Changing Composition*, University of California Press, Berkeley.

Pinchbeck, I.(1930) *Women Workers and the Industrial Revolution*, Frank Cass, London (1969 edition, Routledge and Kegan Paul).

Routh, G. (1980) *Occupation and Pay in Great Britain 1906–1979*, Macmillan, London.

Stewart, C.M. (1961) 'Future Trends in the Employment of Married Women', *British Journal of Sociology*, 12.

Stewart, C.M. (1970) 'The Employment of Married Women in Great

Britain', *Proceedings of International Population Conference*, 1969.
Sweet, J.A. (1973) *Women in the Labor Force*, Seminar Press, New York.
Tarling, R.J. (1976) 'The Labour Force', mimeograph, Department of
Applied Economics , University of Cambridge.

**B. Determinants of Labour Force Participation in a Changing
Economy: Differing Perspectives on Female Involvement in the
Labour Force**

Amsden, A.H. (ed.) (1980) *The Economics of Women and Work,* Penguin
Books, Harmondsworth.
Anyanwu, E.A. (1969) 'The Relationship between Employment and
Unemployment by Region', mimeograph, National Institute of
Economic and Social Research (NIESR), London.
Bancroft, G. (1958) *The American Labor Force: its Growth and Changing
Composition,* Wiley, New York.
Barth, P.S. (1968) 'Unemployment and Labor Force Participation',
Southern Economic Journal, 34.
Bowen, W.G. and Finegan, T.A. (1969) *The Economics of Labor Force
Participation,* Princeton University Press, Princeton.
Bowers, J.K. *et al.* (1972) 'Some Aspects of Unemployment and the
Labour Market, 1966–70', *National Institute of Economic and Social
Research Review,* November.
Bowers, J.K. (1975) 'British Activity Rates: A Survey of Research',
Scottish Journal of Political Economy, 22.
Cain, G. (1966) *Married Women in the Labor Force: An Economic
Analysis,* Chicago University Press, Chicago.
Corry, B.A. and Roberts, J.A. (1970) 'Activity Rates and Unemployment
— The Experience of the UK, 1957–1966, *Applied Economics,* 2.
Corry, B.A. and Roberts, J.A. (1974) 'Activity Rates and Unemployment
— the UK Experience: Some Further Results', *Applied Economics,* 6.
Daniel, W.W. (1974) 'A National Survey of the Unemployed', PEP
Broadsheet No. 546, Political Economic Planning, London.
Elias, P. (1980) 'A Time Series Analysis of the Labour Force Participation
of Married Women in the UK, 1968–1975', Manpower Research Group
Discussion Paper, University of Warwick.
Fleisher, B.M. and Rhodes, G. (1976) 'Unemployment and the Labor
Force Participation of Men and Women: A Simultaneous Model',
Review of Economics and Statistics, 58.
Galambos, P. (1967) 'Activity Rates of the Population of Great Britain: An
Analysis by Regions and Age-Groups', *Scottish Journal of Political
Economy,* 14.
Godley, W.A. and Shepherd, J.R. (1964) 'Long-term Growth and Short-
term Policy', *National Institute of Economic and Social Research
Review,* 29.
Greenhalgh, C. (1977) 'A Labour Supply Function for Married Women in
Great Britain', *Economica,* 44.

Greenhalgh, C. (1979) 'Male Labour Force Participation in Great Britain', *Scottish Journal of Political Economy,* 26.

Greenhalgh, C. (1980a) 'Participation and Hours of Work for Married Women in Great Britain', *Oxford Economic Papers,* 32.

Humphrey, D.D. (1940) 'Alleged Additional Workers in the Measurement of Unemployment', *Journal of Political Economy,* 58.

Hunter, L.C. (1963) 'Cyclical Variations to Labour Supply: British Experience 1951–60', *Oxford Economic Papers,* 17.

Joseph, G. (1982) 'A Stochastic Analysis of Short-term Changes in Labour Market Activity in Great Britain', Discussion Paper in Econometrics, ES119, University of Manchester.

Joshi, H.E. (1978) 'Secondary Workers in the Cycle: Married Women and Older Workers in Employment Fluctuations, Great Britain 1961–1974', Government Economic Service Working Paper, No. 9.

Joshi, H.E. (1981) 'Secondary Workers in the Employment Cycle', *Economica,* 48.

Joshi, H.E. and Owen, S. (1981) 'Demographic Predictors of Women's Work Participation in Post-War Britain', CPS Working Paper, No. 84, Centre for Population Studies, London School of Hygiene and Tropical Medicine.

Layard, R. *et al.* (1980) 'Married Women's Participation and Hours', *Economica,* 47.

McGregor, A. (1978) 'Unemployment Duration and Re-employment Probability', *Economic Journal,* 88.

Mackay, D.I. *et al.* (1971) *Labour Markets under Different Employment Conditions,* Allen and Unwin, London.

Mackay, D.I. and Reid, G.L. (1972) 'Redundancy, Unemployment and Manpower Policy', *Economic Journal,* 82.

McNabb, R. (1977) 'Labour Force Participation of Married Women', *Manchester School,* 45.

Metcalf, D. (1975) 'Urban Unemployment in England', *Economic Journal,* 85.

Mincer, J. (1962) 'Labour Force Participation of Married Women: A Study of Labor Supply', in *Aspects of Labor Economics,* Conference (National Bureau of Economic Research), Princeton University Press, Princeton.

Mincer, J. (1966) 'Labor Force and Unemployment: A Revision of the Recent Evidence', in R.A. Gordon (ed.), *Prosperity and Unemployment,* University of California Press, Berkeley.

Nickell, S.J. (1979b) 'The Effect of Unemployment and Related Benefits on the Duration of Unemployment', *Economic Journal,* 90.

Nickell, S.J. (1980) 'A Picture of Male Unemployment in Britain', *Economic Journal,* 90.

OECD (1976) *The 1974–75 Recession and Employment of Women.*

Rubery, J. and Tarling, R. (1982) 'Women in the Recession', in D. Currie and M. Sawyer (eds), *Socialist Economic Review,* Merlin Press, London.

Shepherd, J.R. (1968) 'Productive Potential and Demand for Labour', *Economic Trends,* August.

Taylor, J. (1972) 'The Behaviour of Unemployment and Unfilled Vacancies: Great Britain — An Alternative View', *Economic Journal*, 82.

Wabe, S. (1969) 'Labour Force Participation in the London Metropolitan Region', *Journal of the Royal Statistical Society*, Series A, 132.

Webb, A.E. (1970) 'The Relationship between Employment and Unemployment', mimeograph, National Institute of Economic and Social Research (NIESR), London.

Woytinsky, W.S. (1940) *Additional Workers and the Volume of Unemployment*, Social Science Research Council, New York.

C. Status of Women Workers in the Labour Market: The Impact of Remuneration, Occupational Segregation and Discrimination

Aigner, D. and Cain, G. (1977) 'Statistical Theories of Discrimination in Labor Markets', *Industrial and Labor Relations Review*, 30.

Arrow, K. (1972a) 'Models of Job Discrimination', in A.H. Pascall (ed.), *Racial Discrimination in the Labor Market*, D.C. Heath, Lexington Mass.

Arrow, K. (1972b) 'Some Mathematical Models of Racial Discrimination', in A.H. Pascall (ed.), *Racial Discrimination in the Labor Market*, D.C. Heath, Lexington Mass.

Becker, G.S. (1957) *The Economics of Discrimination*, University of Chicago Press, Chicago (2nd edition, 1971).

Benet, M.K. (1972) *Secretary: An Inquiry into the Female Ghetto*, Sidgwick and Jackson, London.

Bergmann, B. (1971) 'The Effect of White Incomes on Discrimination in Employment', *Journal of Political Economy*, 79.

Bergmann, B. (1974) 'Occupational Segregation, Wages and Profits where Employers Discriminate by Race or Sex', *Eastern Economic Journal*, 1.

Blau, F.D. and Jusenius, C.L. (1976) 'Economists' Approach to Sex Segregation in the Labor Market', *Signs*, 1.

Blaxall, M. *et al.* (1976) *Women and Workplace: The Implications of Occupational Segregation*, University of Chicago Press, Chicago.

Bosanquet, N. and Doeringer, P. (1973) 'Is there a Dual Market in Great Britain?', *Economic Journal*, 83.

Bosanquet, N. and Standing, G. (1972) 'Government and Unemployment: 1960–1970', *British Journal of Industrial Relations*, 10.

Brown, G.D. (1976) 'How Type of Employment Affects Earnings Differences by Sex', *Monthly Labor Review*, 99.

Chiplin, B. and Sloane, P.J. (1974) 'Sexual Discrimination in the Labour Market', *British Journal of Industrial Relations*, 22.

Chiplin, B. and Sloane, P.J. (1976) *Sex Discrimination in the Labour Market*, Macmillan, London.

Chiplin, B. *et al.* (1980) 'Relative Female Earnings in Great Britain and Impact of Legislation', in P.J. Sloane (ed.), *Low Pay and Women*, Macmillan, London.

Chiswick, B.R. (1973) 'Racial Discrimination in the Labor Market: A Test of Alternative Hypotheses', *Journal of Political Economy*, 81.

Department of Employment (1975) 'Women and Work: A Review', *Manpower Paper*, No. 11.

Department of Employment (1976) 'Teachers Pay — How and Why Men and Women's Earnings Differ', *Department of Employment Gazette*, September.

Doeringer, P.B. and Piore, M.J. (1971) *Internal Labor Markets and Manpower Analysis*, D.C. Heath, Lexington Mass.

Economic Commission for Europe (1980) *The Economic Role of Women in the EEC Region*, United Nations, New York.

Edgeworth, F.Y. (1922) 'Equal Pay to Men and Women for Equal Work', *Economic Journal*, 32.

Edwards, R.C. *et al.* (1975) *Labor Market Segmentation*, D.C. Heath, Lexington Mass.

Fawcett, M.G. (1918) 'Equal Pay for Equal Work', *Economic Journal*, 28.

Fuchs, V.R. (1971) 'Differences in Hourly Earnings between Men and Women', *Monthly Labour Review*, 94.

Fuchs, V.R. (1975) 'A Note on Sex Segregation in Professional Occupations', *Explorations in Economic Research*, 2.

Gordon, D. (1972) *Theories of Poverty and Underdevelopment: Orthodox Radical and Dual Labor Market Perspectives*, D.C. Heath, Lexington Mass.

Greenhalgh, C. (1980b) 'Male–Female Wage Differentials in Great Britain: Is Marriage an Equal Opportunity?', *Economic Journal*, 90.

Hartmann, H. (1979) 'Capitalism, Patriarchy and Job Segregation by Sex', in Z.R. Eisenstein (ed.), *Capitalism, Patriarchy and the Case for Socialist Feminism*, Monthly Review Press, New York.

Hebden, J. (1978) 'Men's and Women's Pay in Britain: 1968–1975', *Industrial Relations Journal*, 9(2).

King, A.G. (1978) 'Industrial Structure, the Flexibility of Working Hours and Women's Labor Force Participation', *Review of Economics and Statistics*, 60.

Layard, R. *et al.* (1978a) 'The Causes of Poverty', The Royal Commission on the Distribution of Income and Wealth, Background Paper No. 5, HMSO, London.

Layard, R. *et al.* (1978b) 'The Effect of Collective Bargaining on Relative Wages', *British Journal of Industrial Relations*, 16.

Lloyd, C.B. and Niemi, B.T. (1979) *The Economics of Sex Differentials*, Columbia University Press, New York.

McAuley, A. (1981) *Women's Work and Wages in the Soviet Union*, George Allen and Unwin, London.

McNally, F. (1979) *Women for Hire: A Study of Female Office Workers*, Macmillan, London.

McNulty, D.J. (1967) 'Differences in Pay between Men and Women Workers', *Monthly Labour Review*, 90.

Madden, J. (1977) 'A Spatial Theory of Sex Discrimination', *Journal of Regional Science*, 17.

Mincer, J. (1974) *Schooling Experience and Earnings*, National Bureau of Economic Research (NBER), New York.

Mincer, J. and Polachek, S. (1974) 'Family Investment in Human Capital: Earnings of Women', *Journal of Political Economy*, 82.

National Union of Teachers (1980) *Promotion and the Woman Teacher*, published jointly with Equal Opportunities Commission (EOC), Manchester.

Niemi, B. (1974) 'The Female–Male Differentials in Unemployment Rates', *Industrial and Labor Relations Review*, 27.

Niemi, B. (1975) 'The Female–Male Differential in Unemployment Rates', in G.B. Lloyd (ed.), *Sex Discrimination and the Division of Labor*, Columbia University Press, New York.

Phelps, E.S. (1972) 'The Statistical Theory of Racism and Sexism', *American Economic Review*, 62.

Phelps Brown, H. (1977) *The Inequality of Pay*, Oxford University Press, Oxford.

Piore, M. (1971) 'The Dual Labor Market: Theory and Implications', in D.M. Gordon (ed.), *Problems in Political Economy: An Urban Perspective*, D.C. Heath, Lexington Mass.

Psacharopoulos, G. and Layard, R. (1979) 'Human Capital and Earnings: British Evidence and a Critique', *Review of Economic Studies*, 46.

Reich, M. *et al.* (1973) 'A Theory of Labor Market Segmentation', *American Economic Review*, 63.

Reynolds, M. (1973) 'Economic Theory and Racial Wage Differentials', Discussion Paper, Institute for Research on Poverty, University of Wisconsin.

Robinson, O. and Wallace, J. (1977) 'National Wage Rates and Earnings Composition: A Note on Potential Sources of Sex Discrimination in Pay', *British Journal of Industrial Relations*, 15.

Royal Commission on the Distribution of Income and Wealth (1979), *Lower Incomes Report*, No.6, Cmnd. 7175, HMSO, London.

Rubery, J. (1978) 'Structural Labour Markets, Worker Organisation and Low Pay', *Cambridge Economic Journal*, 2.

Sloane, P.J. (1980) *Women and Low Pay*, Macmillan, London.

Sloane, P.J. and Siebert, W.S. (1980) 'Relative Female Earnings in Great Britain and Impact of Legislation', in P.J. Sloane (ed.), *Low Pay and Women*, Macmillan, London.

Sloane, P.J. (1981) *The Earnings Gap between Men and Women in Britain*, Social Science Research Council, London.

Spence, M. (1973) 'Job Market Signalling', *Quarterly Journal of Economics*, 87.

Swinton, D. (1978) 'A Labor Force Competition Model of Racial Discrimination in the Labor Market', *Review of Black Political Economy*, 9.

Thurow, L. (1975) *Generating Inequality*, Basic Books, New York.

Turnbull, P. and Williams, G. (1974) 'Sex Differentiation in Teachers' Pay', *Journal of the Royal Statistical Society*, Series A, 137.

UNESCO (1976) *Statistics of Women in Britain*, UK National Commission.

Vinnicombe, S. (1980) *Secretaries, Management and Organisation*, Heinemann, London.

Wabe, S. and Leech, D. (1975) 'Relative Earnings in UK Manufacturing—

A Reconsideration of the Evidence', *Economic Journal*, 88.

Wachter, M.L. (1975) 'Primary and Secondary Labor Markets: A Critique of the Dual Approach', in A.M. Okun and G.L. Perry (eds), *Brookings Paper on Economic Activity*, Volume 3, Brookings Institution, Washington DC.

Woodward, N. and McNabb, R. (1978) 'Low Pay in British Manufacturing', *Applied Economics*, 10.

D. Domestic Labour and Market Work: Familial Aspects of Women's Work

Barker, D.C. and Allen, S. (eds) (1976) *Dependence and Exploitation in Work and Marriage*, Longman, London.

Barrett, M. and McIntosh, M. (1980) 'The "Family Wage": Some Problems in Marxist Feminist Analysis', *Capital and Class*, 11.

Barron, R.D. and Norris, G.M. (1976) 'Sexual Division and the Dual Labour Market', in D.L. Barker and S. Allen (eds), *Dependence and Exploitation in Work and Marriage*, Longman, London.

Becker, G.S. (1960) 'An Economic Analysis of Fertility', in *Demographic and Economic Change in Developed Countries*, (National Bureau of Economic Research), Princeton University Press, Princeton.

Becker, G.S. and Lewis, H.G. (1973) 'On the Interaction between the Quantity and Quality of Children', *Journal of Political Economy*, 81.

Becker, G.S. *et al.* (1976)'Economics of Marital Instability', mimeograph, National Bureau of Economic Research (NBER), New York.

Becker, G.S. and Tomes, N. (1976) 'Child Endowments and Quantity and Quality of Children', *Journal of Political Economy*, 84.

Beechey, V. (1978) 'Women and Production: A Critical Analysis of Some Sociological Theories of Women's Work', in A. Kuhn and A.M. Wolpe, *Feminism and Materialism*, Routledge and Kegan Paul, London.

Ben Porath, Y. (1973) 'Economic Analysis of Fertility in Israel: Point and Counterpoint', *Journal of Political Economy*, 81.

Blake, J. (1968) 'Are Babies Consumer Durables?', *Population Studies*, 22.

Brown, M. (1974) *Sweated Labour: A Study of Homework*, Low Pay Pamphlet, Low Pay Unit, London.

Burke, R.J. and Weir, T. (1976) 'Relationship of Wives' Employment Status to Husband, Wife and Pair Satisfaction and Performance', *Journal of Marriage and Family*, 38.

Cain, G. and Weininger, A. (1973) 'Economic Determinants of Fertility: Results from Cross-Sectional Aggregate Data', *Demography*, 10.

Crine, S. (1979) *The Hidden Army*, Low Pay Pamplet, Low Pay Unit, London.

Daniel, W.W. (1980) *Maternity Rights: The Experience of Women*, Policy Studies Institute, London.

De Tray, D.N. (1973) 'Child Quality and the Demand for Children', *Journal of Political Economy*, 81.

Dickinson, K. (1976) 'Child Care', in G.J. Duncan and J. Morgan, *Five Thousand Families,* Institute for Social Research, University of Michigan, Ann Arbor.

Easterlin, R.A. (1969) 'Towards a Socio-Economic Theory of Fertility', in S.J. Behrman *et al.* (eds), *Fertility and Family Planning: A World View,* Michigan University Press, Ann Arbor.

Equal Opportunities Commission (1980) *The Experience of Caring for Elderly and Handicapped Dependants: A Survey Report,* EOC, Manchester.

Freedman, R. and Coombs, L. (1966a) 'Child Spacing and Family Economic Position', *American Sociological Review,* 13.

Freedman, R. and Coombs, L. (1966b) 'Economic Considerations in Family Growth Decisions', *Population Studies,* 20.

Gardiner J. (1976) 'Political Economy of Domestic Labour in Capitalist Society', in D.L. Barker and S. Allen (eds), *Dependence and Exploitation in Work and Marriage,* Longman, London.

Gardiner, J. (1977) 'Women in the Labour Process and Class Structure', in A. Hunt (ed.), *Class and Class Structure,* Lawrence and Wishart, London.

Gardner, B. (1973) 'Economics of the Size of North Carolina Rural Families', *Journal of Political Economy,* 81.

Gavron, H. (1968) *The Captive Wife,* Penguin Books, Harmondsworth.

Ghez, G.R. and Becker, G.S. (1975) *The Allocation of Time and Goods over the Life Cycle,* National Bureau of Economic Research (NBER), New York.

Gordon, H.A. and Kammeyer, K.C. (1980) 'The Gainful Employment of Women with Small Children', *Journal of Marriage and Family,* 42.

Gramm, W.L. (1975) 'Household Utility Maximisation and Working Wife', *American Economic Review,* 65.

Gronau, R. (1973) 'The Inter-Family Allocation of Time: The Value of Housewives' Time', *American Economic Review,* 63.

Hakim, C. (1980) 'Home Working: Some New Evidence', *Employment Gazette,* October.

Hawrylyshyn, O. (1976) 'The Value of Household Services: A Survey of Empirical Estimates', *Review of Income and Wealth,* 22.

Hoffman, L.W. (1963) 'The Decision to Work', in F.I. Nye *et al.* (eds), *The Employed Mother in America,* Rand McNally, Chicago.

Kaluzyuska, E. (1980) 'Wiping the Floor with Theory: A Survey of Writings on Housework', *Feminist Review,* 6.

Kuhn, A. (1978) 'Structures of Capital and Patriarchy in the Family', in A. Kuhn and A.M. Wolpe (eds), *Feminism and Materialism,* Routledge and Kegan Paul, London.

Land, H. (1976) 'Women: Supporters or Supported', in D.L. Barker and S. Allen (eds), *Sexual Divisions and Society: Process and Change,* Tavistock, London.

Liebowitz, A. (1972) 'Women's Allocation of Time to Market and Non-Market Activities: Differences by Education', unpublished PhD dissertation, University of Columbia.

Murphy, M. (1978) 'The Value of Non-Market Household Production: Opportunity Cost versus Market Cost Estimates', *Review of Income and Wealth*, 24.

Myrdal, A. and Klein, V. (1968) *Women's Two Roles: Home and Work*, Routledge and Kegan Paul, London.

Namboodri, N.K. (1964) 'Women's Work Experience and Child Spacing', *Milbank Memorial Fund Quarterly*, 42.

Nerlove, M. and Razin, A. (1981) 'Child Spacing and Numbers: An Empirical Analysis', in A. Deaton (ed.), *Essays in the Theory and Measurement of Consumer Behaviour in Honour of Sir Richard Stone*, Cambridge University Press, Cambridge.

Nickols, S. (1976) *Women and Housework: Family Roles in Productive Activity*, National Council on Family Relations, New York.

Nye, F.I. (ed.) (1963) 'Personal Satisfactions', in *The Employed Mother in America*, Rand McNally, Chicago.

Preston, S.H. and Richards, A.T. (1975) 'The Influence of Women's Work Opportunities on Marriage Rates', *Demography*, 12.

Ridley, J.C. (1959) 'Number of Children Expected in Relation to Non-Familial Activities of the Wife', *Milbank Memorial Fund Quarterly*, 37.

Rimmer, L. and Popay, J. (1982) 'The Family at Work', *Employment Gazette*, June.

Ryder, N.B. (1973) 'Comment', *Journal of Political Economy*, 81. (A Comment on Economic Theory of Fertility Behaviour.)

Sawhill, I.V. *et al.* (1975) 'Income Transfers and Family Structure', *The Urban Institute Working Party*, 979–03, Washington.

Sawhill, I.V. *et al.* (1977) 'Economic Perspectives on the Family', *Daedulus*, 106.

Schultz, T.W. (1973) 'The Value of Children: An Economic Perspective', *Journal of Political Economy*, 81.

Sloetzel, J. (1948) 'Une Étude du budget — temps de la femme dans les agglomérations urbaines', *Population*, 1.

Smith, R.E. (ed.) (1974) *The Subtle Revolution: Women at Work*, The Urban Institute, Washington DC.

Smith, P. (1978) 'Domestic Labour and Marx's Theory of Value', in A. Kuhn and A.M. Wolpe (eds), *Feminism and Materialism*, Routledge and Kegan Paul, London.

Sobol, M.G. (1963) 'Commitment to Work', in F.I. Nye (ed.), *The Employed Mother in America*, Rand McNally, Chicago,

Turchi, B.A. (1975) *The Demand for Children: The Economics of Fertility in the United States*, Ballinger, Cambridge Mass.

Vanek, J. (1974) 'Time Spent in Housework', *Scientific American*, 231.

Walker, K.E. (1973) 'Household Work Time: Its Implications for Family Decisions', *Journal of Home Economics*, 65.

Willis, R.J. (1973) 'A New Approach to the Economic Theory of Fertility Behaviour', *Journal of Political Economy*, 81.

Yudkin, S. and Holme, A. (1969) *Working Mothers and their Children*, Michael Joseph, London.

E. The Quality of Labour and the Patterns of Work: The Role of Education, Training, Work Experience and Other Relevant Considerations in Determining the Status of Women Workers

Byrne, E.M. (1978) *Women and Education*, Tavistock, London.

Clark, G. (1982) 'Recent Developments in Working Patterns', *Employment Gazette*, July.

Deem, R. (1978) *Women and Schooling*, Routledge and Kegan Paul, London.

Equal Opportunities Commission (1981) 'Job Sharing', *Alternative Working Arrangements*, EOC, Manchester.

Greenhalgh, C.A. and Stewart, M.B. (1982) 'The Training and Experience Dividend', *Employment Gazette*, August.

Kelly, A. (1981) *The Missing Half: Girls and Science Education*, Manchester University Press, Manchester.

Leicester, C. (1982) 'Towards a Fully Part-Time Britain', *Personnel Management*, June.

Liebowitz, A. (1974) 'Education and Home Production', *American Association, Papers & Proceedings*.

Liebowitz, A. (1975) 'Education and Allocation of Women's Time', in F.T. Juster (ed.), *Education, Income and Human Behaviour*, McGraw-Hill, New York.

Polacheck, S.W. (1975) 'Discontinuous Labor Force Participation and its Effects', in C.B. Lloyd (ed.), *Sex Discrimination and the Division of Labor*, Columbia University Press, New York.

Yohalem, A. (1968) 'The Potential of Educated Women', in E. Ginsberg (ed.), *Manpower Strategy for the Metropolis*, Columbia University Press, New York.

F. Women Workers and Trade Unions

APEX, (1979) *Office Technology, the Trade Union Response*, Association of Professional, Executive, Clerical and Computer Staff (APEX), London.

Bain, G.S. (1970) *The Growth of White Collar Unions*, Oxford University Press, Oxford.

Bain, G.S. and Price, R. (1972) 'Union Growth and Employment Trends in the United Kingdom: 1964–1970', *British Journal of Industrial Relations*, 10.

Ellis, V. (1981) *The Role of Trade Unions in the Promotion of Equal Opportunities*, Equal Opportunities Commission (EOC), Manchester.

Harrison, M. (1979) 'Participation of Women in Trade Union Activities. Some Research Findings and Comments', *Industrial Relations Journal*, 10.

Lewenhak, S. (1977) *Women in Trade Unions*, Ernest Benn, London.

Nickell, S.J. (1977) 'Trade Unions and the Position of Women in the Industrial Wage Structure', *British Journal of Industrial Relations*, 15.

Soldon, N.C. (1978) *Women in The Trade Unions, 1874–1976*, Gill and Macmillan, Dublin.

Stageman, J. (1980) 'Women in Trade Unions', Occasional Paper, No.6, Industrial Studies Unit, Adult Education Department, University of Hull.

G. Employment Effects of New Technology: The Position of Women Workers

APEX (1980) *Automation and the Office Worker*, Association of Professional, Executive, Clerical and Computer Staff (APEX), London.

Barker, J. and Downing, H. (1980) 'Word Processing and the Transformation of Patriarchal Relations of Control in the Office', *Capital and Class*, 10.

Barron, I. and Curnov, R. (1979) *The Future with Microelectronics*, Francis Pinter, London.

Bird, C. (1980) *Information Technology: The Impact on Women's Jobs*, Equal Opportunities Commission (EOC), Manchester.

Downing, H. (1980) 'Word Processors and the Oppression of Women' in T. Forester (ed.), *The Microelectronics Revolution: The Complete Guide to the Silicon Chip and its Impact on Society*, Basil Blackwell, Oxford.

Green, K. *et al.* (1980) *The Effects of Microelectronic Technology on Employment Prospects: A Case Study of Tameside*, Gower Press, Farnborough.

Green, K. and Coombs, R. (1981) 'Employment and New Technology in Tameside', *Futures*, 13.

Hirsch, W. (1980) 'Manpower in the Paper and Paper Products Industry', Paper and Paper Products Industry Training Paper.

Jenkins, C. and Sherman, B. (1980) *The Collapse of Work*, Eyre Methuen, London.

Liff, S. (1981) 'New Technology and Women's Work in Manufacturing Industries: The Situation and Experience of Women within Two Food Factories', unpublished manuscript, Department of Liberal Studies in Science, University of Manchester.

Metra (1980) 'Impact of Micro-Chip Technology on Employment', A Report, (summarised in *The Times*, 11th August, 1980, p.2).

Nora, S. and Minc, A. *'L'informatisation de la société'*, Documentation Française, Paris.

Senker, P. (1980) 'Assembly', in N. Swords-Isherwood and P. Senker (eds), *Microelectronics and the Engineering Industry: The Need for Skills*, Francis Pinter, London.

Siemens (1978) 'Internal Report on Impact of Office Technology. Federal Republic of Germany', discussed in D. Dangelmayer, 'The Job Killers of Germany', *New Scientist*, 8th June, 1978.

Sleigh, J. *et al.* (1979) *The Manpower Implications of Micro-electronic Technology*, Department of Employment, HMSO, London.

SPRU Women and Technology Studies (1982) 'Microelectronics and

Women's Employment in Britain', Occasional Paper Series No. 17, Science Policy Research Unit, University of Sussex.

H. Equal Opportunities Legislation and Women Workers

Coote, A. (1978) 'Equality and the Curse of the Quango', *New Statesman*, December.

Department of Employment (1982) 'Equal Pay and Sex Discrimination', *Employment Gazette*, May.

Glucklich, P. *et al.* (1978) 'Equal Pay and Opportunity', *Department of Employment Gazette*, July.

Robinson, O. and Wallace, J. (1975) 'Equal Pay and Equality of Opportunity', *International Journal of Social Economics*, 2.

Snell, M. (1979) 'The Equal Pay and Sex Discrimination Acts: Their Impact in the Work Place', *Feminist Review*, 1.

I. Statistical Sources and Methods

Ashenfelter, O. and Heckman, J. (1974) 'The Estimation of Income and Substitution Effects in a Model of Female Labor Supply', *Econometrica*, 42.

Ashworth, J. and Ulph, D.T. (1977) 'Estimating Labour Supply Constraints with Piecewise Linear Constraints', mimeograph, Department of Economics, University of Sterling.

Atkinson, A. and Stern, N. (1981) 'On Labour Supply and Commodity Demands', in A. Deaton (ed.), *Essays in the Theory and Measurement of Consumer Behaviour in Honour of Sir Richard Stone*, Cambridge University Press, Cambridge.

Becker, G.S. (1965) 'A Theory of Allocation of Time', *Economic Journal*, 75.

Department of Employment (1971) *British Labour Statistics: Historical Abstracts 1886–1968*, HMSO, London.

Duncan, O.D. and Duncan, B. (1955) 'A Methodological Analysis of Segregation Indices', *American Sociological Review*, 20.

Gronau, R. (1974) 'Wage Comparisons — A Selectivity Bias', *Journal of Political Economy*, 82.

Heckman, J. (1974) 'Shadow Prices, Market Wages and Labor Supply', *Econometrica*, 42.

Heckman, J. and Macurdy, T. (1980) 'A Life Cycle Model of Female Labor Supply', *Review of Economic Studies*, 48.

Johnston, J. (1972) *Econometric Methods*, McGraw-Hill, Tokyo.

Kitagawa, E. (1955) 'Components of a Difference between Two Rates', *Journal of American Statistical Association*, 50.

Lancaster, T. (1979) 'Econometric Methods for the Duration of Unemployment', *Econometrica*, 47.

Lee, C.H. (1979) *British Regional Employment Statistics*, Cambridge University Press, Cambridge.

Lewis, H.G. (1974) 'Comments on Selectivity Bias in Wage Comparisons', *Journal of Political Economy*, 82.

Mincer, J. (1963) 'Market Prices, Opportunity Costs and Income Effects', in C. Christ *et al.* (eds), *Measurement in Economics: Studies in Mathematical Economics and Econometrics in Memory of Y. Grunfeld*, Stanford University Press, Stanford.

Mitchell, B.R. and Dean, P. (1962) *Abstracts of British Historical Statistics*, Cambridge University Press, Cambridge.

Nickell, S.J. (1979a) 'Estimating the Probability of Leaving Unemployment', *Econometrica*, 47.

Smith, J. (1979) 'Family Labor Supply over the Life Cycle', *Explorations in Economic Research*, 4.

Wales, T.J. and Woodland, A.D. (1979) 'Labor Supply and Progressive Taxes', *Review of Economic Studies*, 46.

J. Miscellaneous Studies

Andorka, R. (1978) *Determinants of Fertility in Advanced Societies*, Methuen, London.

Bebel, A. (1883) *Women under Socialism*, Schocken, New York (1939 edition).

Becker, G.S. (1975) 'Altruism, Egoism, Genetic Fitness: Economics and Sociobiology', *Journal of Economic Literature*, 13.

Boulding, K. (1970) 'Economics as a Science', in *A Primer on Social Dynamics: History as Dialetics and Development*, Free Press, New York.

Braverman, H. (1974) *Labor and Monopoly Capital*, Monthly Review Press, New York.

Calot, G. and Thompson, J. (1981) 'The Recent Upturn in Fertility in England and Wales, France and West Germany', *OPCS Population Trends*, 24.

Cherlin, A. (1977) 'The Effect of Children on Marital Dissolution', *Demography*, 14.

Dixon, R. (1975) 'Women's Rights and Fertility', *Reports on Population/ Family Planning No. 17*, The Population Council, New York.

Dunell, K. (1979) *Family Formation 1976*, Office of Population, Censuses and Surveys (OPCS), London.

Engels, F. (1884) *The Origin of the Family, Private Property and the State*, International Publishers, New York (1942 edition).

Farid, S.M. (1974a) 'Components of Period Fertility in England and Wales', *Journal of Biosocial Science*, 6.

Farid, S.M. (1974b) 'On the Tempo of Child-bearing in England and Wales', *Population Studies*, 28.

Glick, P.C. (1977) 'Updating the Life Cycle of the Family', *Journal of Marriage and Family*, 39.

Greenhalgh, C. (1981) 'The Taxation of Husband and Wife: Equity, Efficiency and Female Labour Supply', *Fiscal Studies*, 2.

Haines, M. (1979) *Fertility and Occupation: Population Patterns in Industrialisation*, Academic Press, New York.

Hannan, M.T. and Tuma, N.B. (1977) 'Income and Marital Events:

Evidence from an Income-Maintenance Experiment', *American Journal of Sociology*, 82.

Haskey, J. (1982) 'The Proportion of Marriages ending in Divorce', *OPCS Population Trends*, 27.

Hawthorn, G. (1970) *The Sociology of Fertility*, Collier-Macmillan, London.

Hoffman, S. and Holmes, J. (1976) 'Husbands, Wives and Divorce', in G.J. Duncan *et al.* (eds), *Five Thousand Families*, Institute of Social Research, University of Michigan, Ann Arbor.

Humphries, J. (1977) 'Class Struggle and the Persistence of the Working Class Family', *Cambridge Journal of Economics*, 1.

Leete, R. and Anthony, S. (1979) 'Divorce and Remarriage: a Record Linkage Study', *OPCS Population Trends*, 16.

Lenin, V.I. (1934) *The Emancipation of Women*, International Publishers, New York.

Lockwood, D. (1958) *The Black Coated Worker*, George Allen and Unwin, London.

Moore, K.A. *et al.* (1978) 'The Consequences of Age at First Childbirth: Marriage, Separation and Divorce', *Urban Institute Working Paper*, 1146–3, Washington DC.

Morgan, J.N. *et al.* (1966) *Productive Americans: A Study of How Individuals Contribute to Economic Growth*, Institute of Social Research, University of Michigan, Ann Arbor.

Morishima, M. (1970) *Theory of Economic Growth*, Clarendon Press, Oxford.

Mott, F.L. and Moore, S.F. (1977) *The Socio-Economic Determinants and Short-Run Consequences of Marital Disruption*, Population Association Meeting, St. Louis.

Nerlove, M. (1974) 'Towards a New Theory of Population and Economic Growth', *Journal of Political Economy*, 82.

Robinson, J. (1934) *The Economics of Imperfect Competition*, Macmillan, London.

Ryder, N. and Westoff, C.F. (1971) *Reproduction in the United States*, Princeton University Press, Princeton.

Sargent, L. (1981) *Women and Revolution: The Unhappy Marriage of Marxism and Feminism*, Pluto Press, London.

Scitovsky, T. (1976) *The Joyless Economy*, Oxford University Press, Oxford.

Scott, H. (1976) *Women and Socialism: Experiences from Eastern Europe*, Allison and Busby, London.

Sivanandan, A. (1979) 'Imperialism and Disorganic Development in the Silicon Age', *Race and Class*, 22.

Weil, M.W. (1961) 'An Analysis of the Factors Influencing Married Women's Actual and Planned Work Participation' *American Sociological Review*, 1.

Westoff, C.F. and Ryder, N.B. (1977) *The Contraceptive Revolution*, Princeton University Press, Princeton.

Young, M. and Wilmott, P. (1973) *The Symmetrical Family*, Routledge and Kegan Paul, London.

Author Index

270

Subject Index